MODERN WARFARE, INTELLIGENCE AND DETERRENCE

OTHER ECONOMIST BOOKS

Guide to Analysing Companies
Guide to Business Modelling
Guide to Business Planning
Guide to Economic Indicators
Guide to the European Union
Guide to Financial Management
Guide to Financial Markets
Guide to Hedge Funds
Guide to Investment Strategy
Guide to Management Ideas and Gurus
Guide to Managing Growth
Guide to Organisation Design
Guide to Project Management
Guide to Supply Chain Management
Numbers Guide
Style Guide

Book of Isms
Book of Obituaries
Brands and Branding
Business Consulting
Business Strategy
Buying Professional Services
The City
Coaching and Mentoring
Doing Business in China
Economics
Emerging Markets
Mapping the Markets
Marketing
Organisation Culture
Successful Strategy Execution
The World of Business

Directors: an A–Z Guide
Economics: an A–Z Guide
Investment: an A–Z Guide
Negotiation: an A–Z Guide

Pocket World in Figures

The Economist

MODERN WARFARE, INTELLIGENCE AND DETERRENCE

The technologies that are transforming them

Edited by Benjamin Sutherland

WILEY

John Wiley & Sons, Inc.

Published by John Wiley & Sons, Inc., Hoboken, New Jersey.
Published simultaneously in Canada.

Published in Great Britain and the rest of the world by Profile Books Ltd

For general information on our other products and services or for technical support, please contact our Customer Care Department within the United States at (800) 762-2974, outside the United States at (317) 572-3993 or fax (317) 572-4002.

Wiley also publishes its books in a variety of electronic formats. Some content that appears in print may not be available in electronic books. For more information about Wiley products, visit our web site at www.wiley.com.

Library of Congress Cataloging-in-Publication Data:

Modern warfare, intelligence and deterrence : the technologies that are transforming them / edited by Benjamin Sutherland.
     pages cm. − (The Economist ; 104)
    Includes index.
    ISBN 978-1-118-18537-7 (cloth); ISBN 978-1-118-22758-9 (ebk);
ISBN 978-1-118-26517-8 (ebk); ISBN 978-1-118-24044-1 (ebk)
    1. Defense industries−Technological innovations.   2. Artificial intelligence.
    3. Weapons systems.   I. Sutherland, Benjamin, editor of compilation.
    HD9743.A2.M635   2012
    355'.07−dc23

                                          2011046346

Printed in the United States of America
10 9 8 7 6 5 4 3 2 1

Contents

Contributors

Bruce Clark covers law, ethics, religion and international institutions at *The Economist*. He contributed articles to Chapter 15.

Diana Geddes is *The Economist*'s southern Africa correspondent. She contributed an article to Chapter 17.

Alison Goddard is *The Economist*'s education correspondent. She contributed articles to Chapters 4 and 6.

Anton La Guardia is bureau chief of *The Economist*'s Brussels office. He contributed articles to Chapters 3, 7, 8, 11, 12, 14, 15 and 18.

Natasha Loder is a science and technology correspondent at *The Economist*. She contributed articles to Chapters 11 and 16.

Edward Lucas edits *The Economist*'s International section. He contributed articles to Chapter 15.

Paul Markillie is *The Economist*'s innovation editor. He contributed articles to Chapters 2, 5, 8, 10, 13, 16 and 17.

James Miles is a China correspondent at *The Economist*. He contributed articles to Chapter 11.

Oliver Morton is *The Economist*'s energy and environment editor. He contributed an article to Chapter 6.

Andrew Palmer is *The Economist*'s finance editor. He contributed an article to Chapter 15.

Tom Standage is *The Economist*'s digital editor. He contributed articles to Chapters 5 and 12.

Other contributors (and the chapter to which they contributed articles) are Stephen Budiansky (Chapter 7), Saswato Das (Chapter 4), Madelaine Drohan (Chapter 12), Jesse Emspak (Chapter 4), Alistair Gee (Chapter 10), Jim Giles (Chapter 13), Duncan Graham-Rowe (Chapter 9), Katie Greene (Chapter 2), Cheryl Jones (Chapter 16), Konstantin Kakaes (Chapter 6), Matthew Kaplan (Chapter 16), David Landau (Chapter 15), Evgeny Morozov (Chapter 12), Thomas Withington (Chapters 2, 3 and 13).

This book was edited by Benjamin Sutherland; he also wrote the introductions and contributed articles to Chapters 1, 2, 3, 4, 5, 6, 7, 8, 9, 11, 12, 13, 14, 15 and 17.

Introduction

IN THE LARGEST AIR BATTLE of the jet age, beginning June 9th 1982 over the Beqaa Valley in eastern Lebanon, Israeli warplanes destroyed all of Syria's 19 anti-aircraft batteries in the area and shot down 82 Syrian fighter jets. The Israeli air force lost just a single aircraft in the conflict, known as the Lebanon war. "It was a real turkey shoot," says Martin van Creveld, an Israeli military historian. Syria fought with Soviet fighter jets, anti-aircraft guns and radar systems. Israel fought with mostly American and Israeli warplanes and kit.

The rout of Syria's air force with "a concert" of Western military technologies has had far-reaching consequences, says David Ivry, head of the Israeli air force during the war. Syria and other rivals of Israel "lost the illusion that they could win a big war against Israel," says Mr Ivry, also a former ambassador to the United States and now head of the Israeli division of Boeing, an American defence giant. Syria scaled back its ambitions, largely limiting its goal to gaining control of the Israeli-occupied parts of the Golan Heights. No air force has since challenged the Israelis in open battle. With little chance of defeating Israel's armed forces, foes have shifted focus to beefing up arsenals of ground-launched missiles and rockets that could reach cities.

More broadly, the dramatic display of Western military technologies contributed to the demise of the Soviet Union less than a decade later, Mr Ivry says. Soviet officials including Mikhail Gorbachev, leader from 1985, increasingly realised that the Soviet Union and its client states would be at a serious technological disadvantage in conventional warfare against a Western enemy. The *perestroika* reforms failed to reverse the Soviet Union's economic and technological decline. Defence technologies do more than play a big role in determining which conflicts turn bloody and who wins: they reshape the political world.

This book is a collection of articles published in *The Economist* about the workings and repercussions of emerging warfare and intelligence technologies. They encompass a broad range of technologies, from laser guns to weaponised computer worms, and from liquid body armour to intelligence-analysis software. Articles are grouped thematically, in chapters, not chronologically. The chapters themselves are grouped into five parts: "Land and sea", "Air and space", "The computer factor", "Intelligence and spycraft" and "The road ahead". A short introduction precedes each part.

This selection of articles, some lightly edited, provides a unique briefing on war and peace in the electronic age. Examining matters from the technology side, it turns out, brings a range of insights into focus. For a start, the spread of new defence and intelligence technologies will make wars easier to start but generally smaller than the horrific conflagrations of the last century.

During the cold war, the nuclear-arms race made war increasingly unthinkable. In contrast, today's arms races in robotics and computer technologies are making war increasingly thinkable, says John Arquilla, head of a PhD programme in computerised weaponry at the Naval Postgraduate School in Monterey, California. Remotely piloted "hunter-killer" drones, such as America's Reaper, make it far easier to launch an attack without the military or political risks of putting boots on foreign soil. Mr Arquilla, a former adviser to Donald Rumsfeld, a secretary of defence under George W. Bush, is a strong advocate of remote-controlled and automated weaponry. Even so, he urges caution. Robotics bring a "great temptation" – launching attacks without the risk of putting troops on the ground or pilots in the air. Succumbing can end up starting an unwise war.

But technology can also make wars less deadly. Defeating a fighting force that uses rudimentary technology may require killing a large portion of its soldiers – the bloodbaths of America's civil war and the first world war attest to that. As fighting forces modernise, battles are often won with proportionately less killing.

Fighting the system

Technology can transform wars of attrition into less bloody "system against system" fighting, in the words of Richard Rowe, a former American army general who served in both the 1991 and 2003 Iraq wars, and who was stationed in occupied Baghdad. A system only functions if its elements function. Destroy enough elements of that system – a modern army's kit and infrastructure, or specialists needed to operate it – and the force cannot keep fighting. And winning with less fighting, and therefore less destruction, well serves a belligerent seeking to occupy a country, be it with good intentions or bad.

Air power can help disrupt an enemy's fighting system. An attacker may be able to fly behind enemy lines to destroy critical equipment – rather than shoot its way through troops on the ground. In 1991 and 2003 the American-led coalitions blew up Iraqi command-and-control facilities, making it difficult for the enemy to muster a defence. The terrifying accuracy of air strikes in both wars convinced many soldiers to surrender.

In one 2003 incident, recounted to American officials by Iraqi survivors, armoured units that had stalled during a thick sandstorm assumed they could not be seen by American warplanes. But new "synthetic aperture" radar systems mounted on large American aircraft discovered and pinpointed the vehicles. "Lo and behold, bombs started coming through the sandstorm," says Barry Watts, a former US Air Force lieutenant-colonel and Pentagon official. Spooked, many soldiers abandoned their vehicles and melted away into the population. The armoured units had not been completely destroyed, but what had been was the will to fight of many untargeted units, says Mr Watts.

Saddam Hussein's army of 380,000 (not counting reservists) was defeated with only around 10,800 Iraqi combatant deaths. For an imperfect comparison, consider the first world war. Troops in trenches had little communications gear and mobility. Massed together, soldiers were easier to target. Fighting required little specialised technical expertise, so soldiers were mostly interchangeable and fresh conscripts could quickly replace the fallen. And it was hard for discouraged soldiers to surrender or sneak away. The central powers were not defeated until more than half of their 25.2m fielded troops were killed or wounded.

Theorists call the shift from attrition warfare to system-disruption warfare the "revolution in military affairs". Precision weaponry is at its heart. Because military targets are generally small, hitting them with dumb bombs during the second world war was difficult. So cities were bombed instead. Carpet-bombing was justified as an effective way to weaken a country's will to fight. But the practice was progressively abandoned or discredited as accuracy improved. The mere existence of precision munitions may well result in less killing even in conflicts in which no belligerent has them. Standards are higher today, so leaders who fear accusations of war crimes have an added inducement to shun indiscriminate attacks.

Choose your own weapon

Who will benefit from new weaponry? Arms considered "asymmetric" provide advantages for technological underdogs, giving them more opportunities to attack a better-equipped foe – much in the way suicide bombers have been used to kill soldiers wielding more sophisticated weaponry. Weaker forces stepped up efforts to obtain asymmetric weapons following the 1991 Gulf war, when it became clear that it would be difficult to fight Western armed forces on their terms. An exported Russian anti-ship missile and a Chinese anti-ship missile in development epitomise this quest for asymmetric advantages. It is easier to hit a warship than to build and defend one.

Russia's Sizzler missile can be launched from a ship, aircraft, submarine, or land battery. It can fly 300km with its final sprint at three times the speed of sound – farther and far faster than the top Western fare. One arms-market consultant describes the Sizzler as "a future kaboom". The missile manoeuvres to avoid being shot down, and American officials fear it could slip through the defences of a sophisticated warship.

The Sizzler has been exported to India and China (where a souped-up version is being developed). At least four other countries have expressed interest in or purchased the Sizzler. Officials decline to reveal if Iran has Sizzlers, which could be launched from its Russian-made Kilo submarines. However, a naval-systems expert with knowledge of the Israel Defence Forces and their operations says that the indications are that Israel believes Iran has the Sizzler. The manufacturer is marketing a four-missile launch package disguised in a commercial shipping container. A non-state group that installed it on a big lorry would secure what is perhaps the most fearsome rogue firepower in history.

China is developing a large anti-ship missile that could upset the military balance of power even more than the Sizzler. The Dong-Feng 21 (literally, "east wind") ballistic missile, with a range of about 1,500km, is being modified to re-enter the atmosphere, diving at about 2km a second, to destroy an aircraft carrier with conventional explosives. Mark Stokes, a former China and Taiwan expert in the office of the US secretary of defence, says a successful test would "send off shockwaves through the international community".

These anti-ship missiles illustrate the tendency of new weapons to spark arms races. Shooting down the Dong-Feng 21 would be difficult, says Mr Stokes, so America has an incentive to develop better spy technologies and weaponry to quickly locate and destroy mobile ground launchers. Submarine construction has boomed, especially in Asia, as surface ships have become more vulnerable. Investment in anti-submarine technology has produced super-fast torpedoes propelled with a rocket instead of a propeller.

Weaponry can be militarily formidable but a political liability. Robert Gates, America's secretary of defence to the end of June 2011, has expressed reluctance to build new carriers because of the increasing threats from anti-ship missiles. Politically, however, the weapons appear to be strengthening America's hand. To China's dismay, some of America's allies in Asia are pressing the United States to step up its defence co-operation and diplomatic activity in the region, says Ramli Nik, a former Malaysian defence attaché to the UN.

Although asymmetric weaponry is apt to give underdogs an edge, rich democracies stand to benefit most, on balance, from other new defence technologies. Western soldiers, accustomed to greater personal freedom than those from authoritarian societies, tend to be innovative problem-solvers good at seizing fleeting opportunities in combat. This cultural factor would not have given Western forces a big advantage in the trench warfare of old, when courage and blind obedience were paramount. (Infantry in the first world war were often given shots of liquor before orders to charge enemy lines.) But much new defence technology, predominantly designed in the West, will increasingly harness the cultural advantage of Western armies.

The West's forte of individual initiative helps explain the trouncing of Syria's aviation during the Lebanon war, says Mr Ivry, the former head of the Israeli air force. Beyond the handicap of fighting with inferior technology, the Syrian pilots were neither permitted, nor mentally prepared, to deviate from rigid Soviet dogfighting doctrine, he says. Israeli pilots were therefore better able to anticipate Syrian manoeuvres. Intelligence was continuously radioed to Israeli pilots, helping them change tactics as they saw fit.

Getting the picture

Technology will increasingly boost soldiers' ability to assimilate intelligence. The US Navy is developing wearable systems to display tactical intelligence superimposed on the real world. The Battlefield Augmented Reality System, as it is called, displays graphics on a see-through visor. As the wearer moves, a computer uses data from a compass, accelerometer, gyroscope and GPS device to reposition the graphics so they "stick" on the right part of the real world. Information displayed could include street names, colour-coded arrows to facilitate an assault or retreat, information about a building's inhabitants, or the location of friendly soldiers on the other side of a wall.

Even the position of a sniper could be displayed: microphone arrays mounted on vehicles and even helmets can triangulate a shooter's location from the sounds of shots and whizzing bullets. Mark Livingston, head of the research at the Naval Research Laboratory in Washington, DC, calls it "X-ray vision". His team has researched "3-D ink" writing methods that would allow soldiers to paint virtual symbols or text on the real world which could be read by soldiers who arrive later. Researchers at the University of Washington in Seattle are even developing "on eye" augmented-reality displays by embedding light-emitting diodes in contact lenses.

NATO soldiers are now receiving so much tactical intelligence that even command chains are being modified, says Jan van Hoof, formerly the top Dutch commander in Afghanistan. Soldiers at the bottom of command chains are being given more freedom to innovate to squeeze greater advantage from fresh intelligence, says Mr van Hoof, now an official at NATO's Joint Air Power Competence Centre in Kalkar, Germany. Russia's army is making improvements in this area, he says, but armed forces in China, North Korea and authoritarian countries in the Middle East remain at a disadvantage.

The advent of defence technologies can raise weighty questions. The MPR-500, an Israeli bomb, can punch through several storeys of a building and explode on a chosen floor. Now that this bomb exists, should an air force be condemned if it flattens a four-storey building housing a target thought to be on the second floor? What if a country makes little effort to gather this sort of detailed targeting information? More broadly, as new precision bombs are produced, should the sale of dumber bombs be increasingly restricted? If a type of bomb has been banned by a weapons convention, can a signatory fight alongside an allied non-signatory that uses the bomb?

In some instances advancing technologies create opportunities for conflict. Countries thought now to have ground-based lasers powerful enough to temporarily "dazzle" remote-sensing satellites include America, Britain, France, Israel, Japan and Russia. French satellites have been temporarily blinded several times by lasers fired from inside China. It appears that the satellites' sensitive optical sensors were not permanently damaged. But had they been, an act that a culprit might claim to be a laser science experiment could be judged by the victim nation to be an act of war.

Political leaders must keep this in mind. The European Space Policy Institute advises politicians not to publicly define the "red line" between a laser flash that merely dazzles a satellite sensor and a beam that, perhaps lingering, actually damages it. Located in Vienna and funded by the Austrian government, the institute provides independent political consulting on space politics to European governments. Kai-Uwe Schrogl, the institute's director, says maintaining face-saving political wriggle room could prevent a failure in a satellite's electronics from triggering armed conflict.

Advanced technology, for all its prowess, cannot guarantee a decisive advantage. Unsophisticated sea mines, for instance, can threaten an aircraft carrier. A former commander of a US Navy air-craft-carrier group, recounting one tense naval patrol in the Middle East, says that he was more worried about mines – which could be pushed off a fishing boat at night – than anti-ship missiles. If fighting has not begun, he says, a commander cannot "put a bubble around the ship" to keep seemingly civilian boats away.

Even faith in technology can be a problem. Foreign salesmen have sold security forces in Afghanistan and Iraq bomb-detection devices that resemble a car antenna on a handle. The wands are supposed to twitch like a divining rod if pointed at explosives, but American officials have called the gizmo a scam. On October 25th 2009 a bomb explosion in Baghdad killed more than 150 people. It later emerged that the bomb had probably been smuggled past a checkpoint where wands were used.

The wands are marketed by "a whole different level of morally offensive immoral" fly-by-night businessmen, says Hal Bidlack, a retired US Air Force lieutenant-colonel who studied the scientific validity of defence co-operation proposals for America's State Department. But without the customers' unqualified belief in the power of technology, the wands would never have been purchased and used.

Mind over matter

In the summer of 1944 German soldiers in Italy began receiving letters offering free morale-boosting sex when they were back in Germany on leave. Soldiers were instructed to stick a logo from the printed letter on a glass while drinking at bars or cafés near train stations. Patriotic members of the Association of Lonely War Women, the letter read, would notice the logo and offer services to support the soldiers' "heroic struggle". At end of the letter, written in German, soldiers were told there was no need to feel guilty: their wives, lovers and sisters back home were similarly lending themselves to the war effort.

The letters had been printed in Rome by America's OSS, a secret service that later became the Central Intelligence Agency. They were a morale-busting weapon of psychological warfare. But there was a problem. Sneaking the letters into the Wehrmacht's postal system was difficult. One method involved dropping mailbags on bombed supply trains. The subversive letters, it was hoped, would eventually be unwittingly mixed in with authentic letters from Germany.

Electronic communications have helped sidestep such message-delivery snags. In the run-up to the 2003 Gulf war, Iraqi commanders received e-mails suggesting that not fighting would be better than dying. During the 2006 war against Hizbullah forces in Lebanon, Israel sent bogus news flashes to mobile phones to demoralise the militia's supporters. Israel also pirated Hizbullah's al-Manar satellite-TV signal and inserted humiliating programming. In efforts to defeat Muammar Qaddafi's forces in Libya, NATO has replaced regime radio with psychological-warfare broadcasting.

"Munitions of the mind" can partly replace physical attacks. Herbert Friedman, a former US Army sergeant-major and psychological-warfare specialist, says that using "psy-ops" to prep the area of a brewing battle results in more surrendering and less killing. A sustained psychological-warfare campaign, he says, helps explain why Iraqi conscripts "just quit in droves" during the first Gulf war. Psychological operations can provide an even greater edge in irregular wars fought "among the people". In such wars, victory involves winning popular support more than militarily dominating clearly defined battlefields, which often do not even exist.

The pursuit of military supremacy has produced horrific technologies. Russia's "Father of All Bombs", the biggest conventional-explosives device publicly known, would flatten many city blocks. Nuclear warheads threaten greater destruction. One type, designed to emit a pulse of electromagnetic energy from above the atmosphere, could fry computers and electronics across a continent. The pulse itself would not kill people, but many millions would die in the first year of societal breakdown following a single detonation above the central United States, according to the EMP Commission, a group assembled by the American Congress to evaluate the threat. The challenge, then, is to ensure that military know-how leads not to such nightmares, but rather to fewer and less deadly conflicts.

PART 1

Land and sea

A SHALLOWLY BURIED BOMB is more deadly in damp soil than in dry soil. Water molecules, being tightly packed, resist compression, so moisture underneath the blast reflects more of its force upwards. Clay soils provide for a bigger punch, too – clay's fine-grained hydrated aluminium silicates also resist compression. Some insurgents in Afghanistan are figuring out these and other fundamentals of soil mechanics, bomb-emplacements suggest, says Steve Holland, head of SJH Projects, a British company that fits blast-absorption armour to the underside of military vehicles. A bomb blast in dry soil that would lift and drop a vehicle might, in wet soil, toss and flip it, he says.

A type of makeshift bomb that takes a different approach uses an explosion to shape a disc of copper into a lump propelled with enough force to smash through tank armour. The upshot is that with a dose of know-how, less-sophisticated technology can become formidable – and especially so in land warfare.

This is one of the points made in the first part of this book, which is a selection of articles about technologies for war on land and at sea, respectively the first and second domains of warfare. (Air, space and computing became the third, fourth and fifth domains of warfare in the 20th century.) The technologies explored are myriad, be it rubber tracks for tanks, light-emitting-diode camouflage or shoulder-fired missiles. They cast light on a wide range of matters, from the emerging "military-consumer complex" to moral quandaries pushed to the surface by technological one-upmanship – as laser guns and an ingenious type of vehicle armour demonstrate.

For millennia new weapons have spurred the development of counter-systems, which have led to counter-counter-systems. From spears, then, to laser guns – "the big new innovation domain today in defence", says Xavier Rolin, a former admiral in the French navy. Laser weaponry is being developed to detonate roadside bombs from afar, shoot down incoming barrages of artillery shells, and protect ships from ever-faster missiles. In mid-2010 Raytheon, an American defence company, demonstrated a ship-mounted laser gun by shooting down a drone.

The moral of the story

Billed as an inexpensive way to destroy inanimate objects, laser guns have been developed with little protest. But the prospect of an invisible laser beam zapping human targets who are cooked and ripped apart in a burst of vapour is more troubling to some than, say, the thought of old-fashioned bullets doing the job. As military technology advances, it often manages to clamber over political or social scruples such as these. But not always: much biological and chemical weaponry has been banned, and few have shown enthusiasm for manufacturing and deploying non-lethal rifles that would use a laser to blind but not kill. A special type of vehicle armour has similarly led to a moral dilemma.

For extra protection, armoured vehicles can be clad in bricks of plastic explosives that detonate if hit with an incoming armour-piercing warhead. This counter-explosion can prevent the penetrating projectile from reaching the crew compartment. But this generates extra shrapnel, which may kill people outside the vehicle. Thus, a quandary: attach explosive bricks to a vehicle to better protect its crew, or forgo bricks to better protect nearby civilians or friendly infantry.

In this matter, the interests of civilians seem to be prevailing. The reluctance of Western military forces to endanger civilians has even prevented sales of a special metal-free explosive brick that produces less shrapnel, says a spokesman for Dynamit Nobel Defence, a German manufacturer. Such concerns, cynics might suggest, are traceable to another sort of technology. Mobile phones with cameras can, in jujitsu fashion, turn what appears to be excessive violence against the attacker in the court of public opinion.

To prepare for sorties in the run-up to the first Gulf war, the US Air Force needed to quickly retrieve about 500 containers on a logistics ship that carried five times as many. But tactical plans had evolved since loading, so the needed containers were not on top. The ship had become an enormous crane-operated Rubik's cube. The puzzle was complicated by the risk of chain-reaction explosions: some containers could not be placed near other containers. Nor could they be offloaded dockside, for the ship, likened to a big powder keg, was unwelcome in Persian Gulf ports. Digging out the containers required 30 days of expensive, around-the-clock crane work.

Eighteen years later, in 2009, a US Navy contractor hired to solve the problem unveiled a solution. BEC Industries, a Florida company, had developed a container-moving crane system that uses combinatorial-mathematics software to work out efficient shuffling patterns, greatly reducing the number of times containers must be moved. An apparently unsensational breakthrough, then, can matter a great deal. In the same vein, naval folding-bridge systems will make it easier to invade a distant country. An invading force has often needed to convince an ally in the region to provide a land base as staging ground. But "seabasing" equipment – including folding bridges that allow vehicles to be rolled from one bobbing vessel to another – reduces the need for a land base in the first place.

Tech-knowledge

Assessing the military technologies of potential belligerents provides clues about who may be emboldened to attack and who is likely to prevail. Such assessment may also reveal shadowy politics behind the machinery of war – thereby promoting peace by honing diplomacy, arms-trade policy and counter-proliferation efforts. Insight into connivance between FARC guerrillas in Colombia and Basque terrorists in Spain, for example, was gained after explosives experts detected the transfer of bomb-making know-how between the groups, says Thierry Vareilles, a former head of a French-army bomb squad.

Technological sleuthing of this sort revealed that much of Iran's nuclear equipment had "nothing to do with boiling water", says Henry Sokolski, a former Pentagon official and member of a congressional group called the Commission on the Prevention of Weapons of Mass Destruction Proliferation and Terrorism. Crucially, stepped-up research into nuclear forensics, especially in America, might even allow a nuclear blast to be linked to the labs where the exploded device was designed or built. (Isotope combinations could serve as "fingerprints".) Fear of retaliation, it is hoped, will discourage would-be proliferators. Detective efforts will become increasingly important. The advent of small and affordable nuclear-power reactors will tempt more countries to develop potentially dangerous nuclear expertise, says Mr Sokolski.

Small nuclear reactors powered warships and submarines long before they became an option for civilian electricity generation. Now at least half a dozen American utilities hope to replace ageing coal furnaces with small nuclear reactors. Defence spending will continue to fuel innovation. Even the success of Israel's tech industry as a whole is partly attributable to obligatory military service. Beyond learning to operate and maintain advanced technology, soldiers are heavily involved in implementing improvements to defence systems, some of them undertaken at their suggestion.

Defence spending can be especially valuable for developing seemingly niche technologies that the market might not otherwise support – a so-called vegetarian robot, perhaps, or lasers that beam up power to solar panels on drones. EATR, a robot being designed with US Department of Defence funding, will munch leaves and grass to combust for energy during long field missions. It could eventually lead to inexpensive home power generators that feed off garden trimmings. Using lasers to transmit power among devices in an industrial plant could be cheaper and safer than installing electrical wiring or keeping batteries charged.

In the coming years innovation will increasingly flow in the opposite direction, too. Money can be saved by modifying or "ruggedising" products such as Apple gadgets and Sony's PlayStation 3 – be it for delivering intelligence to a foot soldier or building a supercomputer. Taxpayers will benefit. Consumer-tech markets move fast, so militaries will see the pace of progress quicken. That is important, because in matters of war, speedy and clever innovation can mean the difference between death and life. The first of the following articles, "Bombs away", makes the point by relating the story of the efforts of America's Central Intelligence Agency to kill insurgent bomb-makers in Iraq with unique "Darwin patrols".

1   Designing, and countering, new weaponry

Bombs away

Military technology: Elaborate new devices designed to defeat makeshift explosives struggle to gain the upper hand in Iraq and Afghanistan

FOR AMERICA'S CENTRAL INTELLIGENCE AGENCY, the glory days of its "Darwin" patrols in Iraq were short-lived. Following the defeat of Saddam Hussein in 2003, the American-led forces faced clever homemade bombs triggered with the remote controls used to open garage doors. So CIA agents drove around transmitting garage-opening signals to blow up any bombmakers who happened to be nearby. This "survival of the fittest" culling, which gave the scheme its nickname, quickly became less effective when the bombers came up with new and better detonators. "We had to keep going back to the drawing board," says a former senior CIA official.

And still the battle continues, with each new bombing advance met by a new countermeasure. As insurgents and terrorists have improved their handiwork, improvised explosive devices (IEDs) have become their most lethal weapons. In Iraq, IEDs are responsible for two-thirds of coalition deaths. In Afghanistan such attacks have roughly tripled in the past two years.

The bombmakers' skills spread rapidly. Thierry Vareilles, a retired colonel in the French army who led bomb-squad missions in a dozen countries, says as soon as one group has come up with "hoax" wiring designed to trick bomb-disposal experts, even distant groups soon start using the treacherous configurations. International travel and the internet help distribute ideas and designs, and not just among groups that share the same ideology.

The right signal

After garage-door triggers, bombers switched to using mobile-phone components to trigger detonators – and from a greater distance. Next, because mobile-phone signals can be randomly delayed or jammed, they turned to long-range cordless phones which do not pass through a telecoms network. Some jamming equipment can scramble these signals, as well as those from mobile phones, but the best kit devours battery power and costs more than €100,000 ($140,000). Also, jamming sometimes wrecks a security force's own communications, a predicament known as "electronic fratricide".

Switching tactics again, the bombmakers reverted to simple triggers that avoid signals altogether. Cheap light sensors can detonate a bomb in a dark room when a door is opened. Colombian terrorists make bombs that detonate when a foot pushes down a concealed syringe that connects a battery-powered circuit. As Colonel John Adams, a US Marine Corps intelligence officer, puts it: "We're always one step behind them."

Rudimentary "contact" detonators, using two wires or metal plates that are pushed together, are now common in Afghanistan, Iraq and elsewhere. American forces fitted some vehicles with extra wheels that protrude from the front (explosions ahead of a vehicle are less destructive than underneath it). But insurgents started placing contact triggers a few meters beyond the bomb. Using powerful vehicle-mounted air blasters, soldiers can search for contact wires by blowing away leaves, sand and soil. But it is not fail-safe.

BAE Systems, a British defence firm, is devising an alternative. It uses a vehicle-mounted camera, object-recognition software and satellite positioning to create detailed 3-D maps of roads, pinpointing features such as pot-holes. When vehicles subsequently pass along the same road the system can spot any new features, such as a rubbish heap or anything else that might hide a bomb. James Baker of BAE, who is working on the project, says defeating IEDs is now the operational priority for Britain's defence ministry.

Many explosives are made of volatile compounds that readily release particles into the air. Equipment that can sniff these vapours could help find bombs. Lynntech, a company based in Texas, is working on a hand-held sniffer which is expected to cost about $20,000 when it is ready in about 2014. It uses a small spectrometer to bounce infrared light off particles in the sample. By analysing the wavelengths of the reflected light it can identify specific chemicals. The company plans to fit these sniffers on airborne drones, too.

At least this technology has some foundation in science. A few years ago an east European company offered the American army a device that resembled a car antenna on a fancy handle. "The story went that somehow this rod and your body generated static electricity" and the antenna would twitch if pointed toward explosives, says a colonel who tested equipment in Baghdad. Once it became clear that this claim would be tested, the vendor was never heard of again.

Nevertheless, wands of this sort became widely used in Iraq and beyond. According to one tally, the Iraqi government purchased more than 1,500 of them from one company at $16,500–60,000 each. It has since emerged that explosives that killed more than 150 people in Baghdad on October 25th 2009 had probably been smuggled through a checkpoint equipped with these wands. Britain has banned exports of such devices and arrested a businessman who was selling them.

Discovering IEDs, however, is not enough; they must then be neutralised. Robots can move them and place explosives to blow them up. But many robots are too big and heavy to be carried by soldiers on foot. QinetiQ, a British firm which makes the widely used Talon robot, has a new lightweight back-packable version called Dragon Runner. It costs more than $150,000.

An alternative is to zap an IED with a laser. The Laser Avenger, which is being developed by Boeing, is a vehicle-mounted system that can slowly heat explosive material from several hundred metres. This can eventually cause a bomb to explode, but with less than half of its usual force.

A simpler contraption has been crafted by the leader of a bomb squad in Cotabato City in the Philippines. Francis Señoron, an army captain, has built "IED disrupters" out of small blasting caps and a water canister the size of a beer can. When positioned close to a device and detonated remotely with a wire, the canister squirts water into the circuitry of the device to short it out. Curious American officials have asked for more details, but Captain Señoron, who hopes to patent his innovation, is keeping it under wraps for now.

Better blast protection helps, too. Mine-resistant ambush-protected vehicles (MRAPs) have V-shaped underbellies to deflect blasts outward. In 2008 America spent more than $16 billion on MRAPs, according to Visiongain, a market-research firm based in London. But some MRAPs weigh more than 30 tonnes, are unwieldy to drive and can damage roads.

A new generation of MRAPs is on its way. These feature suspended seats to protect riders from shockwaves below. The Ocelot, an MRAP built by Force Protection of South Carolina, is made from lighter and stronger steel. At only a quarter of the weight of some vehicles, it also has a new and more effective V-shaped hull and a removable "crew pod" that allows more of a bombed vehicle to be salvaged.

Kevlar airbags may eventually provide even better protection. Survival Consultants International, a small Florida company, is using several layers of Kevlar and other tough materials to design external airbags that would inflate nanoseconds after a blast and absorb some of its force.

Yet as vehicles get tougher, the blasts get fiercer. Already in Afghanistan, Iraq and Pakistan makeshift "explosively formed projectiles" – disks of copper or other metals that are shaped by a blast into a hurtling lump – can smash through some of the toughest armour.

An endless war?

Can technology really win the fight against IEDs? The bombmakers' equipment may appear to be relatively crude, but it is cunning enough to stymie counter-IED systems, admits Wayne Shanks, a spokesman for NATO's International Security Assistance Force in Kabul. Yet Colonel Adams of the NSA sees something that could tip the balance in the army's favour: predictive-analysis software.

Computers are good at determining how myriad variables might affect events. Bombs, for example, are more likely to be planted in damp ground on dark moonless nights in areas where opposition is high. Bombers tend to communicate frequently with certain clerics, drive slowly through potential attack zones and return home without having got out of their cars. Separately these things mean little, but by combining data from hundreds of different sources, software can calculate how probable it is that IEDs have been placed and possibly the area where they are.

Richard Rowe, an American major general in Baghdad, says predictive software is already helping identify terrorists. For example, he says, bombmakers could be spotted if they rent apartments near potential targets to bring apparently harmless IED ingredients past checkpoints, rather than completed bombs.

Capturing or killing bombers may, however, reduce attacks only briefly. The reason for this, says Kenneth Comer, deputy director of intelligence at the Joint IED Defeat Organisation, an American defence agency, is that taking them out of circulation can actually strengthen terror networks by encouraging the remaining members to jostle for power and experiment with new and more lethal techniques. Predictive analysis, he says, often appears to serve as an "evolutionary algorithm" that replaces the weak with others who may be even more capable. If such "survival of the fittest" is really going on, then the technological leap-frogging in the IED war will sadly continue – and only a political settlement will end it.

This article was first published in *The Economist* in March 2010.

Peril on the sea

Naval warfare: As anti-ship missile and torpedo technologies improve, a new seaborne arms race could be on the horizon

THE WEST HAS SOME FORMIDABLE MISSILES designed to sink warships. Three of the most deadly are America's Harpoon, France's Exocet and the Swedish RBS-15. These all fly close to the speed of sound for up to about 200km (124 miles) using precision-guidance systems to skim over land or water. This makes them difficult to detect. And even if they are spotted, the missiles can fly in unpredictable patterns, which makes it harder to shoot them down. They then punch a warhead, weighing as much as 200kg (440lbs), into a moving ship with devastating consequences.

Despite all this, missile defences can be effective. Shooting at missiles with rapid-firing guns, or anti-missile missiles, can bring them down. The incoming missile's electronics can also be scrambled with blasts of electromagnetic radiation, such as microwaves. And decoys can be fired to trick the missile's homing sensors and lure it away from the vessel under attack. But missile attacks on ships are rare, so it is difficult to know just how safe a ship really is – especially if an attacker launches a dozen or so missiles at once.

One particular anti-ship missile has become especially worrying for Western defence chiefs. This is because it is even more fearsome than anything NATO countries and their allies now use. The Russian-made missile is called the Club and it can carry bigger warheads farther than any anti-ship missile the West can launch.

As is the way of NATO nomenclature, the Club has been designated another name, the Sizzler. In some configurations the Sizzler can deliver about 450kg of explosives as far as 300km. It also carries out defensive manoeuvres – even curving around islands – and some lighter versions perform a unique, nasty trick: the warhead separates a few dozen kilometres away and then accelerates from almost the speed of sound to about three times as fast.

Sizzling targets

In early 2009, Timothy Keating, then an admiral in the American navy, told the House Armed Services Committee that America's ability to defeat the Sizzler was uncertain, not least because the military lacked an adequate dummy stand-in for testing defensive systems against such a fast missile. Now one is in the works. Dan McNamara, a manager with the US Navy group developing what is called the Multi-Stage Supersonic Target, says it will help defeat the "groundbreaking" Sizzler. The new missile is expected to be ready in 2014.

The Sizzler is the leading example of a growing class of supersonic cruise missiles designed by non-Western countries. Versions of it, and its competitors, can be launched from submarines, aircraft and vehicles. The Yakhont, a slightly slower Russian missile that also carries a heavy warhead, has been sold to countries including Indonesia and Vietnam. The BrahMos, a joint Indian and Russian upgrade of the Yakhont, comes even closer to matching the Sizzler's effectiveness.

These non-Western supersonic missiles are changing defence thinking. To begin with, uncertainty about ship "survivability" is increasing as missiles proliferate, says Steve Zaloga, a missile expert at Teal Group, an aerospace consultancy in Fairfax, Virginia. China and India already have Sizzlers and countries that have indicated interest in, or bought, the Sizzler or versions of it include Algeria, Syria, the United Arab Emirates and Vietnam. Some think Iran probably has Sizzlers too.

As a rule of thumb, to hit a well-defended modern warship a volley of more than ten subsonic missiles might be needed, according to an expert at Thales, a French defence contractor. How much deadlier might supersonic ones be? Sinking a warship, especially a big one, is unlikely with a single missile, whether supersonic or not. More probably, attackers would score a "mission kill" that limits a ship's ability to fight. In 2006 a subsonic missile fired by Lebanon's Hizbullah militia seriously damaged an Israeli corvette more than 15km offshore. Four sailors were killed.

Hizbullah's success highlights the so-called "asymmetric" element of anti-ship technologies: striking a warship can be far less expensive and complex than operating and defending one. According to Rafael, an Israeli defence contractor, a ship's protection gear often costs as much as its attack weaponry. Missiles are now the "poor man's way" of obtaining sea power, says Nathan Hughes, an analyst at STRAT-FOR, a consultancy in Austin, Texas.

Iran is one country gaining naval power without much in the way of sophisticated ships. It has large numbers of anti-ship missiles which can be launched from small, fast boats or batteries hidden ashore in buildings or trucks. Defence officials are troubled by the prospect of missiles that can be launched from civilian positions. A product designed by Concern Morinformsystem-Agat, the Russian company behind the Sizzler, may heighten such fears. The firm now offers a four-missile launching package hidden inside a standard commercial shipping container. It could be transported on a ship, train or big lorry. Called the Club-K Container Missile System, it provides dangerous potential to rogue forces, says a Western arms-market consultant who has visited the manufacturer's facilities in Russia.

Defensive technologies, of course, will also improve. Sofradir, a French remote-sensing defence contractor, plans to start making a "multichannel" missile-detection system in late 2010. (Early versions are already being tested by potential customers.) It integrates radar, infra-red and visible-light sensors into a single unit. Software can then better assess the quality of data from one channel by comparing it with data from the other two. Such sensing technology should make it easier to "lock onto" (and therefore shoot down) incoming supersonic missiles, especially when they tend to gain altitude to pinpoint a target before dropping down for a final sea-skimming approach, says Philippe Bensussan, Sofradir's chief executive.

From the deep

But there are also threats from below to deal with. The sinking in March 2010 of a South Korean frigate provides a further example of the asymmetric nature of anti-ship weapons: the evidence suggests that it was sunk by a torpedo fired from a North Korean "midget submarine" small enough to hide in shallow water, where it is hard to detect using sonar. North Korea is thought to have supplied such submarines to Iran.

Torpedoes can still be tricked, in many cases, with decoys that emit sound waves to mimic ships. But torpedoes, like missiles, are getting smarter. Their homing and guidance systems are improving. Many torpedoes, once fired, can be controlled via a long optical fibre that remains attached to the submarine to increase accuracy and prevent jamming. And some torpedoes will now circle back if they miss a target on the first pass. At Rafael, the Israeli defence contractor (and a maker of anti-torpedo countermeasures), a spokesman reckons that torpedo effectiveness has roughly doubled in the past decade, also in part because of work carried out in Russia.

Torpedoes rarely travel faster than 100kph because water friction and turbulence could cause them to veer off course or suffer damage. But now speeds can be doubled or even tripled by "cavitating" torpedoes. The trick involves positioning a flat disk, smaller than a DVD, about 10cm in front of the torpedo's nose tip. At high speed the disc vaporises water, creating a steamy air bubble, called a cavity, which envelops the torpedo. This dramatically reduces water drag.

Cavitating torpedoes remain rare, not least because they are problematic. High speeds can make it hard to decipher the sonar signals used for guidance. Propulsion is provided by a rocket engine, rather than a propeller and rudder, which makes steering difficult: some cavitating torpedoes can travel only in a straight line. High pressures deep underwater pose further difficulties, and may have contributed to the sinking of Russia's *Kursk* submarine in 2000, killing all on board. (It sank after an explosion during the testing of a cavitating torpedo called Shkval, or Squall.) A German cavitating torpedo called the Barracuda is thought to be the fastest, but Russia's Shkval is sold more widely.

As ship vulnerability increases navies are buying more submarines, especially in Asia, says Ramli Nik, Malaysia's defence attaché to the United Nations until 2004. Malaysia will receive its second attack submarine by the end of the year, he says. Other countries plan to buy or build more. Australia expects to double its fleet of six; Indonesia aims to expand its fleet from two to 12 and Singapore expects to double its fleet of four. Vietnam has none but plans to have six by 2025. By then, China may have 70 attack submarines. Mr Nik thinks submarines provide the best naval defence platform. With modern remote-sensing kit, they can stealthily "get all the details" of warships, he adds.

Yet warship-building is far from declining. Naval budgets, broadly speaking, are growing because of a big shift in strategy caused in part by improved missile capabilities. Premvir Das, a former commander of India's Eastern Naval Command, says the availability of fast, powerful and accurate cruise missiles is encouraging forces to restructure so that they are better able to conduct, or support, land warfare from the sea. India, he says, will extend the range of its BrahMos missile "quite substantially" beyond its current 300km range.

Even more exotic new weapons could be just over the horizon. About five years ago Pentagon officials learned that Chinese engineers working on a government missile project appeared to have solved a difficult technical challenge involving manoeuvring with radar data. According to Eric McVadon, a retired American rear-admiral, some defence officials began "running around with their hair on fire". China was modifying a medium-range space-faring ballistic missile, the DF-21, so it could re-enter the atmosphere and nosedive, at about two kilometres a second, into a warship and detonate conventional explosives. The new missile could be ready for testing by 2012.

China's missile might be vulnerable, some experts say, to America's newest Aegis intercept missiles, which are launched from ships. But a different type of countermeasure could be even more effective. America and France are among a few countries developing powerful lasers to shoot down missiles. As a former American battle-group commander notes, a nuclear-powered aircraft-carrier generates enough electricity to power a small city, let alone a powerful laser. "Literally, that's ammunition," he says: "directed energy" which can be delivered by laser. And no missile can travel as fast as light.

This article was first published in *The Economist* in June 2010.

Fighting with photons

The most famous weapon of science fiction is rapidly becoming fact

LIKE SO MUCH ELSE IN SCIENCE FICTION, the ray gun was invented by H.G. Wells. In the tentacles of Wells's Martians it was a weapon as unanswerable by earthlings as the Maxim gun in the hands of British troops was unanswerable by Africans. Science fiction, though, it has remained. Neither hand-held pistols nor giant, orbiting anti-missile versions of the weapon have worked. But that is about to change. The first serious battlefield ray gun is now being deployed. And the next generation, now in the laboratory, is coming soon.

The deployed ray gun (or "directed-energy weapon", in the tedious jargon that military men seem compelled to use to describe technology) is known as Zeus. It is not designed to kill. Rather, its purpose is to allow you to remain at a safe distance when you detonate unexploded ordnance, such as the homemade roadside bombs that plague foreign troops in Iraq.

This task now calls for explosives. In practice, that often means using a rocket-propelled grenade, so as not to expose troops to snipers. But rockets are expensive, and sometimes miss their targets. Zeus is effective at a distance of 300 metres, and a laser beam, unlike a rocket, always goes exactly where you point it.

At the moment, there is only one Zeus in the field. It is sitting in the back of a Humvee in an undisclosed theatre of war. But if it proves successful it will, according to Scott McPheeters of the American army's Cruise Missile Defence Systems Project Office for Directed Energy Applications, be joined by a dozen more within a year.

You fight with light?

If Zeus works, it will make soldiers' lives noticeably safer. But what would really make a difference would be the ability to destroy incoming artillery rounds. The Laser Area Defence System, LADS, being developed by Raytheon, is intended to do just that – blowing incoming shells and small rockets apart with laser beams. The targets are tracked by radar and (if they are rockets) by infrared sensors. When they come within range, they are zapped.

If it works, LADS will be a disruptive technology in more senses than one. It will probably supersede Raytheon's Phalanx system, which uses bullets to do the same thing. Phalanx and its competitors require lots of ammunition, and can be overwhelmed by heavy barrages. By contrast, Mike Booen, vice-president of Advanced Missile Defence and Directed Energy Weapons at Raytheon, observes, as long as LADS is supplied with electricity it has "an infinite magazine".

And LADS is merely the most advanced of a group of anti-artillery lasers under development. Though Raytheon is convinced it is on to a winner and is paying for most of the development costs out of its own pocket, it has received some money from the Directed Energy Weapons Programme Office of the American navy. In August 2008, inter-service rivalry reared its head, when the army handed Boeing a $36m contract to develop a similar weapon, known at the moment as the High Energy Laser Technology Demonstrator.

The army's Space and Missile Defence Command is also in the game. Its Joint High Power Solid State Laser, a prototype of which should be ready in summer 2009, is meant to destroy rockets the size of the Katyushas used by insurgents in Afghanistan and Iraq, and by Hizbullah in Lebanon.

The most ambitious laser project of all, though, is the Airborne Laser, or ABL, being developed by the American Missile Defence Agency and Boeing, Lockheed Martin and Northrop Grumman. The beam is generated by mixing chemicals in a reactor known as a COIL (chemical oxygen-iodine laser) and packs a far bigger punch than the electrically generated beams emitted by systems such as LADS. When mounted in the nose-cone of a specially converted Boeing 747, an ABL should be capable of disabling a missile from a distance of several hundred kilometres.

The aim is to hit large ballistic missiles, including ICBMs, just after they are launched – in the boost phase. The ABL is therefore a son of Ronald Reagan's Star Wars scheme, although in that programme, which dates back to the 1980s, the lasers would have operated from space.

There are many advantages to attacking a missile during its boost phase. First, it is still travelling slowly, so it is easier to hit. Second, it is easy to detect because of its exhaust plume (once the boost phase is over, the engine switches off and the missile follows Newton's law of gravity to its target). Third, if it has boosters that are designed to be jettisoned, it will be a larger target when it is launched. Fourth, any debris will fall on those who launched it, rather than those at whom it was aimed.

Getting the system to work in practice will be hard, though. A missile launch is observed using an infrared detector. Then the missile must be tracked. When the beam fires, the control system must compensate both for aircraft jitter and for distortions in the beam's path caused by atmospheric conditions. And ABL-carrying planes must be in the right place at the right time in the first place. Even so, a number of tests have been carried out, and according to Colonel Robert McMurry, the head of the Airborne Laser Programme Office at Kirtland Air Force Base in New Mexico, there will be a full-scale attempt to shoot down a boost-phase missile off the coast of California in summer 2009.

All of which is good news, at least for countries able to deploy the new hardware. But wars are not won by defence alone. What people in the business are more coy about discussing is the offensive use of lasers. At least one such system is under development, though. The aeroplane-mounted Advanced Tactical Laser, or ATL, another chemical laser being put together by Boeing and the American air force, is designed to "neutralise" targets on the ground from a distance of several kilometres. Targeting data will be provided by telescopic cameras on the aircraft, by pictures from satellites and unmanned aerial drones, and by human target-spotters on the ground. The question is: what targets?

The ATL's supporters discuss such possibilities as disabling vehicles by destroying their wheels and disrupting enemy communications by severing telephone lines. Killing troops is rarely mentioned. However, John Pike, the director of GlobalSecurity.org, a military think-tank in Alexandria, Virginia, who is an expert on ATL, says its main goal is, indeed, to kill enemy combatants.

Surely this is forbidden?

Boeing is unwilling to discuss the matter and John Wachs, the head of the Space and Missile Defence Command's Directed Energy Division, observes that it is "politically sensitive". The public may have misgivings about a silent and invisible weapon that would boil the body's fluids before tearing it apart in a burst of vapour.

That seems oddly squeamish, though. War is not a pleasant business. It is doubtful that being burst by a laser is worse than being hit by a burst from a machine gun. As the Sudanese found out at the Battle of Omdurman in 1898, the year that "The War of the Worlds" was published, that is pretty nasty too.

This article was first published in *The Economist* in October 2008.

All at sea

Foreign military bases have both political and practical difficulties. "Seabasing" may offer a solution

BASING TROOPS AND EQUIPMENT on foreign soil is fraught with difficulty. Even friendly countries can cut up rough at crucial moments, as America found when Turkey restricted the use of its territory and airspace during the invasion of Iraq in 2003. In an occupied country the situation is worse, as a base is a magnet for attacks. Nor can you always put your base where you need it. If a country does not want to host it, and cannot be bribed to, that – short of invasion – is that.

But no one owns the high seas, and partisans rarely have access to serious naval power. So America, still the world's only superpower and thus the one with most need for foreign bases, is investigating the idea of building military bases on the ocean. They would, in effect, be composed of parts that can be rearranged like giant Lego bricks. The armed forces could assemble them when needed, add to them, subtract from them and eventually dismantle them when they are no longer required – and all without leaving a trace.

Constructing such bases is a formidable technological challenge. Not only do you have to provide quarters for servicemen, but you also have to handle, store and retrieve large amounts of supplies and weapons without access to dockside cranes. Shuffling the containers carrying these, so that those needed immediately are accessible, is akin to solving a moving-block puzzle where the blocks weigh many tonnes each. But America seems committed to the idea, and the first seabases should be deployable within a decade.

Basic thinking

The original approach to seabasing was extremely Legolike. Modular rafts – platforms mounted on pontoons – would be linked together by hinges to create large, flattish surfaces that could nevertheless bend with the waves. Such a system was tested in a peacetime operation off the coast of Liberia in spring 2008. Instead of armaments, hospital supplies and the materials to build a school were unloaded from a ship to the platform, and thence to landing craft which disgorged them onto a beach.

The experiment worked, but there are doubts about taking it any further. One question is how such a raft of rafts would stand up to severe weather. There is also scepticism about whether the original goal, a surface large enough to create a floating runway that could accommodate transport aircraft, is either financially or physically feasible. It would be far larger than the largest aircraft-carrier now afloat, and thus expensive to build, and it would have to be both rigid and stable enough to act as a runway and flexible enough to withstand rough seas. The difficulty of squaring these requirements has led designers to abandon the idea of strict modularity in favour of a system that uses an array of more conventional but still specially designed ships. According to Robert Button, a seabasing expert at the RAND Corporation, a think-tank, America's navy plans to build 35 ships designed for seabasing over the next decade.

The core of such a ship-based seabase would be something known, in the strangulated jargon beloved of military men, as the Maritime Pre-Positioning Force (Future). America's marines already use pre-positioning supply ships as floating warehouses. The 14 ships in the new replacement class will continue to store supplies in this way. But, in addition, they will have room to berth 2,000 servicemen, or between 20 and 30 vertical-take-off aircraft, or hundreds of ground vehicles. More impressively, each ship will carry a folding bridge, about 30 metres long, to connect it to its neighbour. These bridges – regarded as the linchpins of seabasing – will remain stable in swells of up to 2 metres. They will allow vehicles the size of lorries to drive from one ship to another.

A second element of this form of seabasing is the "mobile landing platform" (MLP), a ship longer than two football pitches, with a large, flat platform. This will make it easier for other vessels, including pre-positioning ships, to load the MLP at sea using cranes and bridges. It will accommodate almost 1,500 servicemen, and ferry them to combat zones along with at least six small landing craft or hovercraft, numerous tanks and lorries, and a small number of vertical-take-off aircraft. One feature of an MLP will be that it can partially submerge itself by pumping water into tanks within its hull. Hovercraft will therefore be able to embark and disembark easily. And a modern hovercraft can carry an Abrams tank, America's heaviest, at a speed of 40 knots.

The cleverest part of a new type of seabase, though, is the mundane matter of having a place for everything, and everything in its place. Most of the stuff on the base will be kept in standard shipping containers until required. War being war, though, it is not always obvious in advance what will be needed when. And if you find that some crucial piece of equipment is in the middle of the bottom of a stack rather than the edge of the top, and you need it in a hurry, you have a problem.

Logistics, logistics, logistics

To deal with this geometric puzzle the defence department paid BEC Industries, an engineering firm based in Florida, to design a special container-management system. The firm completed this system, known as GRID, in February 2009.

In essence, GRID is a way of unburying containers. A winch shuttles back and forth, and side to side, on a grid of rails above stacks of containers. The equipment works rapidly, repositioning half a dozen containers in ten minutes. (A traditional crane might move that many in an hour.) Software determines the most efficient way to rearrange them. Removing just two dozen containers from stacks aligned in rows can involve hundreds of repositionings. Each decision about which container to move next, and where to place it, has implications for the number of times all the other containers must be moved later. According to Brian Pfeifer, the project's chief engineer, working out the shuffling logic was the most complex part of the project. The first example of GRID will be installed on a warship during 2009.

Cranes will still be needed, though, to load the pre-positioning ships from supply vessels. That is always going to be tricky in anything other than a dead calm. As Ed May, a crane expert at Oceaneering International, an engineering company based in Houston, Texas, observes, the trick is for the crane operator to wait until the ships' movements position the load over the right spot, and then "set it down real quick". Or, in non-technical jargon, drop it.

Dropping it accurately may also be easier in the future. By measuring the motions of nearby waves and vessels with radar and lasers, the software running a crane can predict exactly how a ship will be pushed, and react accordingly. A crane developed by America's Office of Naval Research (ONR) in collaboration with Oceaneering and Siemens, a German industrial giant, automatically adjusts its position to compensate for ship movements the moment they begin. The ONR will test the system at sea in autumn 2009.

"Logistics, logistics, logistics" is a mantra of seabasing. It is, perhaps, a less catchy slogan than "shock and awe". But warfare – or even a formidable threat to attack – begins with the movement and stationing of troops and kit. If you can bring your own base with you, that threat is more credible and easier to make.

This article was first published in *The Economist* in April 2009.

The armour strikes back

Military technology: Better protection systems based on a range of new technologies are helping to keep armoured vehicles in the fight

IN THE FIRST FEW DAYS of the Yom Kippur war in October 1973, Israeli armoured units were attacked by Egyptian forces armed with Soviet-made anti-tank missiles. The Israelis "suffered wholesale destruction", according to an American army manual written soon afterwards to help counter the weapon in question. There was not much that could be done. As the guide noted, the missile system – called Sagger by Western forces – could be carried in a suitcase, launched and steered by a joystick to hit a target 3km (1.9 miles) away. It would then penetrate any vehicle armour in existence.

Tanks had been destroyed with weapons carried by foot soldiers before; America introduced its M1 Bazooka during the second world war. But never had infantry so decimated armoured vehicles. Of Israel's roughly 2,120 tanks, about 840 were destroyed during the 20-day war. The era when "the tank was king" had ended, says Keith Brendley, head of Artis, an American firm that develops protection systems for military vehicles. Since then anti-tank munitions have become even more powerful, but steel armours have improved little. Now, however, aided with new materials and advanced sensors, a promising and eclectic array of alternative and often ingenious new forms of armour is emerging.

Anti-tank missiles and rocket-propelled grenades (RPGs) penetrate armour with a shaped charge. This explodes after the tip of the warhead has sunk into the target. The brunt of the blast is projected straight ahead, forcing a powerful spike of metal, usually copper, into and through the armour. Using steel alone, few vehicles today could carry enough armour to stop even an inexpensive RPG reliably.

Armour that explodes? Yes, really

To provide added protection, engineers have developed explosive-reactive armour. This involves covering parts of a vehicle with bricks of plastic explosives sandwiched between metal plates. When a warhead hits the outer metal plate, the explosives underneath (also specially shaped) detonate and force the sandwich to rapidly bulge as the plates move apart. This can shear the armour-piercing spike into bits, which are then less likely to pierce the underlying armour.

The Israel Defence Forces, shaken by their losses during the Yom Kippur war, developed an early but effective explosive-reactive armour that kept tank losses exceptionally light during the 1982 Lebanon war. The innovation, however, created a new problem: the explosive bricks generate shrapnel which can kill nearby infantry or civilians. As a result, when America's Bradley and Stryker fighting vehicles are clad in explosive-reactive armour they are not used in civilian areas.

Dynamit Nobel Defence, based in Burbach, Germany, is marketing a new metal-free explosive armour, called CLARA, that limits the number of such flying fragments. (The replacement materials are secret.) But no military has purchased it. Defence officials with one western European government have expressed concern that the extra protection to their armoured-vehicle crews would come at too great a cost: even explosive armours that produce less shrapnel could unacceptably endanger people near vehicles. Peter Lehniger of Dynamit Nobel Defence concedes that the armour "may not be, from a moral point of view, a good trade-off".

Engineers are finding ways to use less explosive material. OJSC NII Stali, a Russian manufacturer, claims that by 2008 its reactive armour required only a quarter of the amount of explosives used in its 1999 version, but provided just as much protection. The earlier model's explosives detonated three to five microseconds after a warhead strike. Such "sluggishness", according to the firm, has been eliminated, reducing the penetrating power of the spike. A danger, however, is that faster-reacting, more-sensitive explosives might detonate accidentally if hit by a bullet or another vehicle.

OJSC NII Stali and others are now developing non-explosive

reactive armour, known as NxRA. This uses "energetic" but non-detonating rubber-like materials. Sandwiched between hard plates, they discharge a rapidly expanding gas to absorb energy from a warhead. The gas pushes out the external layer of armour so that it encounters the emerging spike at a glancing angle. "Bulging armour", as this system is sometimes called, also increases the distance a spike must travel to enter the crew compartment.

Non-explosive reactive armours typically provide less stopping power, but they have an advantage in countering "tandem charge" munitions from systems like America's shoulder-launched Javelin and aircraft-launched Hellfire missiles. Once a brick of explosive armour detonates, that spot becomes more vulnerable to a second charge carried towards the rear of the same munition and detonated about 500 microseconds later. Rubbery non-explosive armour, in contrast, often remains partially intact. So-called "cage" armour can provide additional protection against tandem charges: metal bars (or even a strong fabric-like material) can make a warhead's first charge detonate a couple of dozen centimetres away from the vehicle.

With a clean hit, the Russian-made RPG-7, the most widely used anti-tank weapon, can sometimes penetrate more than 25cm of solid steel. A more recent model, the RPG-29, is even more formidable. To counter it, some European Union countries are developing electric armour. This consists of two electrically charged metal plates separated by an insulating layer. The idea is that when hit, the metal in a projectile shorts the two charged plates together, forming a circuit and releasing a surge of electricity which can break the warhead up.

Antoine Vincent, in charge of electric armour for the European Defence Agency (EDA), says it has tested well against RPGs. A study by BMT Defence Services, a British firm, notes that electric armour, being lightweight, makes it easier to airlift vehicles. Even so, neither BMT nor the EDA think the technology will be deployed soon. It has proven difficult to rearm the metal plates from batteries fast enough to zap the second charge of a tandem warhead. Some of the power-management technologies being developed for electric vehicles may help on that front. But, says Mr Vincent, electric armour still does not deliver enough electricity to fry the metal in many kinetic-energy projectiles, which destroy armour with their impact. An RPG warhead may eject a copper spike weighing several hundred grams. Kinetic-energy projectiles can weigh several kilograms.

Another approach is to use new materials. Steel armour performs well against a powerful, broad blast, but if the energy is focused on a small spot the metal can "melt like butter", says an engineer with an American manufacturer of armoured vehicles. To cope with that, scientists have developed hard ceramic composites made from rubber and epoxy resins. Unlike steel, they respond to tremendous pressure by snapping. This action can break up a projectile or a shaped charge. A ceramic armour called Dorchester Level 2, used on British Challenger 2 tanks, is reportedly at least three times as resistant to some strikes as the same weight of steel.

The shockwave from a buried "improvised explosive device" (IED) can tear into or toss a vehicle. SJH Projects, a small British company, has developed a so-called "stone sponge" material that, fixed to a vehicle's undercarriage, partially absorbs the blast. XPT, as it is called, is a roughly 2cm-thick sheet of silica particles glued together with a strong, heat-resistant resin. Small pores, visible with a magnifying glass, channel the blast into mazes of micro-chambers. As they are destroyed, the blast-energy is absorbed. It costs about $17,000 to protect a jeep-sized vehicle using XPT, and it only works once. Steve Holland, the owner of SJH Projects, says NATO trials with crash-test dummies show that the material dramatically reduces spine and skeletal injuries.

Does this mean armour is catching up with weapons technology? Hardly. Armour is getting better, but weapons are getting deadlier. Consider the Panzerfaust 3 (literally, "tankfist"), a shoulder-fired anti-tank guided missile that flies at more than 720kph (450mph). After striking its target, the exploding warhead shoots out a spike of copper at more than 7km a second (25,200kph) with enough energy to blast through a metre of steel, or any armoured vehicle used today, according to its manufacturer, Dynamit Noble Defence. (Like many defence suppliers, it makes both weapons and anti-weapon systems.)

Moreover, some munitions can kill a tank crew without even penetrating the armour. A high-explosive munition known as "squash head", fired by some British tanks, flattens a ball of plastic explosives against an armoured vehicle. It immediately explodes, transmitting a compression shock wave into the crew compartment, where it strips off "spall" – flakes of metal, some the size of a frisbee, that fly into occupants. Summing up the outlook for vehicle survivability, Stuart Wheeler, an armour expert at the Tank Museum in Bovington, England, says: "It looks grim." Armour and vehicle designers, he says, are still looking for a comeback.

Fight fire with fire

It may be on the way. On March 1st 2011 an RPG was fired at an Israeli tank patrolling near the Gaza Strip security barrier. A radar system on the tank tracked the incoming warhead, feeding data to a computerised gun that shot it down with a small burst of projectiles. Israel plans to deploy the system, called Trophy, more widely. Daniel Klein, an armaments official at the EDA, reckons that the foiled attack, probably the first of its kind, bodes well for defending military vehicles. An additional benefit, he believes, is that Trophy and other so-called "active protection" systems are lightweight. Some modern military vehicles have become so heavy with armour that their manoeuvrability is impaired and they are unable to use certain roads and bridges.

Iron Curtain, another active-protection system, has been developed for American forces by Artis. It uses radar and optical sensors to calculate the trajectory of an incoming warhead, and then intercepts it with a projectile fired from a roof-rack. The impact causes the warhead to combust before it hits the armour. Mr Lehniger, of Dynamit Nobel Defence, says that Iron Curtain and its ilk might be able to defeat his firm's Panzerfaust 3 missile. If so, the achievement will be especially instructive to those who, decades ago, considered protecting vehicles to be a doomed endeavour.

This article was first published in *The Economist* in June 2011.

2   Upgrades for combatants

Fluid defences
Body armour can be made lighter and stronger using special liquids

A SUIT OF ARMOUR that is lightweight and flexible, yet capable of absorbing the impact of a bullet, is an idea that seems to come from the future – a bit like the liquid skin of the cyborg in "The Terminator". However, for a number of years researchers have been investigating materials that might be able to provide such protection. Now BAE Systems, a British defence contractor, seems close to turning such "liquid armour" into reality.

In tests at the company's Advanced Technology Centre, in Bristol, liquid armour has been used to construct a material that is thinner than normal body armour and yet is able to stop a low-velocity bullet. Work is now under way to see if it can also stop more powerful bullets. If these tests are successful, liquid armour could furnish soldiers with protective clothing that is more comfortable and less cumbersome than existing body armour, and provides them with greater protection.

Liquid armour relies on the properties of materials called shear-thickening fluids. The molecules in such liquids are closely packed, but loosely arranged. The result behaves like a liquid in normal conditions, and is able to flow. If subjected to pressure, though, the molecules lock together and the result behaves like a solid. The gooey substance produced by mixing cornstarch with a little water is a commonplace example of such a material. This flows like a liquid when poured yet, if hit with a spoon, reacts like a solid.

Researchers at the University of Delaware developed shear-thickening fluids for use as liquid armour almost ten years ago. Several military laboratories and defence firms have worked on them since then. Among them was Armour Holdings, an American company that BAE took over in 2007.

The fluid that Armour Holdings worked on is a liquid polymer containing nano-engineered particles of silica, though BAE is coy about the details of what it is using. The new armour is not pure liquid, of course. Rather, the fluid is sandwiched between layers of Kevlar, a high-strength polymer commonly employed in protective gear. When the sandwich is struck by a bullet, the locking together of the molecules in the fluid spreads the load across a wide area, allowing the material to absorb more of the impact. It also distorts less than conventional body armour when it is hit. That means it is less likely to cause serious injury by deflecting inward.

Standard body-armour contains around 30 layers of Kevlar. The material being tested by BAE has only ten Kevlar layers. BAE therefore thinks it may be possible to build body-protection suits that are only around half as thick as existing ones, but still able to offer greater protection. Soldiers would find that a welcome relief.

This article was first published in *The Economist* in August 2010.

How to disappear

Military technology: Advances in camouflage, concealment and deception are revolutionising an age-old art of warfare

AS A SPECIAL-FORCES AGENT in the French navy, Michel Malalo has clandestinely entered several African countries by sea to extract endangered French nationals. Almost all the enemy fighters he encountered carried the AK-47, a widely used assault rifle renowned for its rugged reliability. But the AK-47 has a serious drawback: glint, which gave Mr Malalo an advantage in firefights. Made with steel, the AK-47 reflects light. "It's flashy – and from afar," says Mr Malalo, who took advantage of glint giveaways when shooting at the enemy. Mr Malalo, who left the special forces uninjured six years ago, says the French assault rifle, the Famas, is superbly non-reflective even in bright light.

Developing new metal alloys to reduce rifle glint is just one facet of the effort to develop better camouflage, concealment and deception technologies that is under way at defence contractors, military research bodies and university laboratories. Most of this research is being conducted in America and Europe. Much is classified. The results are often remarkable.

Even the most common form of camouflage – the coloured patterns printed onto combat fatigues – is being given a high-tech twist, as designers work with new software that incorporates neuroscientists' understanding of human vision. Pattern-generation software analyses a large number of photographs of a given theatre of operations. By crunching meteorological data on typical lighting and visibility conditions, combined with information about the colours and predominance of shapes visible in cities, fields and wilderness areas, the software proposes new, improved patterns. "It really does get technical," says Réjean Duchesneau, a lieutenant-colonel with NATO in Casteau, Belgium, who helped design a Canadian camouflage pattern called CADPAT.

Some camouflage designers, including those at America's Army

Research Laboratory, also study the reflective and light-absorbing properties of materials common to an area, such as sand, cement and foliage. As well as being used by the camouflage-generation software, this information is used to manufacture fabric inks with the desired optical properties. Similar software optimises colours and patterns for vehicles and aircraft. The ability to customise camouflage for particular theatres has increased the use of temporary camouflage, which is painted on hardware before missions and washed off afterwards.

For decades most fatigues, now referred to as battledress uniforms, incorporated wiggly patterns of solid colours known as tiger stripes. But research in the field of "clutter metrics" – the study of how well observers locate and identify objects – has now discredited tiger stripes. With the help of eye-tracking devices that follow iris movements to determine where subjects are looking, researchers have determined that fabrics with small squares of colour, known as pixels, are harder to see. These new pixel patterns are now worn by many Western armies, including those of the United States, Britain, Canada, France and Germany. Canada has improved its camouflage so much in recent years that to spot soldiers in some conditions, observers must be 40% closer than they would have to have been in 2000.

"Adaptive" camouflage that changes rapidly in response to the environment is also in the works. TNO, a Dutch defence contractor based in Soesterberg, is using thin, textile-like plastic sheets embedded with light-emitting diodes (LEDs). A small camera scans the environment, and the colours and patterns displayed on the sheet are changed accordingly. The material is not yet flexible enough to be worn comfortably by soldiers, but it is being tested in Afghanistan with Saab Barracuda, a Swedish maker of camouflage equipment.

Pieter Jacobs, TNO's chief technologist, says the defence ministries of Canada, Germany and the Netherlands, which have funded the development of the technology, consider such "chameleon" sheeting to be an urgent requirement. Maarten Hogervorst, a vision neuroscientist at TNO, says its performance is formidable. A tank draped with the sheeting and parked in front of a grassy slope displays an image of grass on its exposed side, for example.

Another kind of adaptive camouflage is based on flexible plastic decals. A small camera, powered by a solar cell, senses the colours and patterns of the surroundings. The surface of the decal is a crude computer display which then replicates these colours and patterns. The US Army wants to use this approach to wrap artillery and munitions containers. Daniel Watts, who leads the project at the New Jersey Institute of Technology (NJIT), says it works well but is still too expensive for battlefield use.

Some like it hot

Concealing things on the battlefield does not just mean hiding them visually. A lot of research is also being done to reduce thermal signatures, too. Infra-red and thermal-vision equipment can reveal a soldier's heat signature at a large distance. Such equipment is becoming less expensive and is now so readily available that the Taliban in Afghanistan are well equipped with it – unlike a few years ago, says Hans Kariis, a senior technologist at the Swedish Defence Research Agency, a government body in Stockholm.

Fabrics designed to block human heat-signatures are improving rapidly. John Roos, a retired US Army colonel in Newport News, Virginia, observed a night-time test of an infra-red "stealth" poncho developed by AAE, a small defence contractor based in Fullerton, California. It was the most impressive infra-red protection he had seen. The man disappeared like "a black void", Mr Roos says. (The head of AAE, Rashid Zeineh, declined to discuss the fabric's composition.)

America's existing heat-blocking garments already provide a remarkable combat advantage, says Mr Roos. They are similar, but inferior, to the AAE stealth poncho, he says. During some night operations, American soldiers may be heard approaching while remaining concealed in the dark. "You can imagine what that would do to enemy morale," Mr Roos says.

One way to block body-heat signatures is to use particles called cenospheres – tiny hollow spheres of aluminium and silica that can be woven into fabrics. A leader in the field, Ceno Technologies, in Buffalo, New York, is developing a cenosphere body-paint for the face and hands which does not block necessary perspiration. Britain's Ministry of Defence is testing it.

Researchers at the NJIT, meanwhile, have developed insulating decals that can be applied to hot objects – even firing artillery cannons – to mask their heat signatures. Even if the heat signature cannot be concealed entirely, decals can be placed so that they alter the signature's shape. Mr Watts says his team has been successful in partially insulating tanks so that observers with night vision see the shape of a car.

This is a useful trick, because entirely eliminating a vehicle's heat-signature can be extremely difficult. Intermat, a Greek supplier of concealment materials to defence contractors including British Aerospace, Lockheed Martin and Thales, produces a foam coating that also smothers heat signatures. Bill Filis of Intermat says that selectively applying a one-centimetre layer of heat-insulating foam can make an armoured personnel-carrier resemble a motorcycle when viewed through thermal-vision goggles. "Make him wonder, and this buys you time," Mr Filis says.

Some thermal coatings are as thin as a coat of paint, so they can be applied to aircraft. But warplanes present an additional problem. When flying high to avoid anti-aircraft fire, white condensation trails, or "contrails", can form "a giant arrow in the sky pointing to where the plane is," says Charles Kolb, chief executive of Aerodyne Research in Billerica, Massachusetts. Researchers at the firm, which is a contractor to America's air force, are examining the thermodynamic processes that lead to the formation of contrails, in the hope of reducing them using chemical additives.

Even as people, weapons and vehicles become harder to spot, however, new detection technologies are also being developed. In the spring of 1999 NATO warplanes flew more than 38,000 sorties over Serbia, in a bombing campaign that succeeded in pushing Serbian forces out of Kosovo. But surprisingly little damage was done to Serbian materiel. Duped NATO pilots had destroyed dummy tanks, artillery and other items of military hardware made out of wood and tarpaulins. Much of Serbia's real military kit was hidden safely under foliage, which interferes with standard radar.

Engineers at Lockheed Martin, a large American defence contractor, have designed a radar system called FOPEN, short for foliage penetration. It became operational in 2005, but still requires further development and is deployed on just one active American warplane so far. But Lockheed Martin's FOPEN programme manager, Robert Robertson, says the radar "will see whatever man made" under a leafy triple canopy, or under netting designed to foil conventional radar systems.

"Stealth" aircraft, designed to avoid detection by radar, have been around since the 1970s. Radar systems illuminate the target with radio waves and then look for reflections, so absorbing incoming radiation, or deflecting it in a totally different direction, can shrink an aircraft's radar signature dramatically. Half a dozen countries now build stealth aircraft, at great expense.

A new type of radar system, however, is capable of spotting such aircraft. It relies on the proliferation of mobile-phone signals. When a plane flies through an environment filled with such signals, the "aircraft shadow in this chatter" becomes visible, says John Pendry, a radar expert at Imperial College in London. Mike Burns, the president of MSE, a small defence contractor in Billerica, Massachusetts, says stealth bombers have indeed been detected against backgrounds of mobile-phone radiation because "a hole" appears in the constant chatter of signals.

This technique can be used only in populated areas, with lots of mobile phones. But it has an edge over standard radar, in addition to being able to spot previously invisible aircraft. It is "passive", because it uses ambient radiation to illuminate the target. This means the target aircraft cannot tell that it is being watched (whereas it can with traditional radar). In short, it is the radar-detection system, rather than the aircraft, that has become invisible. It is just the latest example of the arms race between concealment and detection.

This article was first published in *The Economist* in September 2008.

Caught in a BEAR hug

Robotics: A newly designed robot can recover casualties from battlefields, and might also be able to make itself useful to soldiers in other ways

KILLING A SOLDIER removes one enemy from the fray. Wounding him removes three: the victim and the two who have to carry him from the battlefield. That cynical calculation lies behind the design of many weapons that are intended to incapacitate rather than annihilate. But robotics may change the equation.

The Battlefield Extraction-Assist Robot, or BEAR for short, is, in the words of Gary Gilbert of the United States Army's Telemedicine and Advanced Technology Research Centre (TATRC), "a highly agile and powerful mobile robot capable of lifting and carrying a combat casualty from a hazardous area across uneven terrain". When it is not saving lives, it can perform difficult and repetitive tasks, such as loading and unloading ammunition.

The current prototype BEAR is a small, tracked vehicle with two hydraulic arms and a set of video cameras that provide a view of its surroundings to its operator via a wireless link. It has been developed by TATRC in collaboration with Vecna Technologies, a company based in Maryland that invented the robot. Daniel Theobald, BEAR's inventor and Vecna's boss, says versatility is at the heart of the robot's design. "It would be completely impractical if you had robots with a sole duty to rescue soldiers, because they would spend most of their time unused," he says. "The whole idea from the start was to design a general-purpose robot."

The BEAR's operator can control the robot in two ways. One, a joystick, can be embedded into the grip of a rifle and manoeuvred by the soldier's fingertip when he is holding his weapon to his shoulder. The advantage of this is that he does not need to put his gun down to rescue his comrades. The other means of control, a special glove designed by AnthroTronix, another Maryland firm, can sense the wearer's hand movements and direct the BEAR accordingly. If, for example, the gloved hand moves to the left, the robot will follow. If the hand moves backwards, the robot will slow down or stop. If the glove's wearer closes his fist, the robot takes that as an instruction to grip an object with its arms.

The BEAR has been tested at the army's Infantry Centre Manoeuvre Battle Laboratory in Fort Benning, Georgia. It has shown that it can travel at around 12mph (19kph) across a flat surface. It can also move over soil, sand and gravel, through trees and inside buildings, albeit at lower speeds. Several more years of tests are planned (this is the army, after all), but Mr Gilbert is optimistic that BEAR will come through them. If it does, soldiers will be able to get on with their primary job of killing the enemy, without having to worry so much about what the enemy has done to their friends.

This article was first published in *The Economist* in March 2011.

Peering into the future

A contact lens that could put names to faces and guide soldiers in combat

SINCE THE LATE 19TH CENTURY, people with imperfect vision have been able to use contact lenses to improve their eyesight. In the early days these lenses were made of glass and could perform only simple visual corrections. Now they are usually made of plastic and can be moulded into the more complex shapes appropriate to those who suffer from astigmatism or who require bifocals. They can also be tinted, for people who wish to change the colour of their eyes. Yet the main purpose of even the most sophisticated contact lens remains what it always has been: to improve a person's sight. That is about to change.

Researchers at the University of Washington, in Seattle, led by Babak Parviz, have incorporated electronic circuitry into a plastic lens, including light-emitting diodes (LEDs) for "on eye" displays, transistors for computing, a radio for wireless communication and an antenna for collecting power from a radio source, such as a mobile phone, in a person's pocket.

Making a "smart" lens like this is not easy. Electronic components are usually manufactured at temperatures which would melt plastic and are made of materials that do not naturally adhere to a contact lens's plastic. Dr Parviz and his colleagues have therefore designed a lens that is peppered with small wells, ten microns deep, that are connected by a network of tiny metal wires. Each well is sculpted so that a component of a particular shape will fit snugly into it and, at its bottom, it contains a small amount of an alloy with a low melting-point. In addition, wells that will accommodate LEDs must be fitted with microlenses to focus the light from the LED in a way that the eye can cope with.

The components are manufactured individually and suspended in a liquid. This suspension is then washed over the lens, allowing the components to blunder into holes of the appropriate shape, where they stay put. The alloy is then gently heated, melting the alloy and connecting the components to the wires and thus to one another.

The researchers say that the resulting circuitry requires so little power that it does not produce enough heat to cause discomfort. And although Dr Parviz has not, himself, worn the lens, he has tested it on rabbits – and the animals do not seem to find it uncomfortable.

So far, the prototype's display is rudimentary: it consists of a single LED. However, Dr Parviz and his colleagues are working on a lens that can accommodate an eight-by-eight array of LEDs. They are also exploring a design which produces images using tiny shutters, in the manner of a liquid-crystal display. The prototype contains a small radio chip and antenna so that it can be powered without wires. The power system taps into the mobile-phone frequencies in the 900-megahertz to 6-gigahertz range and draws about 100 microwatts of power.

What the display will show, of course, is up to the imagination – the name, perhaps, of someone the wearer has met but does not recall, or the street directions in an unfamiliar city. Or, perhaps, the quickest route to a target that needs destroying. For this sort of technology surely has military applications as well.

This article was first published in *The Economist* in September 2009.

3 Powering up, differently

Munching machines

Robotics: A vegetarian robot that forages for fuel and runs on steam power would have a range of military and civilian uses

A ROBOT WITH DIETARY REQUIREMENTS might sound a bit far fetched, but a team of American researchers is developing a machine that will fend for itself by gathering biomass (wood, leaves and grass) to be used as a biofuel to run its steam-driven engine. Who might want such a device? The American army.

The Energetically Autonomous Tactical Robot is known, of course, by its acronym: EATR. It is the brainchild of Robotic Technology of Washington, DC. So far it is only a concept, but a working prototype is in the works. The research, in part funded by America's Defence Advanced Research Projects Agency, is seen as a way to help soldiers reduce their dependence on fuel supplies. The robot could, for instance, forage for biofuel while a unit on a long-endurance mission rested. It could then be used to recharge their electrical devices, carry some of their equipment or even transport the soldiers.

The EATR uses a robotic arm to gather and prepare vegetation, which it feeds through a shredder into a centrifugal combustion chamber, where it is ignited and then heats a series of coils. The coils contain deionised water (to stop them from furring up like a kettle). As the water inside the coils is superheated the steam is piped to a radial steam engine, which consists of six pistons. The steam drives the pistons, turning a generator which produces electricity. This is stored in batteries that power the electric motors which drive the EATR along.

The steam engine is designed to be a "closed-loop" system, in which water escaping from the cylinders through the exhaust valves is captured and cooled in a condensing unit. This turns the steam back into water, which is then returned to the combustion chamber. As well as using biomass, EATR's engine could also run on petrol, diesel, kerosene, cooking oil or anything similar that could be scavenged. The ability to consume a wide range of fuels would be important if the vehicle found itself in areas like deserts, where vegetation may not be available and alternative fuel would be needed.

Image-recognition software linked to a laser and camera would allow EATR to recognise plants, leaves and wood. Robert Finkelstein, Robotic Technology's president, estimates that about 68 kilograms (150 pounds) of vegetation would provide enough electricity for the machine to travel around 160km (100 miles). The company recently received EATR's engine, which has been developed by Cyclone Power Technology of Florida. The next stage is to integrate the EATR technology into a military vehicle to prove that the idea works. The type of vehicle that will be used has not yet been decided, although it could be a High Mobility Multipurpose Wheeled Vehicle, popularly known as a Humvee, modified to drive itself under robotic control. Dr Finkelstein thinks an EATR prototype could be scurrying around woodland by around 2013.

Such a machine would be extremely useful for the army. With no dependence on external fuel supplies, an EATR would be able to perform long reconnaissance missions in areas which might be deemed too dangerous for soldiers to venture. There are also civilian applications, such as a forestry patrol over large swathes of territory where traditional fuel may be hard to find, but where there is plenty of biomass to keep the EATR going. An agricultural version might navigate around farmland, checking for weed and insect infestations, and feeding itself as it went. It would be a return, in a way, to a time when old-fashioned steam engines once worked in the fields.

This article was first published in *The Economist* in June 2010.

Beam it up

Energy: Laser beams can deliver energy to machines through thin air. This might be a good way to power drone aircraft or a space elevator

THE *PELICAN*, a small, remotely controlled helicopter drone weighing less than a kilogram, is powered by a battery that provides about 20 minutes' flying. And yet, one evening in October 2010, the *Pelican* took off, rose ten metres and hovered throughout the night. It was brought down in the morning only because the exhibition hall near Seattle, where it was airborne, was about to open for business.

This remarkable feat was achieved with the ingenious use of a laser beam. The laser, aimed from the ground at photovoltaic cells mounted on the *Pelican*'s underside, charged the chopper's battery, keeping it aloft for an unprecedented 12 hours and 27 minutes. An optical-tracking system kept the laser beam on target, creating a "scientifically exciting, yet a little boring" experience, according to Michael Achtelik of the Pelican's German manufacturer, Ascending Technologies, after a long night monitoring flight data.

Keeping drones aloft is not the only putative application of power beaming, as this technology is known. In 2005 NASA, America's space agency, offered prize money to any team that could build a remotely powered robot able to climb quickly up a cable. Only in 2009, however, were the first of these prizes claimed, when three teams from America and Canada demonstrated climbing robots powered by lasers on the ground. LaserMotive, the Seattle company that designed the *Pelican*'s laser system, won $900,000 by powering a 5kg robot up almost a kilometre of cable dangling from a manned helicopter. LaserMotive's beam struck a photovoltaic panel on the robot, generating electricity that turned a set of wheels gripping the cable.

Conventional photovoltaic cells, made of silicon, are designed to collect energy from sunlight. LaserMotive uses special cells made with arsenic and gallium, which are better able to capture the near-infrared wavelengths of its laser beam. The panel on the climbing robot, about the size of a coffee tray, harvested enough power to run a small lawnmower. One of LaserMotive's founders, Jordin Kare, reckons that a similar laser could deliver about as much energy 20km up if the panel were only a few times larger.

One reason NASA supports power beaming is that it hopes the technology could be used to help run a space elevator. This is a machine, familiar from science fiction, which some engineers think could be made science fact. In essence, it would be a giant cable reaching tens of thousands of kilometres into space to an orbiting satellite. Cable-climbing robots, powered by laser beams shot upward from the ground, or downward from space, would take payloads to orbit. Rockets would thus become redundant. Indeed, Andy Petro of NASA's technology office in Washington, DC, says power beaming might change the economics of space exploration completely. Lasers beamed from landing craft could, he says, power rovers in sunless areas of the moon or Mars, such as craters where water might be found.

Power beaming is also becoming more efficient. A few years ago lasers typically converted less than 40% of the electrical energy used to run them into beam power. The figure is now about 60%, and costs have dropped – the result of efforts to develop better laser printers, CD burners and even hair-removal devices. Moreover, engineers have worked out how to make laser beams more intense by using short lengths of optical fibre to narrow the beam. Such intense lasers are better suited to power-beaming because the cells that collect the laser light can be smaller.

The *Pelican*'s successful flight probably means that the first big application for power beaming will be supplying energy to drones. At the moment, most small drones rely on battery power, so their flights are short. LaserMotive reports that American army officials, including some responsible for special-forces kit, have expressed an interest in power-beaming systems for drones. DARPA, the American Defence Department's technology agency, is also sponsoring research into power beaming. British readers of a certain age may remember that the spaceships flown by Dan Dare, Britain's answer to Buck Rogers, were powered by "impulse waves", beamed from Earth. That piece of science fiction, too, may prove not to have been quite so wide of the mark.

This article was first published in *The Economist* in March 2011.

Greenery on the march

Clean technology: Finding alternative sources of energy is becoming a pressing military necessity for America's armed forces

THE AIR AROUND Bagram airfield, the main American base in Afghanistan, is thick with the smell of jet fuel, the roar of aircraft taking off on bombing missions and the constant drone of electricity generators. Outside the ramparts, a snakelike convoy of brightly coloured lorries waits to unload fuel hauled from Pakistan and Central Asia. These are the modern equivalents of the pack mules that once carried military supplies – much of it fodder for the beasts themselves. The British army calculates that it takes seven gallons of fuel to deliver one gallon to Afghanistan.

Modern warfare would be impossible without vast quantities of fossil fuel. It is needed to power everything from tanks to jets to electricity generators that run the communications networks on which Western armies depend. In the punishing climate of Iraq and Afghanistan, moreover, soldiers' accommodation must be kept cool in hot weather, and warm in the cold. American forces consume more than 1m gallons of fuel a day in Afghanistan, and a similar quantity in Iraq.

Until recently military planners had assumed that fuel would be plentiful and easily available. A Humvee with added armour does just four miles per gallon; an Abrams tank burns four gallons to move a mile, in some conditions. These days, though, America's armed forces want to reform their gas-guzzling ways; green is no longer just the colour of army uniforms.

What has changed? During the invasion of Iraq in 2003, America's marines often found themselves outrunning their fuel supplies. "Unleash us from the tether of fuel," their then commander in Iraq, General James Mattis, later pleaded. As insurgency engulfed the Americans, supply convoys became a favourite target. In July 2006 General Richard Zilmer, the marine general then in charge of American forces in western Iraq, sent out an urgent request for solar panels, wind turbines and other devices to reduce the need for liquid fuels. His troops were being placed "in harm's way each time we send out a convoy", he said; protecting supply convoys was drawing forces away from other tasks. And in 2008 the spike in oil prices played havoc with military budgets: the Pentagon's fuel bill rose from $13 billion in 2007 to about $20 billion.

So it is not a question of preventing climate change, reducing dependence on imported oil, or even complying with President Barack Obama's green agenda. The need for alternative sources of energy is a military necessity.

In Iraq and Afghanistan about 40% of fuel is used to run electricity generators. A successful quick-fix to reduce energy consumption was to coat military tents with a thick layer of commercial insulating foam, of the kind used for cavity walls in homes, covered with a sealant to protect it from ultraviolet light. Joseph Sartiano, a Pentagon official, says this treatment halves the energy needed for air-conditioning and pays for itself within three to six months, depending on how the price of fuel is reckoned.

If the various generators on a base are linked together in a "smart grid" system, which optimises their operation and distributes power to priority areas, such as communications equipment, a further 20% saving is possible, he adds. Such a grid is being tested at the army's model forward operating base (FOB) in Fort Irwin, California, along with prototypes of a mobile, hybrid power station that combines solar panels and wind turbines with a conventional generator. America's marines are creating a smaller model FOB at their base in Quantico, near Washington, DC, to test systems for deployment in Afghanistan by mid-2010.

Another idea, already being tried out at Camp Victory, the main American base in Baghdad, is to convert rubbish into electricity. A battalion of about 500 men typically produces about a tonne of waste every day. A machine called the Tactical Garbage to Energy Refinery (TGER), heats solid waste to produce syngas (synthetic gas, a mixture of carbon monoxide and hydrogen), ferments food slops to produce alcohol, and chemically processes the two to make biodiesel that powers a generator. TGER produces as much as 64 kilowatts of power – enough to run the command post of a battalion.

Such measures should reduce the amount of fuel needed to produce electricity. Much of the Pentagon's fuel goes to the air force, however, and reducing the consumption of jet fuel is much more difficult. The air force is working to certify all its aircraft to use synthetic fuels made from gas derived from coal or biomass, using the Fischer-Tropsch method used by Germany during the second world war. By 2016 the air force seeks to use a 50:50 blend of synthetic and ordinary jet fuel for half of its aviation requirements within America. But the shift towards synthetic fuel has provoked criticism, because when such fuel is made from coal and then burned in an aircraft engine, more greenhouse gases are emitted overall than would be produced if the aircraft simply burned conventional fuel derived from oil. Nor does it help reduce demand in war zones.

The American navy, for its part, is placing its faith in biofuels. It has tested a biofuel made from the camelina plant in its F-18 Hornet jet. Next it will test biofuels in ship turbines. It is also installing stern flaps on its amphibious vehicles that can reduce fuel use by 2–3%, and developing better coatings to prevent the growth of algae and barnacles on hulls that cause drag and increase fuel consumption.

In October 2009 the USS Makin Island, an amphibious assault ship, was the first of 12 hybrid-powered ships to take to the water. It saved nearly $2m in fuel costs on its maiden voyage alone. At slow speeds, it runs only on an electric motor powered by the ship's auxiliary turbine. At higher speeds, the main turbine takes over. This is a step on the way to the navy's ambition to develop all-electric ships. When fully dedicated to missile defence, some ships already devote 40% of their power to electrical systems, says Rear-Admiral Philip Cullom, in charge of the navy's fleet readiness. "With an all-electric ship it will be a bit like 'Star Trek', in which the captain can order power to be moved to the weapons or to the engines," he says.

For the foreseeable future, clean technology will flow mainly from the commercial to the military sector. But over time, new technologies, such as "blended wing" aircraft and new composite materials, may come out of military-funded laboratories. At the very least, the armed forces could act as crucial early adopters for costly new green technologies.

They are also promoting one important conceptual change: the pricing of fossil fuel. Liquid fuel ordinarily sells for $2–3 a gallon, but by the time it reaches a war zone the cost is much higher: about $15 for delivery to a big FOB in Afghanistan and as much as $400 to an outpost that, say, has to be resupplied by helicopter. This "fully burdened" cost of fuel is seeping into the calculations of military planners. It tries to capture the cost of military logistics, rather than environmental impact. But if military leaders are ready to put a more realistic price on fuel, perhaps other Americans will follow suit.

This article was first published in *The Economist* in December 2009.

4   New materials, new capabilities

Return of the blob

Robotics: Amoebas have provided the inspiration for new, squishy kinds of robot capable of squeezing into confined spaces

TRAPPED UNDER A PILE OF RUBBLE, you wait for rescue. Then, to add to your troubles, you see a small blob ooze through a nearby crack. Soon afterwards it is followed by the emergency services digging down to find you. This scene is science fiction now, but it might not be for much longer. Traditionally, people have thought of robots as whirring bits of metal, but there are those in the field who ask why that need be so. Instead of trying to build a robot that looks like a human, an insect or even a tank, some roboticists have decided to look to the humble amoeba for inspiration.

America's Department of Defence has taken the idea seriously enough to provide a $3.3m grant via its research arm, the Defence Advanced Research Projects Agency, to iRobot (a firm best known for its vacuum-cleaning robot, the Roomba). Chris Jones of iRobot says DARPA's criterion for the robot was that it had to fit through an opening half its full diameter.

The result is the blob-like Chembot, which moves by deforming one side. To achieve this, iRobot's engineers used a concept called "jamming", which takes advantage of the fact that some particulate materials are quite stiff when compressed but, given space, flow like liquids. Dr Jones says the phenomenon is much like that observed in a vacuum-packed coffee brick. An unopened brick is stiff and strong because the external air pressure is compressing it. When the foil is cut, however, air gets in, equalising the pressure. The coffee then acts like the pile of particles it is, and the brick can change shape.

The Chembot is a vaguely spherical structure made of soft triangular panels, each of which is filled with particles. The control system, which uses tiny compressors to pump air in and out of the panels, is in the centre. The triangular panels remain stiff until a small amount of air is pumped into them. That lets the particles move around and allows the panel to deform. Increasing the pressure inside a panel on one side of the robot's base makes it bulge and causes the robot to roll over slightly; many such inflations and deflations make the robot roll along. The deformability also allows the robot to enter any space no smaller than its fully compressed state, more or less regardless of the shape of that space.

Nor is the Chembot the only contender for the artificial-amoeba crown. Dennis Hong, a mechanical engineer at Virginia Tech, has taken a different approach. He has looked at the way amoebas move and tried to replicate it. The Chembot moves by pushing itself along. Real amoebas, however, pull themselves. They extend a pseudopod in the direction they wish to travel, and the rest of the amoeba then flows forward into the pseudopod.

Dr Hong could not exactly duplicate that, but he came up with something similar: the idea of an extended torus, or doughnut shape, which turns itself inside out. For large robots, he accomplishes this with a series of hoses, arranged like ribs, to form the torus. Each hose can be expanded and contracted independently. Doing so in sequence along the length of the torus generates forward motion.

For small robots Dr Hong has used rings made of a polymer that changes shape in response to a specific chemical stimulus. The result is a robot that scuttles along when an appropriate chemical is brushed on one end. Dr Hong will not yet say which chemicals he uses, but the robot moves impressively fast. It can also, like the Chembot, squeeze through openings smaller than its initial diameter.

Search-and-rescue is one obvious application for robots like this. Another is endoscopy – the process by which doctors insert a camera into someone through an orifice to perform an internal examination. At the moment, the camera has to be fitted to the end of a stiff, yet flexible cable. A soft, squishy robot, sufficiently small, could be an alternative. How patients would feel about having an autonomous blob roaming around inside them is another matter.

This article was first published in *The Economist* in June 2010.

Quiet, please

Military technology: Using rubber rather than steel tracks on military vehicles could reduce wear and tear on both soldiers and equipment

RATTLING ALONG in the "washing-machine environment" of an armoured personnel-carrier (APC) on steel tracks can shake the soldiers inside to the point of exhaustion, according to Dan Goure, a military analyst at the Lexington Institute, a think-tank in Arlington, Virginia. And J.G. Brunbech, an APC expert at the Danish Army Material Command in Oksboel, observes that the crew's limbs are prone to becoming prickly and numb, and their hands get tired, because they must grip the vehicle's safety handles tightly. The vehicle itself suffers, too. The vibrations cause rapid wear and tear – not to mention outright damage, especially to electronics.

In the past, engineers have tried to reduce these vibrations by fixing rubber pads to the treads. The pads wear out quickly, however, and often get torn or even melted. But now tough, new rubbers have come to the rescue. Moreover, these rubbers are not being used just as pads. Instead, they are crafted into enormous rubber bands that replace the steel tracks completely. The Danes are converting their entire APC fleet to rubber tracks. This will increase the amount of time a soldier can safely spend on board from just one and a half hours to ten hours.

Details of how the new super-rubbers are made are still classified, but the results are not, and they are impressive. Rubber tracks weigh less than half as much as their steel counterparts. That, in turn, allows the weight of the suspension system to be reduced by 25%. All this can cut fuel consumption by as much as 30%, says TACOM, the American army's Tank-Automotive and Armaments Command.

Rubber tracks also provide more traction, in part because, being lighter, they can be made wider than steel tracks. That means vehicles fitted with them do not get stuck in the mud. The vehicles accelerate faster, too, and drivers say they handle almost as well on paved roads as wheeled vehicles do. On top of this, they are quieter. That has two benefits. One is that crews are often able to talk to each other without resorting to intercoms. The other is that it is harder for the enemy to hear them coming. According to Curt Aspelund, the head of tracks and suspension development at BAE Systems, a British defence firm that is collaborating with TACOM to design a new APC called the Manned Ground Vehicle (MGV), rubber tracks will reduce the distance from which the vehicle can be heard by 40%.

Rubber tracks are more reliable, too. Tracked military vehicles are notorious for breaking down. On average, the segments of a steel track must be repaired or replaced after just 400km (250 miles) of use. Carrying spare segments adds to a vehicle's weight. Rubber tracks, by contrast, usually last more than 3,000km.

They are also kinder to roads. Traditionally, of course, that did not matter much. The whole point of a tank or an APC is that it is the ultimate off-road vehicle. But the growth of peacekeeping operations, in which showing the flag to the locals is an important tactic, means that road-friendly vehicles are becoming more desirable. The locals will certainly not love you if you chew up their tarmac and make their streets impassable.

As a result of all this, Soucy International of Drummondville, Quebec, one of the firms that makes the tracks, reports booming business. The armed forces of both Canada and Norway have converted almost all their APCs to tracks made by Soucy. Those of several other countries, including Britain, Germany, Italy, the Netherlands, Singapore and Sweden, are following suit or are in the advanced stages of testing the tracks. France plans to start tests next year. And although America has not sent APCs with rubber tracks into action, they form part of Future Combat Systems, the Department of Defence's main modernisation programme.

At the moment, rubber tracks can support only vehicles weighing less than 20 tonnes. They are not strong enough for 50-tonne battle tanks. But this is changing. The MGV, for example, will weigh 30 tonnes, and Canada has begun a trial of rubber tracks on the Mobile Tactical Vehicle Light (MTVL), a 22-tonne APC. If the MTVL passes muster it will join Canada's rubber-tracked 20-tonne M113 APCs in Afghanistan. Soucy, meanwhile, is developing rubber tracks for full-sized tanks. Warfare, it seems, is about to get quieter.

This article was first published in *The Economist* in December 2008.

Liquid radio

America's navy is developing an antenna made of seawater

A BIG AMERICAN WARSHIP bristles with more than 100 large copper antennae that send and receive signals for its weapons, its radar and its voice and data communications. A lot of aerials, then, but still not enough. The navy wants its ships to carry even more of them. Fulfilling that desire has, however, stymied experts for decades. If placed too close together, antennae interfere with each other's signals. They also get in the way of aircraft and weapons. And, crucially, naval antennae – many of them more than 20 metres tall – make warships more easily visible to enemy radar.

At the American navy's Space and Naval Warfare Systems Command (known as SPAWAR for short), in San Diego, a team of more than 30 engineers is trying to solve such problems. In 2007 the team's leader, Daniel Tam, thought of a possible answer, appropriately enough, while taking his morning shower. The sodium and chloride ions in salt water conduct electricity. Could a spout of seawater, he mused, replace a metal antenna?

After a trip to a hardware store, Mr Tam discovered that indeed it could. With an $80 water pump, a $15 rubber hose and a $20 electrical device called a current probe that was easily plugged into a hand-held radio, he produced a spout roughly four metres tall from the waters of San Diego Bay. With this he could send and receive a clear signal. Over the intervening years his invention, dubbed the "pee antenna" by incredulous colleagues, has been tweaked and improved to the point where it can transmit over a distance of more than 50km (30 miles).

To make a seawater antenna, the current probe (an electrical coil roughly the size and shape of a large doughnut) is attached to a radio's antenna jack. When salt water is squirted through the hole in the middle of the probe, signals are transferred to the water stream by electromagnetic induction. The aerial can be adjusted to the frequency of those signals by lengthening or shortening the spout. To fashion antennae for short-wave radio, for example, spouts between 18 and 24 metres high are about right. To increase bandwidth, and thus transmit more data, such as a video, all you need do is thicken the spout. And the system is economical. The probe consumes less electricity than three incandescent desk lamps.

A warship's metal antennae, which often weigh more than 3½ tonnes apiece, can be damaged in storms or combat. Seawater antennae, whose components weigh next to nothing and are easily stowable, could provide handy backups – and, eventually, more than backups. Not all of a ship's antennae are used at once, so the spouts could be adjusted continuously to obtain the types needed at a given moment. According to SPAWAR, ten such antennae could replace 80 copper ones.

Fewer antennae mean fewer things for enemy radar to reflect from. Seawater is in any case less reflective of radar waves than metal. And if a ship needed to be particularly stealthy (which would mean keeping its transmissions to a minimum), her captain could simply switch the water spouts off altogether.

One disadvantage of water spouts is that they can be torn apart by the wind. SPAWAR's researchers have, however, found that their antennae work just as well if encased in a plastic tube. The tube can be sealed at the top so that the water goes up the middle, bounces off the top and then trickles down the inside of the tube's wall to the bottom, where it may be recycled.

That innovation also means that SPAWAR's invention need not be restricted to the navy. The closed-tube design allows saline aerials to be deployed on land, too. Indeed, one has already been tested successfully by a group of marines. It worked, as expected, with brine made from fresh water and a few pinches of salt. But if salt is not to hand, never fear. It also worked fine when the spout was fed with Gatorade.

This article was first published in *The Economist* in January 2011.

Sound reflections

How to stop echoes giving you away

IN GREEK MYTHOLOGY, Echo was a mountain nymph who lost her voice and was condemned to repeat only the words of others. Now science is poised to silence the sprite completely. A group of physicists, led by Steven Cummer of Duke University in North Carolina, has devised plans for a cloak that would shield objects from sound, preventing its reflection. Such a device could be used to hide submarines.

Sonar, the technique employed to detect subs, uses a transmitter to emit a pulse of sound – usually a distinctive "ping" – and a receiver to listen for its reflection. That reflection indicates the presence of an object and the time that elapses between the sound's being emitted and its being detected indicates how far away it is. A second ping allows the object's direction, speed and location to be calculated.

Dr Cummer, however, has devised a plan to surround a submarine with a shell that directs sound waves to flow around it as though the vessel were not there. The proposal relies on two properties of the material used to make the shield – its density and its "bulk modulus", a measure of its springiness. It should be possible to tailor these so that sound waves are bent such that no echo results. The design would also avoid absorbing sound, ensuring no acoustic "shadows" were cast.

Dr Cummer's method, reported in the current issue of *Physical Review Letters*, is akin to an existing design for an invisibility cloak that would work for light waves, proposed by Sir John Pendry of Imperial College, London. (Sir John is also one of the authors of the new paper.) Yet the acoustic version has a distinct advantage over its optical counterpart. Making an invisibility cloak would be tricky because the device would work only at certain wavelengths. An aeroplane shrouded in such kit might be invisible to the human eye, for example, but would be picked up readily by radar, which works at radio wavelengths.

An acoustic cloak, however, would work for a wider range of wavelengths, making it far harder to spot. That is possible because light and sound are rather different sorts of waves. As Einstein observed, light in a vacuum travels at the greatest speed possible, around 300m metres a second. Even when it is slowed by air and water, its progress usually remains close to this limit. That means light must obey the rules of Einstein's special theory of relativity. When light is bent by an invisibility cloak, certain components of the wave are allowed to stretch the laws of physics and travel faster than the nominal speed of light, but only under strict conditions. The energy and the information that the wave carries, for example, cannot exceed the speed of light. The effect is to narrow the range of wavelengths that can be bent by an optical shroud.

Sound, meanwhile, travels at a sedate 300 metres a second. Because this is a million times shy of the relativistic limit, the behaviour of sound waves is not restricted in the same way. Under non-relativistic conditions, many different wavelengths can be bent simultaneously by the same acoustic shield, making it far more effective at concealing an object.

It was unrequited love that made the Echo of Greek mythology fade away until only her voice remained. Although Dr Cummer and his colleagues are still some way from transforming their design into a working device, they reckon precisely engineered materials may soon erase her final utterances.

This article was first published in *The Economist* in January 2008.

A good yarn

Nanotechnology: Cotton fibres coated with carbon nanotubes could be used to make clothing that glows, or detects bleeding

MANY SCIENCE-FICTION STORIES portray a time when warring generals monitor their forces on computer displays that are linked to special suits worn by their soldiers. Information about any injuries are sent to the command station immediately, so the generals can tell that, say, Sergeant Johnson has a fractured ankle or that Corporal Caley has lost 1.2 litres of blood. Such a day may not be too far off. Researchers have been able to produce cotton fibres capable of detecting blood and of signalling its presence electrically.

Intelligent textiles have a lot of appeal. For both soldiers and doctors, clothing that adapts to changing conditions could provide adjustable levels of protection from such things as microbes, chemicals and radiation. Commercial manufacturers see huge potential in clothes that glow, do not wrinkle or overcome body odour. Materials can already be made to do some of these things, but they are too bulky, rigid or complicated for practical use. So the aim is to manufacture a light material that can be easily woven but is also highly durable and, in order to transmit information, can conduct electricity.

A team of researchers led by Nicholas Kotov, a chemical engineer at the University of Michigan, has come up with a way in which this might be done by coating cotton threads with carbon nanotubes. These tubes are cylindrical carbon molecules with a unique honeycomb-like arrangement of atoms. They are regarded as among the most versatile nanomaterials available because of their mechanical strength and electrical properties.

Nanotube composites are often made into solid structures or sheets, although flexible versions, such as electrically conductive films and electronic inks, can be prepared from dilute nanotube solutions. Some electronic devices, such as field-emission displays in some flat panels, are made from nanotube yarns. But the weaving of these yarns, which may be only one-thousandth of a millimetre thick, is complicated and expensive. Creating garments with electrical properties has not been considered practical.

However, Dr Kotov and his colleagues have reported in *Nano Letters* a simple process for coating standard cotton threads with carbon nanotubes. Being much thicker than nanotube yarns, such threads can be woven more easily. The researchers dispersed carbon nanotubes in a dilute solution of a mixture of Nafion, a commercial synthetic polymer, and ethanol. They then repeatedly dipped cotton threads, 1.5mm in diameter, into the solution, letting them dry between each dip. This allowed the nanotubes to cover individual cotton strands and to adhere strongly to the surface of the cellulose fibres in the strands. The process also encouraged the nanotubes to arrange themselves along the axis of the cotton fibres, which increased electrical connectivity. After several dips, Dr Kotov found that the cotton threads were conductive enough that they could be used to wire up a light-emitting diode.

In a further test the researchers added molecules of a material that reacts with human serum albumin, an essential component of human blood, to the dipping solution. Then they immersed more cotton threads. This time they ran an electrical current through the thread while exposing it to different concentrations of albumin. They found that the threads' electrical conductivity varied according to the level of albumin. The researchers propose that such material could be used to detect bleeding if suitably woven into military clothing – just as the science-fiction writers predicted.

This article was first published in *The Economist* in March 2009.

5 iPod militaries

The military-consumer complex

Military technology used to filter down to consumers. Now it's going the other way

THE EARLIEST COMPUTERS were used to crack codes and simulate nuclear explosions. The internet grew out of a military research project. In-car navigation systems rely on satellites that were put into orbit to guide ships, troops and missiles. The Boeing 747, with its raised cockpit, was designed as a military transporter. In each case a technology created for military use has gone on to become widely used by civilians. That this happens so often is not surprising: the military is, after all, a deep-pocketed customer prepared to fund the development of expensive new technologies. As gizmos become smaller and cheaper – and they invariably do – they are then able to percolate from the soldier on the battlefield to the man in the street.

But lately some kinds of technology have been moving in the other direction, too. In early December 2009, the United States Air Force placed an order for 2,200 Sony PlayStation 3 video-game consoles, which will be the building-blocks of a supercomputer. Soldiers in Iraq and Afghanistan are using Apple iPods and iPhones to run translation software and calculate bullet trajectories. Xbox video-game controllers have been modified to control reconnaissance robots and drone aircraft. Graphics chips that power PC video-cards are being used by defence firms to run simulations.

What has caused this shift? Global defence spending, at about $1.5 trillion a year, far exceeds sales of consumer-electronics, at around $700 billion a year. But only a small fraction of defence spending is devoted to developing electronics. The consumer-electronics industry can therefore outspend the military in research and development, and spread out those costs over a far larger market: more than a billion mobile phones are sold every year, for example. Electronics firms also move much faster than the slow, multi-year grind of military procurement programmes, with few products remaining on the market for more than a year before being replaced by something better or cheaper. And the emergence of open standards and open-source software makes it easier to repurpose off-the-shelf technologies or combine them in novel ways. (All those PlayStation 3s will have a customised version of Linux, an open-source operating system, installed on them and will be wired up using Gigabit Ethernet, the networking technology commonly used in offices.)

So much for the $1,000 screwdriver

All this is to be applauded. Where consumer technology can be used, it is much cheaper and quicker to do so. The air force's new supercomputer will cost around one-tenth as much as a conventional supercomputer of equivalent power. Using an iPod to run translation software in Iraq makes much more sense than designing and building a dedicated device. America's armed forces are also using commercially available green technologies to reduce their demand for fuel. Of course, there are limits to this off-the-shelf approach: it is no way to procure tanks, helicopters or missile systems. But the selective use of existing technology allows military planners to focus their spending on the development of new technologies, rather than reinventing the wheel. The consumer-electronics industry has been taking advantage of military innovations for years. It seems only fitting that it should now return the favour.

This article was first published in *The Economist* in December 2009.

War games

Consumer products and video-gaming technology are boosting the performance and reducing the price of military equipment

VIDEO GAMES have become increasingly realistic, especially those involving armed combat. America's armed forces have even used video games as recruitment and training tools. But the desire to play games is not the reason why in early December 2009 the United States Air Force issued a procurement request for 2,200 Sony PlayStation 3 (PS3) video-game consoles. It intends to link them up to build a supercomputer that will run Linux, a free, open-source operating system. It will be used for research, including the development of high-definition imaging systems for radar, and will cost around one-tenth as much as a conventional supercomputer. The air force has already built a smaller computer from a cluster of 336 PS3s.

This is merely the latest example of an unusual trend. There is a long tradition of technology developed for military use filtering through to consumer markets: satellite-navigation systems designed to guide missiles can also help hikers find their way, and head-up displays have moved from jet fighters to family cars. But technology is increasingly moving in the other direction, too, as consumer products are appropriated for military use.

Traditionally the military has preferred to develop and control its own technology, not just for tactical advantage but also to ensure that equipment was tough and reliable enough for those whose lives would depend on it. That began to change after the cold war as defence budgets became constrained and the development of sophisticated industrial and consumer products accelerated. As some of these technologies have become commoditised products which are available to everyone – friend and foe alike – there seems less reason not to buy them and use the savings for more critical equipment that needs to be built-to-order. And consumer products can often be tweaked to make them more rugged or secure when necessary.

Hands off the Xbox

A new piece of military kit can take years to specify, test and acquire using a traditional procurement process, only to arrive already outdated. So, where possible, it is quicker and cheaper to buy commercial off-the-shelf items. These range from industry-standard components, like processor chips incorporated into military equipment, to products that consumers would recognise. Sometimes these are made more rugged, like Panasonic Toughbook computers, or converted for other uses, like Xbox 360 video-game controllers adapted to operate small robotic ground vehicles used for reconnaissance.

Apple's iPod and iPhone are among the latest additions to a soldier's kit. American forces in Afghanistan and Iraq are using them for translation and to view intelligence information, such as pictures transmitted from unmanned reconnaissance drones. An iPhone app called Bullet Flight enables snipers to calculate range and trajectory for their shots, and built-in satellite-positioning allows local weather conditions to be taken into account. The basic version costs $3.99 and the full military one – which even calculates how the Coriolis effect from the rotation of the Earth will influence a bullet's flight – costs $29.99.

In the fast-moving consumer-electronics industry, where some products are lucky to have a shelf life of more than a year, companies can spread their research-and-development costs across a global mass market. Defence contractors, however, usually supply only a limited amount of equipment designed to meet the specific requirements of a particular customer. Exports can help spread costs, but different countries demand different specifications, which pushes costs back up. Consumer-electronics companies also adopt aggressive pricing strategies to grab market share. The PS3, which now costs $300 in America, was initially sold at a loss by Sony in order to boost its popularity. (The company hopes to recoup its losses by taking a cut from the sale of each game for the console.)

In many cases it is probably now impossible for companies outside the consumer-electronics industry to match the price and performance of mass-market components. BAE Systems, a British aerospace and defence contractor, has calculated that a £300 ($500) video card from NVIDiA, a Californian company which is a leader in gaming graphics, can replace £30,000 worth of other computing equipment used for engineering simulation.

What has changed in the past two years, says David Standingford, group leader of electromagnetic modelling at BAE, is that products such as the PS3 and NVIDiA graphics cards have become immensely powerful computers in their own right. He adds that the emergence of new industry standards and a leap in power from the use of multi-core processors, which contain several number-crunching engines working in parallel, has made it easier to incorporate and link up such devices to tackle much bigger tasks.

In 2008 an IBM supercomputer called Roadrunner, based at the Los Alamos National Laboratory in New Mexico, established a new record by operating at more than one petaflop (1,000 trillion calculations a second). Roadrunner is the world's first "hybrid" supercomputer, having been assembled in part from off-the-shelf equipment, including 12,960 Cell processor chips like those found inside the PS3. It will be used to simulate the behaviour of nuclear weapons.

In Britain, BAE Systems, Airbus, Rolls-Royce, Williams (a Formula 1 racing team) and others have set up a not-for-profit laboratory based in Bristol called CFMS to evaluate consumer products and components that could reduce the cost of engineering simulations. Jamil Appa of BAE, who is involved in the project, says one aim is to see how easily the internal architecture of video-games consoles can handle the complex algorithms used in simulations. The lab will provide feedback to consumer-product suppliers, he adds.

NVIDIA already recognises that it is not just gamers who are interested in its products. In September 2009, when Jen-Hsun Huang, NVIDIA's CEO, unveiled the company's latest graphics technology, he described it as the "soul of a supercomputer" with applications beyond gaming.

Nor is it just the military that is keen to employ consumer technology in sophisticated applications. The Swedish police are already using a virtual autopsy system based on gaming technology to help solve crimes. And Siemens, a German electronics and engineering giant, launched an ultrasound scanner in early December 2009 which allows expectant mothers to see their unborn child in 3-D. It uses an

NVIDIA graphics card and 3-D glasses devised for gaming. Soldiers have also been spotted wearing 3-D glasses, which will add another dimension to modern warfare.

This article was first published in *The Economist* in December 2009.

MBAs are for wusses

Military service makes Israeli techies tougher

MANY ISRAELI START-UPS should pay royalties to the army, says Edouard Cukierman, a venture capitalist in Tel Aviv. He is only half joking. Despite the recession, Israel's technology exports grew by more than 5% in 2009. Mr Cukierman thinks military service deserves some of the credit. Israel's army does not just train soldiers, he says; it nurtures entrepreneurs.

Teenagers conscripted into high-tech units gain experience "akin to a bachelor's degree in computer science", says Ruvi Kitov, co-founder and chief executive of Tufin Technologies, an Israeli software firm. Almost all of Tufin's employees in the country are, like Mr Kitov himself, veterans of the Israel Defence Forces (IDF). One of the firm's cash cows is software that finds spam servers and blocks their transmissions. It is based on IDF cyberwarfare technologies that developers first used as soldiers.

Traditional armies drill unquestioning obedience into their grunts. Israel's encourages creativity. An IDF spokesman says it is "highly acceptable" for soldiers to point out problems and pitch ideas to superiors. That is why veterans are snapped up by start-ups, says Alan Baker, president of the Israel-Canada Chamber of Commerce in Tel Aviv. They also do well raising money, he says, because investors assume the IDF has already weeded out the dishonest and irresponsible. In other countries, employers rely on the college-entry obstacle course to select the brightest and best. In Israel, thanks to conscription, most job applicants have tackled real obstacle courses.

Like Americans, Israelis are quick to challenge authority, says Shlomo Maital, the author of "Global Risk/Global Opportunity", a management book published in 2010. In the IDF, which he served as a reservist for nearly a quarter of a century, soldiers are encouraged to improvise, lest they lose the initiative in the fog of battle. This culture helps ex-army entrepreneurs solve civilian problems, Mr Maital says. He points to Check Point, a large developer of internet-security software. Its founders used to build firewalls to protect systems run by Israeli intelligence.

Optibase, a company based in Herzliya in greater Tel Aviv, sells video technology. Its founders cut their teeth tinkering with video technologies used in the IDF's intelligence and weapons systems. The firm might not exist without the IDF, says Eli Garten, a vice-president (who commanded 34 soldiers in an air-force intelligence agency when he was 20). Ironically, tech companies such as Optibase are now poaching talent from the IDF with higher salaries.

This article was first published in *The Economist* in August 2010.

6 Nukes

On target, finally

A machine for testing nuclear weapons opens for business

WHAT DO YOU GET when you focus 192 lasers onto a pellet the size of a match head and press the "fire" button? The answer, hope physicists at the National Ignition Facility (NIF) in Livermore, California, is: the most powerful machine on the planet. The NIF, scheduled to go into operation on May 29th 2009, is designed to create conditions like those found in stars – and also in the explosions of hydrogen bombs. To do that requires, for the brief instants when it is operating at full tilt (a total of three thousandths of a second a year), that it has a power of 500 trillion watts, about 3,000 times the average electricity consumption of the whole of planet Earth.

The pellets at which this energy is directed are made of frozen hydrogen. The aim is to make those pellets undergo nuclear fusion – the process that causes stars to shine and hydrogen bombs to explode. Although the justification for building the NIF has changed over the years (originally there was talk of it being a prototype for fusion-based power stations), it is the resemblance to bombs which has saved the project from the budgetary chop. For the NIF provides America with a way to carry out nuclear-weapons tests without actually testing any weapons.

Had the NIF been a purely scientific project, it would almost certainly have been cancelled. It has cost $4 billion so far, almost four times the original estimate, and is running more than five years behind schedule. Construction started in May 1997 but the initial design proved impractical and was sent back to the drawing board. In 2000 the Department of Energy, which is responsible for the Lawrence Livermore National Laboratory, the NIF's host, altered the design and

revised its budget and deadlines. And in July 2005 Congress actually voted to suspend construction of the machine – relenting only
when extra money was found to compensate for cost overruns that
had threatened to penalise the work of two other energy-department
laboratories that drew their cash from the same pot.

Testing, testing

What ultimately saved the NIF from cancellation was that its backers
persuaded politicians it was vital to the "stockpile stewardship" programme for America's nuclear bombs. Although America has not rati-
fied the Comprehensive Test-Ban Treaty, it suspended the testing of its
nuclear weapons in 1992. Instead of weapons development, nuclear-
weapons scientists are now engaged in a programme intended to
ensure that the country's existing warheads will continue to function
predictably as they age. This work uses "subcritical" tests that do not
involve full nuclear detonations, and computer simulations of how a
weapon would explode.

Such simulations are all well and good, but they must, from time
to time, be tested against the real world. That is where the NIF comes
in. It will, if it works, create real nuclear explosions, not subcritical
phuts. These explosions will be too small to count as nuclear tests
within the meaning of the treaty (which America tries to abide by,
even though it has not signed). They will, however, be big enough to
yield information useful to nuclear-weapons scientists.

Each laser pulse will begin as a weak infra-red beam. This is split
into 48 daughter beams that are then fed into preamplifiers which
increase their power 20 billion times. Each of the daughters is split
further, into four, and passed repeatedly through the main amplifiers.
These increase the beams' power 15,000 times and push their wavelengths into the ultraviolet.

The pellet itself contains a sphere of deuterium (a heavy form
of hydrogen, with nuclei consisting of a proton and a neutron) and
tritium (even heavier hydrogen, with a proton and two neutrons) that
is chilled to just a degree or so above absolute zero. The beams should
compress the sphere so rapidly that it implodes, squeezing deuterium and tritium nuclei together until they overcome their mutual

repulsion and fuse to form helium (two protons and two neutrons) together with a surplus neutron and a lot of heat. If enough heat is generated it will sustain the process of fusion without laser input, until most of the nuclear fuel has been used up.

Physicists hope that in a year or so the NIF will become the first machine to achieve a nuclear-fusion reaction that produces more energy than it takes to ignite, albeit for only a fraction of a second. Sceptics reckon that the machine may not be capable of such a feat. Creating a sustained nuclear-fusion reaction that could generate power is the goal of another mammoth experiment, the International Experimental Thermonuclear Reactor, which is being built in Cadarache, France. Plenty of people are sceptical about the likely success of that project, too. Like the NIF, it appears to be slipping behind schedule. Full experiments to test nuclear fusion as a power source seem likely to be delayed until 2025.

If the NIF does work, the bomb-scientists will be ecstatic. Astrophysicists will be pretty pleased, too. Although they will get only about 200 of the annual budget of between 700 and 1,000 runs, they will be able to use their time on the machine to simulate the interiors of giant planets, stars and exploding supernovae, by varying the compositions of the pellets to match what they think those things are made of. Bombs or no bombs, astronomy will start to move from being an observational to an experimental science. At a mere $140m a year, then, the NIF is a snip.

This article was first published in *The Economist* in May 2009.

Who wins, nukes

Preventing nuclear trafficking is easier than policing it

NO NUCLEAR MATERIAL, no bomb. It's as simple as that. Hence the renewed, unanimous call by the United Nations Security Council for Iran to cease its suspect uranium-enriching and plutonium work. The same is true for terrorist groups such as al-Qaeda, known to be seeking nuclear materials and other weapons of mass destruction as a "religious duty". The difference is that Iran can produce its own fissile material; terrorists have to steal theirs.

Keeping nuclear weapons out of the hands of terrorists therefore involves a lot of gumshoe work to clamp down on traffickers. But it would surely be better to plug the security holes that allow the stuff to leak out in the first place. Changing the nuclear industry's security culture is the immodest aim of the newly launched World Institute for Nuclear Security (WINS).

One measure of the scale of the plugging needed comes from the nuclear trafficking database of the International Atomic Energy Agency (IAEA), the UN's nuclear guardian. From 1993, when the IAEA first started counting, to the end of 2007, there had been 1,340 recorded incidents of the misuse, theft or loss of nuclear materials; 18 of these involved highly enriched uranium (HEU) or plutonium, some in quantities as large as kilograms (it takes up to 25kg of HEU or 8kg of plutonium to make a bomb).

Most such cases have involved material filched from ill-guarded sites in Russia after the collapse of the Soviet Union. The number of serious incidents recorded has been falling. That may not be as comforting as it sounds. Traffickers are probably getting cleverer; by its nature, illicit trade goes largely undetected. But it helps that America has been assisting Russia and others with security upgrades, including better fences, surveillance equipment and radiation monitors, as well as security training, at military and civilian sites where nuclear materials are used or stored.

Now two things are about to change. Security upgrades in Russia are to be completed by the end of 2008. It remains to be seen whether improvements will last once the dollars and the chivvying stop. Meanwhile an industry using deadly materials spread across more than 40 countries may be about to expand farther and wider, as from Venezuela to Vietnam governments contemplate nuclear power as a source of cleaner energy.

The international legal apparatus to deal with this looks robust. The UN's resolution 1540 obliges all governments to stop nuclear (and chemical and biological) bomb-making materials falling into terrorist hands. Some 75 countries have banded together in a supporting Global Initiative to Combat Nuclear Terrorism. The IAEA, meanwhile, can help governments with advice: protecting the Olympics, for example, against radiological attack, disposing of radioactive materials found in factories and hospitals, and fixing security breaches. It is also boosting the academic study of nuclear security.

But the weakest links will always be sites where materials are kept. WINS is a place where for the first time those with the practical responsibility for looking after nuclear materials – governments, power plant operators, laboratories, universities – can meet to swap ideas and develop best practice.

Start-up cash comes from America's Department of Energy, the Nuclear Threat Initiative, a private Washington-based group that has long promoted nuclear clean-up activities around the world, and the Norwegian government. Eventually WINS will have to live on support from those who find its services useful.

It took the Chernobyl nuclear disaster in Ukraine for the nuclear industry to focus collectively on reactor operating safety. Preventing security lapses that would mean an even bigger catastrophe ought to be a winning cause.

This article was first published in *The Economist* in October 2008.

Thinking small

Nuclear power: Combining several small reactors based on simple, proven designs could be a better approach than building big ones

WHEN THE TWO BIG NUCLEAR REACTORS under construction at Flamanville in France and Olkiluoto in Finland come on stream, each will boast enough electricity-generating capacity to light up a city of 1.5m. But despite the best efforts of EDF and Areva, which are building the reactors, both are behind schedule and, at over $5 billion apiece, well over budget. With results like these, it is little wonder that the vaunted "nuclear renaissance" has failed to materialise. In fact, the number of operating reactors is in decline, spurring the nuclear-power industry to look for new approaches. Rather than relying on huge, traditional reactors costing billions, it is turning to small, inexpensive ones, many of which are based on proven designs from nuclear submarines or warships.

A global race is under way to develop small-reactor designs, says Paul Genoa of the Nuclear Energy Institute, an industry body in Washington, DC. He estimates that more than 20 countries have expressed serious interest in buying mini-reactors.

At least eight different approaches are being developed, mainly in America and Asia, by an army of 3,000 nuclear engineers, according to Ron Moleschi of SNC-Lavalin Nuclear, an engineering firm based in Montreal. Regulatory and licensing procedures are lengthy, so little will be built until around 2017, he says. But after that the industry is expected to take off. The International Atomic Energy Agency (IAEA) estimates that by 2030 at least 40 (and possibly more than 90) small reactors will be in operation. It reckons that more than half of the countries that will build nuclear plants in coming years will plump for these smaller, simpler designs.

Nuclear deliveries

Russia is an early adopter. Rosatom, the state nuclear-energy giant, is building a floating, towable power station in a St Petersburg shipyard. The Akademik Lomonosov, due to set sail in 2012 for waters near Russia's far-east town of Vilyuchinsk, will be followed by at least four other floating nuclear plants for the country's Arctic regions. Such power stations are less prone to earthquakes and avoid the difficulties of erecting nuclear facilities on frozen land, which can melt, jeopardising foundations, says Vladimir Kuznetsov of the IAEA. And at a mere $550m a pop they cost a fraction of what a traditional reactor does (though they also provide less power).

Rosatom hopes its plants will appeal to energy-hungry coastal or river cities all over the world. By manufacturing in Russia, the firm sidesteps some of the regulatory controls a client country would impose on a plant built and installed on its own soil. Another selling point is Russia's willingness to bring home the nuclear waste. Demand for floating plants may also help Russia broaden, or at least retain, its nuclear expertise, which has suffered as engineers have gone abroad or retired.

"Engineers of small reactors stress their similarity to proven, existing designs such as those found in nuclear-powered ships and submarines."Similar concerns are driving efforts to develop small reactors elsewhere. No new nuclear plant has come on stream in America since 1996. The industry was dealt a blow in October 2010, when Constellation Energy, a utility, dropped a joint plan with EDF to build a large nuclear plant in Maryland. In spite of strong political support and a reported $7.5 billion in government loan guarantees, Constellation balked at the initial capital outlay. Steven Chu, America's energy secretary, sees miniaturisation as a way to revive the country's once-mighty nuclear industry.

One advantage of small reactors is their modularity. Extra units can be added to a plant over the years, incrementally boosting output as capital becomes available and electricity demand rises. NuScale, of Corvallis, Oregon, offers "scalable" nuclear plants with reactors delivered by truck. A plant with 12 reactors, each with its own electricity-generating turbine, would cost about $2.2 billion and produce roughly a third as much power as a big facility. Since large plants can cost roughly three times as much, the cost of electricity would be about the same. Moreover, a modular facility would generate revenue as soon as the first reactor is fired up, after a few years of construction. A big reactor traditionally takes a decade to erect.

Hyperion Power Generation, a firm based in Santa Fe, New Mexico, is building components for what it calls a "nuclear battery". The refrigerator-sized Hyperion Power Module (HPM) reactor will shift much of the building from field to factory, where a controlled environment reduces costs. Also, fewer workers and families must be moved, at great expense, to distant building sites. HPMs would be delivered by truck with enough uranium to run for about ten years. They would be constructed in batches with interchangeable parts and cost about $100m each. And they need little human oversight to operate. "Forget huge – let's make a hand-held version of a power plant," says John Deal, the firm's boss. Five companies, located in America, Britain, Canada, China and India, have put down deposits for an HPM.

Engineers of small reactors stress their similarity to proven, existing designs such as those found in nuclear-powered ships and submarines, or, in Rosatom's case, icebreakers. And some small-reactor designs have an important advantage over bigger reactors. Because less heat is generated, small water-cooled reactors can use simpler designs relying not on pumps, but on natural convection. And eliminating moving parts should make the new small reactors both safer and cheaper. For instance, Hyperion's HPM dispenses with elaborate valve systems by using a molten metal as a coolant because, unlike water, it doesn't need to be kept under pressure to absorb large amounts of heat.

Christofer Mowry, who heads civilian power at Babcock & Wilcox, a maker of nuclear-propulsion systems for the US Navy, says the company's small reactor offers another source of savings. Because it can use existing power-transmission lines without overloading them, the mPower can act as a "drop-in replacement" for ageing coal furnaces without the need for costly refurbishment. The Tennessee Valley Authority, America's biggest public utility, hopes to put two of the firm's reactors into an old coal plant. Five other American utilities are also considering replacing coal furnaces with nuclear reactors, according to Philip Moor of the American Nuclear Society, an industry group. He estimates that in America alone perhaps 100 old coal plants could be converted to nuclear within a decade – a trice by the industry's standards.

Not all nuclear nations have entered the fray. France has studied micro-reactors' potential in spaceship propulsion, but for generating power on Earth, big reactors are best, says Christophe Béhar, in charge of nuclear energy at the country's Atomic Energy Commission. New markets for large plants are opening up as developing countries strengthen their grids to cope with the huge amounts of power they produce. China is building two small helium-cooled reactors, but the electricity they produce will never be as cheap as that from big reactors, according to Mr Béhar. Just in case, the Chinese have also commissioned French firms to build two large nuclear plants.

In Japan, too, utilities' interest in small reactors appears scant for now. Tatsujiro Suzuki, the vice-chairman of the Atomic Energy Commission in Tokyo, hopes it will grow. Today's broad trend to loosen government controls on electricity prices may do the trick. Utilities are more willing to make massive investments if they can accurately predict future income. As prices are allowed to fluctuate more widely, shorter-term investments for smaller reactors will become more attractive. At least one Japanese engineering giant sees promise in the market for such devices. Toshiba says its 4S ("super-safe, small and simple") reactor is capable of running for three decades without refuelling.

Small comfort

Sceptics fear that these small, cheap reactors will not be enough to revive the nuclear industry. Mycle Schneider, a nuclear-energy expert who is an external lecturer at École des Mines, an engineering school in France, and also an adviser to Germany's environment ministry, says licensing and building small plants will take far too long to be profitable. As the costs of solar, wind and biogas power continue to fall, investors will increasingly favour household energy-producing kit and transmission technologies that let consumers sell excess production to neighbours and utilities, he says. South Africa's decision in September 2010 to abort construction of a small reactor, even though about $1.3 billion had been spent, illustrates the sort of financial risk the sector faces.

Others fret that lots of small reactors, rather than a few big ones, will be more vulnerable to a terrorist attack. Hyperion's Mr Deal insists that neither a rocket-propelled grenade nor a tank round could smash a small reactor. Small reactors can be shielded by a heavy layer of concrete and buried, in effect making them safer than big ones, whose protective concrete domes can only be so thick, lest they collapse under their own weight.

What if a rogue government tries to take advantage of an affordable reactor to acquire nuclear expertise or materials for weapons work? Henry Sokolski, a former Pentagon official who heads the Nonproliferation Policy Education Centre, a think-tank near Washington, DC, says that Western intelligence agencies have overestimated their ability to monitor the spread of nuclear equipment and know-how. If new enrichment facilities are built to supply a slew of small nuclear reactors, materials and expertise useful in bomb-making may spread as a result.

TerraPower, an American firm backed by Bill Gates, thinks it has the solution. It is designing a small "travelling wave" reactor that, once kick-started with a tiny amount of enriched uranium, would run for decades on non-enriched, depleted uranium – a widely available material. This will be possible because the nuclear reaction, eating its way through the core at the rate of about one centimetre a year, would gradually convert the depleted uranium into fissionable plutonium – in effect "breeding" high-grade fuel and then consuming it.

Mr Gates points out that nuclear power has historically been dogged by five worries: safety, proliferation, waste, cost and fuel availability. "This thing is a miracle that solves all five," he says. John Gilleland, TerraPower's boss, says that a single enrichment plant would then suffice to produce all the enriched uranium needed to spark up the world's mini-reactors.

The prospects for mini-reactors, like those for large reactors, depend on a combination of technical, commercial and regulatory factors. The stars do not seem to be aligning for large reactors. But they are no longer the only game in town.

This article was first published in *The Economist* in December 2010.

A weighty matter

How to analyse smuggled uranium

BETWEEN 1992 AND 2007, according to Ian Hutcheon of the Lawrence Livermore National Laboratory, in California, 17kg of highly enriched uranium was seized from smugglers around the world, along with 400 grams of plutonium. In neither case is that enough for a proper atom bomb, but it is still worrying. Presumably, more is out there. Even if it is not, the material that has been found could have been used to make a "radiological" weapon, by blowing it up and scattering it around a city using conventional explosives. Dr Hutcheon is one of those charged with analysing this captured material, to discover how dangerous it really is and where it came from – and thus whether it has been stolen from legitimate nuclear projects or made on the sly. He showed off some of the tricks of his trade at a meeting organised by the American Association for the Advancement of Science in February 2010 in San Diego.

His main tool is a device called a secondary-ion mass spectrometer. This measures the flight path of ions (electrically charged atoms) through a magnetic field. The lighter an ion is, the more the field bends its trajectory. The spectrometer can thus distinguish between, say, ^{235}U (the fissile sort, from which bombs are made) and ^{238}U (which has three extra neutrons in its nucleus and is much less fissile). Natural uranium has only seven atoms per thousand of the former. Weapons-grade uranium is 95% ^{235}U. The "depleted" uranium used in armour-penetrating shells, by contrast, is almost pure ^{238}U.

Uranium that has been in a reactor, though, has other isotopes in it, ^{233}U and ^{236}U, for example. The quantities of these, plus isotopes of elements such as plutonium that are also created in reactors, vary from one reactor to another. The isotopic signature is changed, too, by the centrifuges used to separate ^{235}U from ^{238}U during the process of enrichment, and radioactive decay after processing creates yet further elements that can be detected this way. These give some idea of a sample's age.

The result is a profile that is often characteristic of a particular type of reactor or centrifuge, and sometimes of an individual machine – and can also indicate how long ago the processing took place. That enables the good guys to improve security in the case where something has been pinched, the bad guys to be admonished if they have been up to something they should not have been doing, and everyone else to sleep more easily in their beds.

This article was first published in *The Economist* in February 2010.

PART 2

Air and space

SHORTLY AFTER SUNRISE on April 6th 2003, a mechanised unit of about 150 Iraqi forces near the northern town of Debecka attacked a smaller detachment of American soldiers and their Kurdish Peshmerga allies. Half an hour later, two US Navy F-14 fighter jets arrived. One, after a flyover, dropped a bomb not on the Iraqi enemy, but on Kurdish troops who had retreated behind their American allies. More than a dozen were killed. Accidents in the fog of war, however tragic, are nothing new. However, the commander who called in the air strike does not attribute the blunder to a lack of high technology, but rather to an excess of it.

Fighter jets fly so fast the pilot has only a few seconds on a flyover to identify the target, says Frank Antenori, a US Army sergeant at the time. Slow and inexpensive low-tech propeller warplanes would often be better and safer for attacking ground forces, says Mr Antenori, now an Arizona state senator. Numerous air forces, including America's, are coming to a similar conclusion.

The story illustrates one of the main themes of this second part of the book, which is about air and space technologies for defence and intelligence. Cheaper and less-sophisticated aircraft and satellite technologies are often better. Drones and even militarised blimps increasingly outperform costlier conventional warplanes and satellites when it comes to spying, conducting electronic warfare, and delivering or guiding precision ordnance.

The following articles explore a broad range of technologies. Rocket boosters that accelerate bunker-smashing bombs could reduce collateral damage. Explosives-sniffing drones may help detect roadside bombs. Shoebox-sized satellites, called "cubesats", can piggyback on launch vehicles for big satellites very cheaply by replacing ballast that a rocket would otherwise carry to improve its weight distribution. Grouping these articles together brings a few broad themes into clearer focus.

For a start, poor or small countries can use less-sophisticated or cheaper kit to obtain significant air or space capabilities. The advent of cubesats allowed Norway to launch its first government satellite in July 2010. Thanks to cubesats, many student groups have begun to build satellites.

"Less is more" technologies will provide some countries with more operational independence. Afghanistan lacks the expertise and infrastructure to operate conventional warplanes. But propeller warplanes are far easier to maintain and can take off or land in small fields. (One expert says only half jokingly that they can be "flown and maintained by plumbers".) By supplying them to Afghanistan, America will find it easier to set up an Afghan air force and gradually withdraw in the next few years. Another benefit is that rival countries are less likely to consider this sort of defence co-operation as a threat.

Rise to power

New technologies are also greatly increasing the value of air power itself. Improvements in drone technology are illustrative. US Marine Corps colonel John Adams, a former National Security Agency expert on gathering intelligence with drones, says that during the first Gulf war America had only one model, the RQ-2 Pioneer, which sported a wooden propeller. Although its fuselage was only about the size of a man, the reconnaissance drone was so loud and conspicuous it resembled "a flying lawnmower", says Colonel Adams. It remained in service, with upgrades, until 2007.

A much larger but stealthier bat-winged drone gathered intelligence above Osama bin Laden's Abbottabad, Pakistan, compound before and during the May 2011 US Navy Seals attack. Reportedly

Lockheed Martin's more than 20m-wingspan RQ-170 Sentinel, it loitered undetected in airspace near sensitive Pakistani army and nuclear facilities protected with air-defence radar. (President Barack Obama and top national-security officials watched live imagery it provided during the raid.) Some spy drones in development will be little bigger than a large insect. Drones as big as a manned aeroplane launch missiles.

Remote-sensing capabilities for aircraft have become formidable. A Canadian-made turret not much larger than a motorcycle helmet can read a licence plate from a distance of 10km, work out the vehicle's location and speed, and mark it with a targeting laser. Thanks to a new and clever configuration of envelopes for helium and ethane gases, a blimp in development could loiter in the stratosphere for months, surveying an area the size of France at far less cost than a satellite. Adversaries hounded by this sort of equipment are at a big disadvantage.

When armed forces with control of the air obtain more sophisticated capabilities, they are increasingly likely to consider, for good or ill, bombardment as a viable option. Better targeting technologies can reduce bombing blunders such as killing friendly forces or civilians. And new types of aircraft beget new opportunities for attacks.

Cessna, a Kansas maker of propeller warplanes, says booming deliveries are providing many countries without the budget or expertise for "sledgehammer" bombers with a new and inexpensive "flyswatter" option, in the words of Pat Sullivan, head of government sales. America's Sikorsky, maker of the Black Hawk attack helicopter, has built a test model with extra rotors that is extremely fast. A collapsible mechanical cushion to protect helicopter passengers during a crash is being developed. And remote-controlled aircraft can keep pilots out of harm's way entirely.

Unholy sanctuary

A perverse result of all this is that underdog forces have increasingly strong motivations to fight from civilian areas. Using non-combatants as human shields can help compensate for a lack of air power. In Libya, forces loyal to strongman Muammar Qaddafi were using civilian vehicles in a bid to avoid being killed by NATO aviation. Their armoured vehicles offered little protection against the ordnance anyway.

Despite the beguiling attractions of bombardment weaponry, time after time it has been shown that air supremacy provides no assurance of victory. Some fighting forces have little material or infrastructure that could be bombed. Distinguishing an enemy from civilians is often difficult. And a fighting force that accidentally kills civilians may strengthen an opponent's resolve and public support.

Tricky legal issues have emerged along with new bombing technologies. Indiscriminate cluster munitions scatter bomblets over wide areas. Duds can explode after battles. A majority of the world's nations banned cluster bombs in the Convention on Cluster Munitions, which became legally binding on August 1st 2010. Colonel Qaddafi's regime was roundly criticised by America and other countries in April 2011 after its forces fired bomblets into the besieged city of Misrata, killing civilians. But the United States has not signed up, in spite of early indications that Mr Obama would push for a ban if he became president.

America has used cluster bombs in recent years in at least Afghanistan, Iraq and Yemen. This could pose problems for America's signatory coalition partners. But new "sensor fused" bomblets with self-destruction mechanisms can improve targeting and reduce post-battle casualties. Calls for exceptions to the ban have increased accordingly.

The militarisation of space, another theme of this part of the book, raises new challenges. Space technologies provide great strength to space-faring nations, and the United States in particular. America is designing ground-launched hypersonic and non-nuclear "Prompt Global Strike" missiles that, guided by satellite, could hit almost any spot on Earth in less than an hour. But a nuclear power could conceivably mistake a non-nuclear ballistic missile zooming towards a target in a nearby country for an incoming nuclear strike on itself.

Beyond this additional risk of escalation, the more a country relies on space technology the greater are its vulnerabilities. At least half a dozen countries now have the technology to shoot down spacecraft, and India and Iran may soon join them. America, China and Russia have successfully destroyed orbiting satellites, and the debris can endanger spacecraft for decades. Efforts to protect spacecraft increase the cost of satellite services that have civil as well as military purposes. Crucially, efforts to control space weaponry have stumbled. As in the realm of cyberwar, verifying compliance would be extremely difficult. For good or ill, new know-how is further militarising the skies and space. As the technologies unfold, so does the future of warfare.

7 Attacks from above

The calibration of destruction

Smaller, cleverer and more accurate munitions are changing warfare

The Perseus, a 900kg (2,000lb) bomb made in Greece, incinerates almost everything in an area larger than a dozen football fields. Farther out, oxygen is sucked from the air and people may be crushed by a pressure wave. The inferno is similar to that caused by napalm – a jellied-petrol explosive heavily restricted by a United Nations weapons convention.

Modified with new technologies, however, the Perseus is increasingly considered legitimate. Mark Hiznay, a bombs-control expert at Human Rights Watch, a humanitarian group based in New York, has gone so far as to say it has become a necessary weapon. With a stronger steel casing and backup shock-resistant triggering mechanisms, the Perseus can smash through several metres of reinforced concrete and detonate only after it has gone into a bunker. This makes the bomb a good way to destroy and sterilise germ- and chemical-warfare laboratories while limiting damage nearby, says Mr Hiznay.

The Perseus is part of a new generation of diverse and advanced bombardment systems that can make bombing campaigns safer for civilians. During the first Gulf war, in 1991, lasers beamed from American warplanes were used to guide bombs. A decade or so later, during the overthrows of Afghanistan's Taliban government (2001) and Saddam Hussein's regime in Iraq (2003), American bombers had the additional option of using satellite-guidance systems. Better technology and targeting intelligence (provided by more satellites, large radar aircraft and lower-flying drones) meant that fewer and sometimes smaller bombs could be dropped from higher altitudes and in poor weather, says Barry Watts, a former US Air Force officer who helped prepare a Pentagon study on bombing effectiveness during the first Gulf war.

Greek fire

Much of this revolution, as Mr Hiznay terms it, is due to guidance kits that can be attached to existing "dumb" bombs. An upgraded bomb, when falling, uses data from the global-positioning system in combination with laser and infra-red sensors to adjust a set of fins that work like aeroplane flaps. This steers the bomb towards its target – even if that target is moving. The AASM, a French navy and air-force guidance system, has fins that can guide and glide bombs for 50km (31 miles) and hit a target within a metre of the bullseye. The LJDAM, a system made by Boeing and first exported in 2008, can land a bomb on a vehicle that is travelling at 110kph.

The market for add-on guidance systems is booming. More than a dozen countries, including South Africa, make them. Two dozen – including India, Pakistan and Turkey – buy them. They are not cheap: $23,000 per bomb will get you one at the bottom of the range. It is not just a more effective weapon, but also a safer one for the bomber. He can fly higher, meaning that he is at less risk from ground fire.

Moreover, these bombs continue to be clever even after arriving at the target. Their fuses can set off explosions at precisely the right moment. One defence contractor, Israel Military Industries, makes a 225kg bomb, the MPR-500, that can hammer through several storeys of a building and explode on a chosen floor. This feat means triggering the detonation about two milliseconds after the bomb hits the ceiling above the doomed storey. The bomb can be programmed to do this just seconds before it is dropped. Such precision means it is sold as a replacement for ordnance two or more times its size.

Bomb-makers are also finding cleverer ways of destroying deeply buried bunkers. Almost five years ago, America's Congress cut research funding for a controversial bunker-busting nuke called the Robust Nuclear Earth Penetrator. Today the bulk of effort to develop bunker-smashers in Western countries employs conventional weaponry. In a classic attack, a succession of big bombs is dropped on the same spot. Such "drilling", however, may require numerous warplanes and inflict great damage on the surrounding area.

Souping up bombs with rockets that speed up their impact might provide an alternative. Bunker-busters work best if they detonate after burrowing into the ground. This helps "couple" the explosion to the ground so that shockwaves designed to collapse a bunker travel deeper. Israel Military Industries is studying a rocket that would ignite just before the bomb hit, digging it deeper than ever before exploding.

That, according to Meir Geva, head of aerial munitions at Israel Military Industries, can be very deep indeed. His firm makes a bunker-buster which weighs about as much as a small car. "To my great sorrow", Mr Geva says, its shockwave ranges cannot be revealed.

Whatever the bunker-buster's destructive power, the next generation of bombs will dwarf it. The Massive Ordnance Penetrator, an American bunker-buster scheduled for deployment at the end of the year, weighs 15 times as much.

On April 2nd 2003, during the second Gulf war, a hundred or so Iraqi armoured vehicles approached a far smaller American reconnaissance unit south of Baghdad. Responding to a call for help, a B-52 bomber attacked the first 30 or so vehicles in the column with a single, historic pass. It dropped two new CBU-105 bombs, and the result shocked the soldiers of both sides – and, soon enough, military observers everywhere.

While falling, the CBU-105 bombs popped open, each releasing ten submunitions which were slowed by parachutes. Each of these used mini rockets to spin and eject outward four discs the size of ice-hockey pucks.

The 80 free-falling discs from the pair of bombs then scanned the ground with lasers and heat-detecting infra-red sensors to locate armoured vehicles. Those discs that identified a target exploded dozens of metres up. The blast propelled a tangerine-sized slug of copper down into the target, destroying it with the impact and the accompanying shrapnel. The soldiers in the 70 vehicles farther back in the column surrendered immediately.

A kinder, gentler future

The CBU-105, however frightening, may actually point the way toward less violent warfare. Cluster munitions – which release bomblets to cover a wide area – are banned or tightly restricted by an international convention. But the CBU-105 and its cousins, known as sensor-fused weapons, are considered legal because very few discs remain unexploded on the battlefield. Those that fail to detect a target are supposed to self-destruct in the air. The trigger batteries of those that do not will quickly die, so duds are unlikely to kill civilians later.

Crucially, the manufacturer of the CBU-105, Textron Defense Systems, of Wilmington, Massachusetts, is improving sensors to allow the weapon to distinguish the heat signatures of cars, buses and homes from those of military hardware. If there is such a thing as a humanitarian bomb, this might be it.

By contrast, consider another sort of new weapon. The explosion of Russia's "Father of All Bombs" approaches that of a small nuclear weapon; it would flatten many city blocks. In 2007, the government showed it off proudly on prime-time television. To most military men, such a bomb is not a PR coup, but an embarrassment.

This article was first published in *The Economist* in January 2010.

Collateral damage

America won't sign a treaty banning cluster bombs. But can it use them now?

IMAGINE A NEW WAR INVOLVING NATO. At the combined air-operations centre, the Americans want to destroy a concentration of enemy forces, or a column of vehicles, with cluster bombs, which rain bomblets over a wide area. The tactic has often been used in American-led operations, including those in Afghanistan and Iraq.

This time, though, several European allies have signed a treaty banning the use of cluster bombs; they have vowed not to "assist" others in using cluster munitions and pledged to make their "best efforts to discourage" their use. What would happen in the heat of battle? Would allied commanders bicker over the legality of the weapons; would Europeans turn a blind eye to their use by America (through a separate American chain of command), accepting the political opprobrium that would follow; or would America yield to its allies' qualms and choose a different weapon, perhaps a big bomb?

Nobody really knows. The treaty was signed in Oslo on December 4th 2008 by 94 countries – among them American allies like Britain, Germany, France, Japan and even, unexpectedly, Afghanistan. It includes an exemption for signatories to conduct operations alongside non-signatories, such as America, that "might engage in activities prohibited" by the treaty. NATO says the clause provides the necessary flexibility for all sides to operate together.

Legally this may be so, but the issue is political: the price of using cluster munitions has been raised. "We are pretty confident that it's going to be extremely difficult for the United States to use cluster munitions in future," says Thomas Nash, co-ordinator of the Cluster Munition Coalition, an umbrella body of groups wanting a ban. At the signing ceremony in Oslo, Britain's foreign secretary, David Miliband, said the treaty set a new global norm. One Western diplomat says the weapons could now be used only "in extremis".

The Convention on Cluster Munitions, negotiated in Dublin in

May 2008, is a natural successor to the 1997 convention to ban land-mines. Opponents of cluster munitions say they are an indiscriminate weapon when they go off; and that unexploded bomblets turn the target area into a virtual minefield. The unstable explosives are often brightly coloured; this is supposed to warn adults, but attracts children, who may be killed or maimed.

Mr Nash says there is "a nice little race" to be among the first 30 countries whose ratification would bring the treaty into force (four did so immediately). Britain is among those that have started destroying stockpiles; it has asked America to remove cluster munitions stored in Britain within the treaty's eight-year deadline.

As with the landmine ban, America stands with Russia and China in opposing the move to outlaw cluster munitions. Other holdouts include countries nervous of Russia, like Poland and Finland, and states that fear future wars, like Israel, Egypt, Syria and the Koreas. Russia, which used cluster munitions in its war with Georgia (which also used them), opposes "unjustified restrictions" on the weapons.

For American officials, the treaty is self-righteous nonsense. They say its impact could be "perverse" if it makes countries use bigger bombs and more of them. They insist that the impact on operations with allies could be "quite bad" and that solving this problem will require political will.

Still, America has had to give ground. It voices sympathy with the humanitarian motives of the treaty. In July 2008 the Pentagon set out a new policy to get rid of cluster weapons by 2018 if they have a failure rate greater than 1%. America wants a similar protocol to be adopted by all countries at the United Nations' talks on a Convention on Certain Conventional Weapons.

Lobby groups hope Barack Obama will back the treaty. As a senator in 2006, he backed a failed move to stop the weapons being used near civilians. His team says he will "carefully review" the treaty. Yet Mr Obama has asked Robert Gates to stay on as defence secretary. One Pentagon insider says Mr Obama will find it hard to change American policy once he realises that cluster munitions make up more than half the country's bomb stockpile.

This article was first published in *The Economist* in December 2008.

An enduring illusion

Israel hoped that air power would avoid the need for a ground war against Hizbullah. It was not the first to be beguiled by bombs

VICTORY IS NOT A MATTER OF SEIZING TERRITORY, Dan Halutz once explained. It is a matter of "consciousness". And air power, continued Israel's chief of staff, affects the adversary's consciousness significantly. Indeed, the very concept of the land battle is "anachronistic". Lieut-General Halutz, an air-force man, is said to have persuaded Israel's militarily inexperienced prime minister, Ehud Olmert, that the task of destroying Hizbullah in Lebanon was the perfect job for aircraft.

It did not quite work out that way. Yet the seductive idea that air power can provide swift victory with light casualties has been around almost as long as the aeroplane itself.

The belief that a few bombs could spare all the bloody butcher's bill of infantry fighting proved especially appealing to many of the military men – and politicians – who had witnessed the horrors of the trenches in the first world war. Even if it meant inflicting civilian casualties, the prospect of a short, decisive war waged from the safety of the skies was far preferable to the spectacle of "morons volunteering to get hung in the wire and shot in the stomach in the mud of Flanders," argued Arthur Harris, an airman who rose to become head of British bomber command in the second world war, earning himself the name of "Bomber" Harris for his relentless obliteration of German cities.

Airmen like Harris argued in the 1920s that armies could fight only other armies, whereas aircraft could strike right to the heart of the enemy's territory, crippling its ability and, more important, its will to wage war. Success, it was claimed, would come mostly through influencing the psychology of the enemy. The first chief of Britain's Royal Air Force, Hugh Trenchard, repeatedly asserted that the "moral effect" of bombing "stands in a proportion of 20 to one" to any physical destruction it might cause. Trenchard once even said that not bombing a town could be as effective as bombing it: "The anxiety as to whether an attack is likely to take place is probably just as demoralising as the attack itself."

Although it was the potential of air power in large wars that galvanised such thinking, airmen were also quick to argue that aircraft could be equally potent in small wars against irregular or guerrilla forces. An early opportunity to put this to the test presented itself in 1919 when the Emir of Afghanistan declared *jihad* against Britain's forces in the North-West Frontier Province. The RAF shipped a single Handley Page biplane bomber to Karachi. It flew over Kabul and dropped four 112lb bombs and 16 20-pounders. The emir sued for peace shortly thereafter.

The political capital and prestige which the RAF reaped from the incident were enormous. Basil Liddell Hart, a military writer, declared that "Napoleon's presence was said to be worth an army corps, but this aeroplane seems to have achieved more than 60,000 men did."

The RAF repeated its triumph to much éclat the next year. This time the target was Mohammed bin Abdullah Hassan, the "Mad Mullah" of Somaliland. The mullah, a precocious Muslim fanatic, had been a thorn in the side of the British for decades. He had adopted a particularly puritanical form of Islam after a pilgrimage to Mecca, which inspired him on his return home in 1895 to emulate the Mahdi who had defied the British in Sudan. The British army then sent four expeditions to Somaliland to try to deal with the mullah, the last one involving 15,000 troops. Each time the mullah regrouped. In 1909 his men, waging a *jihad* against local tribesmen who had accepted British rule, slaughtered a third of the territory's inhabitants.

When the War Office balked at repeating the effort yet again, the war minister, Winston Churchill, proposed to have the RAF do it. Six small aircraft were ferried to East Africa on warships, the mullah's fort was bombed for two days, and a month later it was all over. Churchill crowed in Parliament that the previous land expedition had cost the Treasury £6m – about £120m ($220m) in today's money; the RAF had done the job for £77,000.

But there were hints even amid the glee that the truth was murkier. The mullah was never captured. He and 700 riflemen slipped out of the country only after being pursued by ground forces, whose commander dismissed the airmen's claims of victory as "something of a hoax". The bombing, he said, had actually made his work harder by dispersing the enemy.

Something approaching a mystique, though, soon began to surround the claims of the airmen. When, in 1922, the RAF was given the job of maintaining British authority in Iraq by similar means – by then the formal name had become air control or air policing – the airmen insisted that only they were qualified to judge just when and where to strike to achieve the exact psychological effect required to bring insurgents to heel. The local British army commander sarcastically described the RAF "appearing from God knows where, dropping their bombs on God knows what, and going off again God knows where." He had a point. Although the RAF claimed it could hit the house of a particular sheikh in a particular village, the airmen often failed to get even half their bombs to land within the village at all.

But the saving in money and lives of troops swept aside most criticism. To the objection that little logic seemed to lie behind their choice of targets, the air commanders merely insisted that their real target was a concept – enemy morale and will – rather than any particular physical object. That proved to be a remarkably resilient theme over the decades. "Bomber" Harris, more honest than many of the Allied air commanders of the second world war when it came to acknowledging the imprecision of the bombing technology of the day, conceded that it was not possible accurately to destroy from the air any targets smaller than a few square miles. For that reason, he argued, the right targets to hit were the only things that were bigger – ie, entire cities. This, he insisted, would win the war.

The possibility that air power would make a ground invasion of France unnecessary tantalised some American politicians right up to the Normandy landings. Harris, too, continued to press his case, even during the final planning for D-day. "Harris told us how well he might have won the war had it not been for the handicap imposed by the existence of the other two services," commented General Alan Brooke, an army compatriot, after one pre-invasion conference of top commanders.

Similarly, 20 years on, when some of Lyndon Johnson's advisers objected that bombing North Vietnam's factories and rail lines would not do much harm to an agrarian country in which industry accounted for only 12% of its minuscule GNP, America's air-force chiefs argued that since its industrial sector was so small, the country was that much more dependent on it, and would suffer all the more if it were destroyed. In fact, the North Vietnamese responded to the bombing of their oil tanks and railways by dispersing fuel across the country in small drums and hauling supplies around on bicycles. But zapping railways, factories and oil tanks was something the air force knew how to do.

By that time bombing, whether effective or not, seemed much more attractive than sending in more troops. As America's ground forces in Vietnam found themselves increasingly impotent against an elusive and resourceful foe, the military commanders proposed endless variations on the same bombing strategy that had so far failed. Johnson one day dressed down the army chief of staff in front of his underlings: "Bomb, bomb, bomb, that's all you know. Well, I want to know why there's nothing else. You're not giving me any ideas for this damn little *pissant* country. Now, I don't need ten generals to come in here ten times and tell me to bomb."

The coming of age of precision guidance did sharply change conventional warfare involving conventional armies, as the two Gulf wars showed: aircraft were able to destroy hundreds of armoured vehicles and paralyse Saddam Hussein's ground forces well before they could engage American or British ground troops. And as NATO's air campaign against Serbia showed in 1999, precision weapons can nowadays destroy selected targets, even in the heart of cities, without causing a thousandth of the civilian casualties that were routine in the second world war.

But when it comes to rooting out guerrillas and insurgents, wishful thinking still tends to outweigh technological capabilities. A study of the use of air power in small wars over the past century by James Corum and Wray Johnson, two former professors at the American air force's School of Advanced Airpower Studies, concluded that insurgents and terrorists "rarely present lucrative targets for aerial attack". Air power has been used to greatest effect in such campaigns only indirectly: to gather intelligence, move troops or maintain communication.

And as others besides the Israelis have found, trying to wage an air campaign against irregular forces is especially vulnerable to the backlash that invariably arises as civilian casualties mount. Since terrorists and guerrillas blend into the civilian population, fight in small units and rely on surprise and mobility, accurate and timely intelligence is crucial, and bad intelligence always results in civilian casualties, sometimes lots of them. Moreover, dropping a bomb in an urban area, even when the intelligence is correct, and even when the bomb is precision-guided, is likely to kill innocent neighbours.

Israel's excellent intelligence in the occupied territories has enabled it to carry out lethally successful precision air strikes against the leaders of Hamas and other outfits there. But even these attacks have often resulted in casualties to bystanders. In Lebanon the Israeli air force found itself in the worst of both worlds, killing civilians without achieving military objectives. No crucial Hizbullah leaders were killed and almost none of their mobile rocket-launchers were destroyed. Only the fixed launchers for their longer-range missiles north of the Litani river appear to have been much damaged.

Not by bombs alone

Israel was hoping, through its use of air power in Lebanon, not just to hammer an irregular guerrilla force; it was also seeking to put pressure on the Lebanese government and others to disarm Hizbullah and secure its southern border. In this General Halutz was said to have been strongly influenced by NATO's war of psychological pressure against Slobodan Milosevic, which aimed to force the Serb dictator to take a specific action – pull out of Kosovo and halt his ethnic cleansing – through an air campaign that kept ratcheting up the costs by destroying power plants, bridges, factories and other bits of infrastructure.

But, in the end, Israel found that even in a war that hinged on psychology and "consciousness", air power had inherent limitations. In the 48 hours before the ceasefire went into effect, Israel sent a surge of ground troops into southern Lebanon to engage in the "anachronistic" pursuit of seizing territory – precisely in order to create the conscious perception of tangible military victory that air power alone had failed to deliver. The truly smart bomb remains as elusive as the silver bullet.

This article was first published in *The Economist* in August 2006.

8 The growing drone dimension

Attack of the drones

Military technology: Smaller and smarter unmanned aircraft are transforming spying and redefining the idea of air power

IN 2004, in the mountainous Afghan province of Baghlan, NATO officials mounted a show of force for the local governor, Faqir Mamozai, to emphasise their commitment to the region. As the governor and his officials looked on, Jan van Hoof, a Dutch commander, called in a group of F-16 fighter jets, which swooped over the city of Baghlan, their thunderous afterburners engaged. This display of air power was, says Mr van Hoof, an effective way to garner the respect of the local people. But fighter jets are a limited and expensive resource. And in conflicts like that in Afghanistan, they are no longer the most widespread form of air power. The nature of air power, and the notion of air superiority, have been transformed in the past few years by the rise of remote-controlled drone aircraft, known in military jargon as "unmanned aerial vehicles" (UAVs).

Drones are much less expensive to operate than manned warplanes. The cost per flight-hour of Israel's drone fleet, for example, is less than 5% the cost of its fighter jets, says Antan Israeli, the commander of an Israeli drone squadron. The Israel Defence Forces' fleet of UAVs tripled in size between 2007 and 2009. Mr Israeli says that "almost all" IDF ground operations now have drone support.

Of course, small and comparatively slow UAVs are no match for fighter jets when it comes to inspiring awe with roaring flyovers – or shooting down enemy warplanes. Some drones, such as America's Predator and Reaper, carry missiles or bombs, though most do not. (Countries with "hunter-killer" drones include America, Britain and

Israel.) But drones have other strengths that can be just as valuable. In particular, they are unparalleled spies. Operating discreetly, they can intercept radio and mobile-phone communications, and gather intelligence using video, radar, thermal-imaging and other sensors. The data they gather can then be sent instantly via wireless and satellite links to an operations room halfway around the world – or to the hand-held devices of soldiers below. In military jargon, troops without UAV support are "disadvantaged".

The technology has been adopted at extraordinary speed. In 2003, the year the American-led coalition defeated Saddam Hussein's armed forces, America's military logged a total of roughly 35,000 UAV flight-hours in Iraq and Afghanistan. In 2008 the tally reached 800,000 hours. And even that figure is an underestimate, because it does not include the flights of small drones, which have proliferated rapidly in recent years. (America alone is thought to have over 5,000 of them.) These robots, typically launched by foot soldiers with a catapult, slingshot or hand toss, far outnumber their larger kin, which are the size of piloted aeroplanes.

Global sales of UAVs in 2009 are expected to increase by more than 10% over the previous year to exceed $4.7 billion, according to Visiongain, a market-research firm based in London. It estimates that America will spend about 60% of the total. For its part, America's Department of Defence says it will spend more than $22 billion to develop, buy and operate drones between 2007 and 2013. Following the United States, Israel ranks second in the development and possession of drones, according to those in the industry. The European leaders, trailing Israel, are roughly matched: Britain, France, Germany and Italy. Russia and Spain are not far behind, and nor, say some experts, is China. (But the head of an American navy research-laboratory in Europe says this is an underestimate cultivated by secretive Beijing, and that China's drone fleet is actually much larger.)

In total, more than three dozen countries operate UAVs, including Belarus, Colombia, Sri Lanka and Georgia. Some analysts say Georgian armed forces, equipped with Israeli drones, outperformed Russia in aerial intelligence during their brief war in August 2008. (Russia also buys Israeli drones.)

Iran builds drones, one of which was shot down over Iraq by

American forces in February 2009. The model in question can report-edly collect ground intelligence from an altitude of 4,000 metres as far as 140km from its base. In 2009 Iranian officials said they had developed a new drone with a range of more than 1,900km. Iran has supplied Hizbullah militants in Lebanon with a small fleet of drones, though their usefulness is limited: Hizbullah uses lobbed rather than guided rockets, and it is unlikely to muster a ground attack that would benefit from drone intelligence. But ownership of UAVs enhances Hiz-bullah's prestige in the eyes of its supporters, says Amal Ghorayeb, a Beirut academic who is an expert on the group.

Eyes wide open

How effective are UAVs? In Iraq, the significant drop in American casu-alties in the roughly 18 months to September 2009 is partly attribut-able to the "persistent stare" of drone operators hunting for insurgents' roadside bombs and remotely fired rockets, says Christopher Oliver, a colonel in the American army who was stationed in Baghdad until mid-2009. "We stepped it up," he says, adding that drone missions will continue to increase, in part to compensate for the withdrawal of troops. In Afghanistan and Iraq, almost all big convoys of Western equipment or personnel are preceded by a scout drone, according to Mike Kulinski of Enerdyne Technologies, a developer of military-com-munications software based in California. Such drones can stream video back to drivers and transmit electromagnetic jamming signals that disable the electronic triggers of some roadside bombs.

In military parlance, drones do work that would be "dull, dirty and dangerous" for soldiers. Some of them can loiter in the air for long periods. The Eagle-1, for example, developed by Israel Aerospace Industries and EADS, Europe's aviation giant, can stay aloft for more than 50 hours at a time. (France deployed several of these aircraft in 2009 in Afghanistan.) Such long flights help operators, assisted with object-recognition software, to determine normal (and suspicious) patterns of movement for people and vehicles by tracking suspects for two wake-and-sleep cycles.

Drones are acquiring new abilities. New sensors that are now entering service can make out the "electrical signature" of ground vehicles by picking up signals produced by engine spark-plugs, alternators, and other electronics. A Pakistani UAV called the Tornado, made in Karachi by a company called Integrated Dynamics, emits radar signals that mimic a fighter jet to fool enemies.

UAVs are hard to shoot down. Today's heat-seeking shoulder-launched missiles do not work above 3,000 metres or so, though the next generation will be able to go higher, says Carlo Siardi of Selex Galileo, a subsidiary of Finmeccanica in Ronchi dei Legionari, Italy. Moreover, drone engines are smaller – and therefore cooler – than those powering heavier, manned aircraft. In some of them the propeller is situated behind the exhaust source to disperse hot air, reducing the heat signature. And soldiers who shoot at aircraft risk revealing their position.

But drones do have an Achilles' heel. If a UAV loses the data connection to its operator – by flying out of range, for example – it may well crash. Engineers have failed to solve this problem, says Dan Isaac, a drone expert at Spain's Centre for the Development of Industrial Technology, a government research agency in Madrid. The solution, he and others say, is to build systems which enable an operator to reconnect with a lost drone by transmitting data via a "bridge" aircraft nearby.

In June 2009 America's Northrop Grumman unveiled the first of a new generation of its Global Hawk aircraft, thought to be the world's fastest drone. It can gather data on objects reportedly as small as a shoebox, through clouds, day or night, for 32 hours from 18,000 metres – almost twice the cruising altitude of passenger jets. After North Korea detonated a test nuclear device in May, America said it would begin replacing its manned U-2 spy planes in South Korea with Global Hawks, which are roughly the size of a corporate jet.

Big drones are, however, hugely expensive. With their elaborate sensors, some cost as much as $60m apiece. Fewer than 30 Global Hawks have been bought. And it is not just the hardware that is costly: each Global Hawk requires a support team of 20–30 people. As the biggest UAVs get bigger, they are also becoming more expensive. Future American UAVs may cost a third as much as the F-35 fighter jet (each of which costs around $83m, without weapons). The Neuron, a jet-engine stealth drone developed by France's Dassault Aviation and partners including Italy's Alenia, will be about the size of the French manned Mirage fighter.

Small drones, by contrast, cost just tens of thousands of dollars. With electric motors, they are quiet enough for low-altitude spying. But batteries and fuel cells have only recently become light enough to open up a large market. A fuel cell developed by AMI Adaptive Materials, based in Ann Arbor, Michigan, exemplifies the progress made. In 2006 AMI sold a 25-watt fuel cell weighing 2 kilograms. Today its fuel cell is 25% lighter and provides eight times as much power. This won AMI a $500,000 prize from the Department of Defence. Its fuel cells, costing about $12,000 each, now propel small drones.

Most small drones are launched without airstrips and are controlled in the field using a small computer. They can be recovered with nets, parachutes, vertically strung cords that snag a wingtip hook or a simple drop on the ground after a stall a metre or two in the air. Their airframes break apart to absorb the impact; users simply snap them back together.

With some systems, a ground unit can launch a drone for a quick bird's-eye look around with very little effort. Working with financing from Italy's defence ministry, Oto Melara, an Italian firm, has built prototypes of a short-range drone launched from a vehicle-mounted pneumatic cannon. The aircraft's wings unfold upon leaving the tube. It streams back video while flying any number of preset round-trip patterns. Crucially, operators do not need to worry about fiddling with controls; the drone flies itself.

Send in the drones

Indeed, as UAVs become more technologically complex, there is also a clear trend towards making their control systems easier to use, according to a succession of experts speaking at a conference in La Spezia, Italy, held in April 2009 by the Association for Unmanned Vehicle Systems International (AUVSI), an industry association. For example, instead of manoeuvring aircraft, operators typically touch (or click on) electronic maps to specify points along a desired route. Software determines the best flight altitudes, speeds and search patterns for each mission – say, locating a well near a hilltop within sniping range of a road.

In 2010 Lockheed Martin, an American defence contractor, will begin final testing of software to make flying drones easier for troops with little training. Called ECCHO, it allows soldiers to control aircraft and view the resulting intelligence on a standard hand-held device such as an iPhone, BlackBerry or Palm Pre. It incorporates Google Earth mapping software, largely for the same reason: most recruits are already proficient users.

What's next? A diplomat from Djibouti, a country in the Horn of Africa, provides a clue. He says private companies in Europe are now offering to operate spy drones for his government, which has none. (Djibouti has declined.) But purchasing UAV services, instead of owning fleets, is becoming a "strong trend", says Kyle Snyder, head of surveillance technology at AUVSI. About 20 companies, he estimates, fly spy drones for clients.

One of them, a division of Boeing called Insitu, sees a lucrative untapped market in Afghanistan, where the intelligence needs of some smaller NATO countries are not being met by larger allies. (Armed forces are often reluctant to share their intelligence for tactical reasons.) Alejandro Pita, Insitu's head of sales, declines to name customers, but says his firm's flights cost roughly $2,000 an hour for 300 or so hours a month. The drones-for-hire market is also expanding into non-military fields. Services include inspecting tall buildings, monitoring traffic and maintaining security at large facilities.

Drone sales and research budgets will continue to grow. Raytheon, an American company, has launched a drone from a submerged submarine. Mini helicopter drones for reconnaissance inside buildings are not far off. In China, which is likely to be a big market in the future, senior officials have been talking about reducing troop numbers and spending more money developing "informationised warfare" capabilities, including unmanned aircraft.

There is a troubling side to all this. Operators can now safely manipulate battlefield weapons from control rooms half a world away, as if they are playing a video game. Drones also enable a government to avoid the political risk of putting combat boots on foreign soil. This makes it easier to start a war, says P.W. Singer, the American author of "Wired for War", a bestseller about robotic warfare. But like them or not, drones are here to stay. Armed forces that master them are not just securing their hold on air superiority – they are also dramatically increasing its value.

This article was first published in *The Economist* in September 2009.

Robo raider

A new drone emerges with the ability to fight back

SOME HOVER LIKE INSECTS, and are not much bigger. Some can be pulled from a rucksack and launched by hand. Others require runways in order to take off. Without the need for an expensively trained pilot and all his supporting gear, the market for unmanned aerial vehicles (UAVs) has quickly turned into a $5 billion business. And it will not stop there. In July 2010, on the eve of the Farnborough Air Show near London, BAE Systems, a British defence contractor, unveiled Taranis. Named after the Celtic god of thunder, this is a drone that takes robotic warfare to a new level.

Taranis is about the size of a small jet trainer, but with the look of a stealth bomber to make it hard to detect on radar. Capable of being operated by remote control from anywhere in the world via a satellite link, it can fly from one continent to another, carrying out surveillance or dropping bombs and firing missiles at ground targets. But it is also capable of another trick: the ability to defend itself, like a jet fighter, if it is attacked by another drone or by a manned aircraft.

It is, as BAE says, "a prelude to the next generation of fighting capacity." More UAVs are coming. Boeing, for one, has a hydrogen-powered UAV called the Phantom Eye that will fly for four days at 20,000 metres (66,000 feet). Some of the pilots showing off their skills at Farnborough may be the last of their kind.

This article was first published in *The Economist* in July 2010.

Unmanned and dangerous

Aviation: Unmanned aerial vehicles are a vital tool of modern warfare. Once-harmless drones are now deadly attack aircraft. Where did the technology come from, and where is it going?

DUSK FALLS OVER BAGHDAD AND KABUL, and the Predators take their places in the skies overhead, ready for action. Western soldiers prefer to fight in the dark, when their night-vision gear gives them the advantage over insurgents. They know that with drone aircraft scanning the ground, with unblinking eyes able to see by day or night and radars that can see through cloud, they "own the night".

For the Predators' pilots, however, it is still bright daylight. Sitting in cramped metal containers in bases across America, they fly their machines by remote control from thousands of miles away, via satellite links. The video from the drones is gathered in a makeshift operations centre in the Nevada desert and distributed to leaders in the Pentagon and commanders on the ground. In the Predator operations centre, one screen monitors the weather around the Arabian Sea (Predators do not like rain or high winds), another shows the location of each aircraft on a map, and a third projects a mosaic of video images from each plane. One image shows a house under close observation in a palm grove in Iraq; another shows a road being scanned for hidden bombs. A laptop computer system known as Rover allows troops on the ground to watch the footage, and will soon let them mark out targets.

First flown in 1995, the Predator is a flimsy drone that flies as slowly as a Cessna and can carry far less weight. Yet it has become one of the most prized assets in today's wars in Iraq and Afghanistan. Initially a surveillance drone, the Predator was given a laser designator to enable it to guide precision-guided weapons from other aircraft, and then acquired its own weapons in the form of Hellfire missiles. It has thus shortened the process of finding, identifying and destroying a target – known in military jargon as the "kill chain" or the "sensor-to-shooter" cycle – to a matter of seconds if necessary. The 432nd

Wing, which flies the Predators, is one of the fastest-growing units of the American air force. In 2006 it flew more than 50,000 hours, and fired Hellfires roughly every other day.

The Predator is far from being the only unmanned aerial vehicle (UAV) in use today, though it is probably the best known. The success of military UAVs is helping to push them into mainstream civil uses all over the world, in applications including border patrol, police surveillance, scientific research and disaster response. And there is a growing community of hobbyists who attach satellite-positioning units, cameras and other sensors to remote-controlled aircraft, turning them into UAVs.

Not everyone approves. Civil regulators are worried about unmanned aircraft sharing the sky with the usual manned variety, since UAVs have previously been limited to war zones or remote areas. And air forces may be reluctant to lose the mystique of the combat pilot. "There's going to be resistance," says Colonel John Montgomery, vice-commander of the 432nd Wing. "When I first saw a briefing on the Predator three years ago [in 2004], I saw one of my mission sets disappear. I miss the thrill of flying. But hanging around for hours in a plane is a waste of manpower."

Mad as a kite

Unmanned flying machines go back a long way. Kites were used in the late 19th century to carry cameras aloft to take pictures of battle-fields. And even before the Wright brothers succeeded in building a heavier-than-air flying machine, the physicist and inventor Nikola Tesla speculated that it would be possible to build a remote-controlled flying bomb – a premonition perhaps of German V-1 flying bombs and modern cruise missiles. Yet aviation history is littered with the wrecks of unmanned-aircraft projects – some of them barmy, others simply too far ahead of their time – that were given a variety of names, including "aerial torpedo" and "remotely piloted vehicle".

Occasionally UAVs found a valuable niche, for instance as targets for anti-aircraft gunnery. The first such machine, a radio-controlled "Fairey Queen" biplane, was catapulted into the air in 1933 and survived two hours of live fire from a British warship. The following year the Air Ministry ordered 420 such aircraft, known as the Queen Bee. This gave rise to the word "drone", which is still used to describe unmanned planes. But this was a rare success. More often, UAVs were defeated by the immaturity of the available technology, changing needs, soaring costs and, above all, the successful development of rival technologies.

Pilots wanted

For decades a human pilot's eyes, sense of balance and hands were simply the best way to guide a flying machine, stay on course and cope with problems. Orbiting satellites were better at spying on enemies than wayward reconnaissance drones, and rockets destroyed targets more reliably than temperamental flying bombs did. The success of modern UAVs such as the Predator is not due to a single technological breakthrough, but to the combination of innovations in several areas – faster computers, fly-by-wire controls, satellite navigation, miniaturisation of sensors and fast data-transmission – into a workable and affordable whole.

Early attempts at unmanned guidance involved gyroscopes. During the first world war a flying bomb known as the Kettering Bug was developed. It was an unmanned biplane with player-piano bellows to power its gyroscope and a cash-register mechanism that calculated distance flown by counting the rotations of a propeller-like rotor. But it proved unreliable and inaccurate, not least because the catapult launches upset the sensitive gyroscopes, and it never saw action.

The development of radio (for remote control), radar (to gauge height from the ground) and television (to provide final aim when nearing a target) revived the idea of flying bombs. In the second world war the American navy experimented with TV-guided drones controlled from another aircraft, but these were little more than side-shows in the Pacific, where air power came mainly from aircraft carriers. In Europe attempts to fly old American bombers packed with explosives were a failure. If anything it was the Axis powers that made the breakthrough. The Japanese used suicide *kamikaze* pilots to direct flying bombs with deadly effect against American ships,

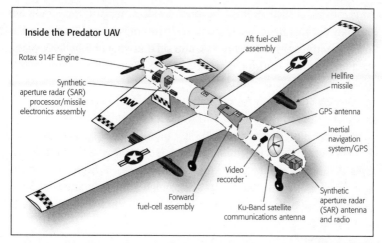

Inside the Predator UAV

Rotax 914F Engine

Synthetic aperture radar (SAR) processor/missile electronics assembly

Aft fuel-cell assembly

Hellfire missile

GPS antenna

Inertial navigation system/GPS

Video recorder

Forward fuel-cell assembly

Ku-Band satellite communications antenna

Synthetic aperture radar (SAR) antenna and radio

Source: AFCESA

FIG 8.1 Under the hood

proving the superior guiding ability of the human brain, and the Germans successfully used the V-1 flying bomb as a weapon of terror against London – a large target a short distance away that was hard to miss.

At the end of the war General Henry "Hap" Arnold, the chief of America's army air forces declared: "We have just won a war with a lot of heroes flying around in planes. The next war may be fought by airplanes with no men in them at all." It was not to be. The advent of nuclear weapons relaxed the need for pinpoint accuracy, but early American cruise missiles designed to carry them – such as the navy's Regulus and air force's Matador – suffered from the perennial problem of guidance. The initial launch using rockets upset the gyroscopes, and radio guidance was unreliable because vacuum tubes suffered under high acceleration.

Radar mapping was attempted on Matador, but suffered from the limitations of 1950s computers. Another UAV, the Snark, was supposed to have intercontinental range and used a stellar guidance system that weighed one ton. "It is possible to build a transoceanic missile right now," said one official at the time, "but we don't know whether it will land in Spain, Portugal or France." One test shot ended up in the

Amazon. As nuclear bombs became smaller, ballistic missiles won the day. Rockets flew much faster and required inertial guidance for just a few minutes to put the weapon on a predictable ballistic path. And unlike radio-controlled aircraft, rockets were all but invulnerable to jamming or interception.

Drones sometimes found a useful role in reconnaissance, especially as improvements in surface-to-air missiles made manned spy flights risky. The loss of a U2 spy plane piloted by Francis Gary Powers over the Soviet Union in 1960 led to the search for alternatives. A reconnaissance UAV known as Red Wagon did not fare well, and funding went instead into a fast, high-altitude plane that later became known as the SR-71 Blackbird, and the first Corona surveillance satellites.

But America's air force continued to experiment, converting a small jet-powered target drone, the Firebee, into an unmanned spy plane called the Lightning Bug. This was launched from another plane, took photographs of its target, and released a parachute upon its return so it could be picked up by a helicopter. It was flown over China in 1964 and then used in the Vietnam war. It was also used as bait to activate North Vietnamese anti-aircraft missile defences and transmit the resulting signals to a manned aircraft before being destroyed. Navigation progressively improved, from inertial systems to a camera with a video link, but by 1973 the drone still missed about half its targets.

The development of integrated circuits and better data links promised a bright future for UAVs in the 1970s. But the shift of military attention to the Soviet Union, the refusal of European civil authorities to allow unmanned planes in their airspace, arms-control agreements and the perennial problem of accurate navigation over long distances conspired against UAVs. Once again, rival technology for manned aircraft stole the thunder: stealthy designs to reduce the radar signature, precision weapons such as cruise missiles and laser-guided munitions and new sensors such as synthetic-aperture radar that could look through clouds.

Ultimately it was Israel, not America, that revived the use of drones in warfare. It had seen at first hand in the 1973 Arab-Israeli war the damage that modern air defences can cause. In the 1982 Lebanon war, the clever use of small Israeli-built UAVs (incorporating technology developed in America's disappointing programmes) helped win a startling air campaign in which Syria's anti-aircraft batteries in the Bekaa valley were destroyed and up to 100 Syrian jets shot down against no losses for Israel. In carefully choreographed moves, drones were used to spy on the Syrian defences, fool their radars and gather the electronic intelligence needed to destroy them.

Unlike America, which sought to operate large UAVs at long distances through hostile air space, Israel's drones operated from its own defended territory, and real-time video was transmitted through short line-of-sight data links. Israeli UAV technology became all the rage in the Pentagon, especially after the American navy lost three aircraft over Lebanon in 1983. Predator is in fact derived from a design devised by a former Israel Aircraft Industries engineer. It also benefited from the advent of the satellite-based Global Positioning System in the 1990s, which finally resolved the problem of accurate navigation. And the Predator's ability to stay aloft for a whole day helped to overcome the main shortcoming of satellites and jets: they can only glimpse a target, rather than watch it over time.

But the Predator is slow and vulnerable, requiring full mastery of the air so it can loiter without being shot down. Like Israeli machines, it was designed for benign weather conditions. In the Balkans, where Predators were first deployed, their wings tended to ice over. Pilots still say it is "skittish" to fly, and UAVs of all kinds are much more prone to crashing.

Removing the pilot from the cockpit means the UAV has to be wirelessly connected to its controllers by vulnerable data links, whether via satellites or ground-based receivers. The Pentagon buys as much as four-fifths of its bandwidth from commercial satellite operators, and the launch of a new generation of military-communications satellites is unlikely to satisfy the demand for capacity, given the need to pipe full-motion video back from UAVs. Against the Taliban and Iraqi insurgents, these problems are manageable. But against a more sophisticated state foe, particularly one able to wage electronic warfare, the benefits of such UAVs could quickly fade.

The technology of UAVs has already moved beyond the Predator, however. There are now hundreds of models under development, from vast flying wings intended to stay aloft for five years using solar power (acting more like a satellite than a plane) to tiny bug-like flying machines that could swarm and interact wirelessly.

Beyond the Predator

The cost of building UAVs is falling, making them more attractive for civilian use. It may be a long time, though, before they become as safe and reliable as civil aircraft. Allowing UAVs to fly alongside airliners will require them to develop the means to "sense and avoid" other planes; new air-traffic-control systems, based on electronic rather than voice communications, will also be needed. Even in war zones, the American air force is starting to worry about the danger of aircraft colliding with smaller UAVs. Predator pilots say it is not unusual to abort a Hellfire missile strike when an army helicopter unexpectedly comes into view.

Military UAVs are evolving quickly. Predator's big brother, called Reaper, went into service in Afghanistan in 2007; it recorded its first "kill" in October 2007. Reaper can fly twice as fast as Predator and can carry about ten times the payload, including 500lb (225kg) precision bombs. Future UAVs will carry other weapons, such as air-to-air or anti-radar missiles. Support aircraft such as unmanned air-to-air refuelling tankers are already being considered; so too are unmanned "wingmen" to accompany, and be directed from, manned fighters.

Global Hawk, a large reconnaissance drone, has demonstrated the ability to take off, cross oceans and land without guidance. More processing power on board UAVs will make them more autonomous and reduce the demand for bandwidth. Surveillance drones could, for example, alert operators only when an area under observation has changed. But UAVs' growing complexity could make them as expensive as manned planes.

On the ground, control systems are becoming more sophisticated. As UAVs become more autonomous, pilots will be able to control more aircraft at once, by giving each one occasional instructions. New displays will fuse video from UAVs seamlessly with computer-generated "synthetic" scenery (generated from maps and surveillance imagery), to create the feeling of being in a real cockpit, rather than looking through a "soda-straw", as pilots describe today's experience.

Might UAVs eventually replace manned combat aircraft altogether? The Centre for Strategic and Budgetary Assessments, an influential American think-tank, advocates cutting back the next generation of manned jets – the Joint Strike Fighter – in favour of unmanned stealth bombers that would operate from aircraft carriers. Much of the work of modern air-defence involves long-distance missile shots rather than acrobatic dog-fights. And when extreme agility is required, the limiting factor on an aircraft's performance is often the need to keep the pilot alive and conscious under high G-forces.

If manned combat aircraft do vanish, however, human pilots will still be needed. Even people developing UAVs doubt that computers will entirely replace the brain in as dynamic, unpredictable and horribly human an activity as war. "Can you still win a medal flying a UAV?" asks Colonel Montgomery, himself a jet pilot. "You may not have the fear of death, but all the other fears are still there: the fear of the unknown and the fear of failure."

This article was first published in *The Economist* in December 2007.

9 Air ops, for less

Air power on the cheap

Small, slow and inexpensive propeller-driven planes are starting to displace fighter jets

JET FIGHTERS MAY BE SEXY in a Tom Cruise-ish sort of way, but for guerilla warfare – in which the enemy rarely has an air force of his own with which to dogfight – they are often not the tool for the job. Pilotless drones can help fill the gap. Sometimes there is no substitute for having a pilot on the scene, however, so modern air forces are starting to turn to a technology from the yesteryear of flying: the turboprop.

So-called light-attack turboprops are cheap both to build and to fly. A fighter jet can cost $80m. By contrast the 208B Caravan, a light-attack turboprop made by Cessna, costs barely $2m. It also costs as little as $500 a hour to run when it is in the air, compared with $10,000 or more for a fighter jet. And, unlike jets, turboprops can use roads and fields for takeoff and landing.

Nor is it only jets that light-attack turboprops can outperform. Armed drones have drawbacks, too. The Reaper, made by General Atomics, can cost $10m or more, depending on its bells and whistles. On top of that, a single drone can require a team of more than 20 people on the ground to support it, plus satellite communications. A manned turboprop can bomb an insurgent for a third of the cost of using a drone, according to Pat Sullivan, the head of government sales at Cessna. And there are strategic considerations, too. Many countries' armed forces rely on allies such as America for the expertise and satellite networks needed to run drones. Such allies can let you down in a pinch. Piloted light-attack planes offer complete operational independence – and, being lower-tech than many drones, are less subject to restrictions on exports in the first place.

They are also better, in many ways, than helicopters. To land a chopper safely in the dirt requires sophisticated laser scanners to detect obstacles hidden by dust thrown up by the downdraught of the rotors. On top of this, such dust makes helicopter maintenance even more difficult than it is already. Maintaining turboprops, by contrast, is easy. According to Robyn Read, an air-power strategist at the Air Force Research Institute near Montgomery, Alabama, they can be "flown and maintained by plumbers". Thrush Aircraft, a firm based in Albany, Georgia, is even more expansive. It claims that the Vigilante, an armed version of its cropdusting plane that costs $1m, can be disassembled in the field with little more than a pocket screwdriver.

Turboprops are also hard to shoot down. Air Tractor, another firm that makes cropdusters, branched out into warplanes last year. One reason was that a fleet of 16 unarmed versions of its aircraft had been used by America's State Department to dust South American drug plantations with herbicide – an activity that tends to provoke a hostile response from the ground. Despite the planes' having been hit by more than 200 rounds, though, neither an aircraft nor a pilot has been lost.

In part, this is because of the robust mechanics of turboprops and in part because Air Tractor's fuel tanks have rubber membranes which close around bullet holes to slow leaks. Add extra fuel tanks, which let the plane stay aloft for ten hours, six 225kg precision-guided bombs and more than 2,000kg of missiles, rockets and ammunition for two 50-calibre machineguns, and you have the AT-802U, a formidable yet reasonably cheap (at $5m) warplane.

Light-attack aircraft also now sport much of the electronics used by fighter jets. The MX-15, an imaging device made by L-3 WESCAM, a Canadian company, allows a pilot to read a vehicle's license plate from a distance of 10km. It is carried by both the AT-802U and the AT-6, a top-of-the-range light-attack plane made by Hawker Beechcraft.

Not surprisingly, then, many countries with small defence budgets are investing in turboprops. Places that now fly them, or are expected to do so, include Brazil, Chile, Colombia, the Dominican Republic, Ecuador, Indonesia, Iraq, Lebanon, Morocco and Venezuela. And the United States. For the biggest military establishment in the world, too, recognises the value of this new old technology. The American air force plans to buy more than 100 turboprops and the navy is now evaluating the Super Tucano, made by Embraer, a Brazilian firm.

In aerial combat, then, low tech may be the new high tech. And there is one other advantage that the turboprop has over the jet, at least according to Mr Read – who flew turboprops on combat missions in Cambodia during the 1970s. It is that you can use a loudspeaker to talk to potential targets before deciding whether to attack them. As Winston Churchill so memorably put it: "When you have to kill a man, it costs nothing to be polite."

This article was first published in *The Economist* in September 2010.

Spies in the sky

Military technology: Blimps equipped with remote-sensing electronics are cheaper than drone aircraft, and have many other advantages

SPYING IS A SOPHISTICATED AND EXPENSIVE BUSINESS – and gathering military intelligence using unmanned aircraft can be prohibitively so. Predator and Global Hawk, two types of American drone frequently flown in Afghanistan and Iraq, cost around $5,000 and $26,500 an hour respectively to operate. The aircraft themselves cost between $4.5m and $35m each, and the remote-sensing equipment they carry can more than double the price. Which is why less elegant but far cheaper balloons are now being used instead.

Such blimps can keep surveillance and ordnance-guiding equipment aloft for a few hundred dollars an hour. They cost hundreds of thousands, not millions, of dollars. And they can stay in the air for more than a week, whereas most drones fly for no more than 30 hours at a time. They are also easy to deploy, because no airfield is needed. A blimp can be stored in the back of a jeep, driven to a suitable location, launched in a couple of hours and winched down again even faster.

Unlike other aircraft, blimps, also known as aerostats, do not need to form a precise aerodynamic shape. This means they can lift improbable objects into the sky, such as dangling radar equipment. At altitudes of just a few hundred metres, a blimp carrying 20kg of remote-sensing electronics (including radar and thermal-imaging cameras) can identify, track and provide images of combatants dozens of kilometres away, by day or night. It can also help commanders aim the lasers that guide their missiles.

Blimps often operate beyond the range of machine-guns and rocket-propelled grenades. Even if they are hit, though, they do not explode because the helium gas that keeps them airborne is not flammable. (Engineers abandoned the use of hydrogen in 1937 after the *Hindenburg*, a German airship, was consumed by flames in less than a minute.) Moreover, they usually stay aloft even when punctured: the pressure of the helium inside a blimp is about the same as that of the air outside, so the gas does not rush out. Indeed, towards the end of 2004, when a blimp broke its tether north of Baghdad and started to drift towards Iran, the American air force had trouble shooting it down.

At least 20 countries use blimps – both global military powers, such as America, Britain and France, and smaller regional ones, including Ireland, Pakistan, Poland and the United Arab Emirates. Many are employed in Iraq. In November 2008 Aerostar International of Sioux Falls, South Dakota, began filling a $1.8m order for 36 blimps to be deployed by the American armed forces in Iraq. But Afghanistan may prove a bigger market. That is because it is difficult to pick up satellite signals in the valleys of that mountainous country. As a result blimps, adjusted to hover at appropriate heights, are often used to relay data to and from satellites.

As politicians around the world seek to cut public spending, the attractions of blimps are growing. In January 2009 America's defence secretary, Robert Gates, told the Senate's armed-services committee that the Department of Defence would pursue greater quantities of "75% solutions" that could be realised in weeks or months instead of "99% exquisite systems" that take more than a decade to develop. Barry Watts, an analyst at the Centre for Strategic and Budgetary Assessments, a think-tank in Washington, DC, says America's air force has been criticised for not providing enough aerial data to "insatiable" ground forces. Blimps, Mr Watts reckons, will help them sate that appetite.

This article was first published in *The Economist* in June 2009.

Bladder control

A way to fly a balloon in and out of the stratosphere

ACCORDING TO THE OLD ADAGE, what goes up must come down. But in the case of balloons, the descent sometimes comes sooner than expected. Although helium-filled weather balloons regularly launch instruments high into the stratosphere, at altitudes of 20km (65,000 feet) the air is 15 times less dense, causing the balloons to expand and ultimately burst.

This problem has long vexed the American military, which would like to use lighter-than-air dirigibles as atmospheric satellites, or stratellites. From 20km a blimp would be able to continuously survey an area the size of Texas for months at a time, but in greater detail and at much lower cost than geostationary satellites or those moving in low Earth orbit.

Despite the problems, dirigibles are coming back into service. Global Telesat Corporation, an American supplier of unmanned aerial vehicles, recently purchased its first SkySat. This 38 metre-long remotely operated airship is designed to carry communications and monitoring equipment for intelligence, surveillance and reconnaissance missions. With its familiar cigar-shaped design, however, it will rise only so far – 14km, to be precise. And at this altitude ferocious winds require a SkySat to burn through its fuel supply just to stay still. As a result it can remain aloft for only a few days at a time.

The ultimate goal is to find a way to slip above the jet stream and into the virtually windless stratosphere for an even better vantage point, says Dan Erdberg of Sanswire, a Florida company which developed SkySat. Over the years the company has looked at various solutions, and it is now working with Global Telesat to develop a novel, snakelike airship called the STS-111. It is made up of four connected and articulated inflatable sections.

Each section of the STS-111 contains two gas envelopes – one inside the other. The inner envelope holds helium in the head section of the blimp and an ethane fuel gas in the three tail sections. The outer envelope of all four sections contains air maintained at atmospheric pressure. Although the airship starts off flaccid, the helium and the ethane expand as it gains altitude. As it does so, the air in the outer envelope is released to allow these gases to fill the void left behind. This approach gives the gases more room to expand without stretching the envelope of the airship too much.

Venting gases is not a new idea, says Mr Erdberg, but usually it involves releasing helium, which reduces the buoyancy of the craft, so that making a safe descent or maintaining a steady altitude becomes extremely difficult. What makes Sanswire's design unique is that it allows the airship to have the same weight on landing as it did when it took off.

This is because air is pumped back into the tail envelopes as the ethane fuel is burned by the craft's thrusters, and is also pumped into the tail and head during descent as the inner envelopes contract. The serpentine aerofoil shape is designed to face into what little wind there is, generating a small amount of lift. And since ethane has roughly the same density as air, the fuel in effect weighs nothing, further reducing the amount of helium needed to create buoyancy.

That is the theory, at least. So far, apart from some low-altitude test flights, the only stratospheric tests have involved a scaled-down version tethered to a weather balloon. Tests of a full-sized STS-111 at high altitude are not expected to begin until next year. So the military will have to wait a bit longer to see if Sanswire's ideas hold up – or its claims are inflated.

This article was first published in *The Economist* in May 2010.

10 Aircraft and flight, enhanced

Crash, bang, cushion

Aviation: How a collapsible mechanical cushion, borrowed from a space capsule, could help protect a crashing helicopter

UNLIKE FIXED-WING AIRCRAFT, helicopters tend to spend a lot of time flying close to the ground, especially during military and emergency missions. Anything that helps occupants survive a collision with the ground is therefore to be welcomed. Hence the interest in a new system that NASA, America's space agency, is testing to make helicopters safer.

The idea comes from an expandable honeycomb cushion which Sotiris Kellas, an engineer at the agency's Langley Research Centre in Hampton, Virginia, came up with to help absorb the impact of landing a space capsule. It has since been tried out by fitting the structure under the fuselage of an MD-500 helicopter, donated by the American army, strapping four crash-test dummies inside and then using a special rig to swing the helicopter forward at 53kph (33mph) and drop it from 10.7 metres (35 feet). The preliminary results show that it worked rather well.

The mechanical cushioning system that Mr Kellas has designed has flexible hinges at the junction of each cell in the honeycomb. This allows the structure, which is made of stiff and strong carbon-fibre-based materials, to be folded flat. When it is deployed, using either wires to snap it into place or an explosive charge like an airbag (or a combination of both), the longer sides of the cells face downward. In the same way that the end of a cardboard tube offers more resistance to being stamped on than the same tube would if laid on its side, this presents the strongest aspect of the cell to the outside world during an impact, allowing it to absorb the maximum amount of energy as it deforms.

In the test, the honeycomb cushion absorbed the impact to the extent that if the occupants had been people they would have suffered little or no injury, says Martin Annett, a researcher involved in the project. In fact, the helicopter was so lightly damaged that it is being repaired so that the test can be repeated – but this time without the cushion – in order to obtain comparable data.

External airbags have been used in the past to help unmanned space landers, including *Mars Pathfinder*, touch down. They have also been fitted under some helicopters, and development work in this area continues. But the researchers at Langley think their mechanical system has a number of advantages.

It is the rapid deflation of an airbag after it has first inflated that actually absorbs the impact, so its position, size, the moment it is fired and its inflation pressure are all crucial. In a car, where the occupants are sitting in known positions, the airbags can be deployed at the optimum time after sensors detect an impact. But in what can be the wildly gyrating final seconds of a helicopter crash, that is harder to achieve. To protect a helicopter in this way would require a multiplicity of specialised external airbags. Covering a machine with honeycomb is simpler.

Indeed, though it is unlikely to replace airbags in cars, Mr Kellas's honeycomb may end up supplementing them by providing additional energy-absorbing areas. Whether it ends up on Mars as well remains to be seen.

This article was first published in *The Economist* in March 2010.

More rotors, more speed

A new type of helicopter breaks speed records

THE ABILITY OF A HELICOPTER to hover and land almost anywhere makes it an enormously useful machine. But helicopters have their limitations, particularly when it comes to flying fast. In a recent series of test flights, a new type of chopper has begun smashing speed records.

The X2 is an experimental helicopter being developed by Sikorsky, the American maker of Black Hawk helicopters, at a test-flight centre in Florida. It recently flew at more than 430kph (267mph), according to a report in *Spectrum*, published by the Institute of Electrical and Electronics Engineers. The present record is held by a souped-up Westland Lynx helicopter, which managed 400kph in 1986. But most helicopters can't fly at anything like these speeds and are typically flat out at 270kph.

To make an official attempt on the record, Sikorsky will need to have the flight monitored by the Fédération Aéronautique Internationale, which compiles airspeed records. But that is unlikely to happen until the X2 is going even faster. By the end of 2010, Sikorsky hopes it will be zipping along at more than 460kph. The company, however, is interested in more than just breaking speed records. It plans to use the technology developed for the X2 in commercial helicopters.

What limits the speed of a helicopter is the same thing that allows it to hover – the air flowing over its spinning rotor blades. The rotor blades work like the wings of an aeroplane, with an aerofoil shape providing lift. But unlike an aircraft, when a helicopter is flying forwards the air passing over its rotor blades does so at different speeds. The air passing across the blade that is advancing to the front of the helicopter and into the oncoming air is going faster than the air passing over the blade that is retreating to the rear of the helicopter. And the faster the helicopter goes, the greater this difference. At 300kph, the air passing over the advancing blade could reach 1,100kph while that over the retreating blade would be about 500kph. This difference in lift can make it hard to maintain level flight. And to make matters worse for the pilot, as the tips of the rotor blades approach the speed of sound (around 1,200kph at lower altitude temperatures), shockwaves produce huge vibrations.

The X2 gets around these problems in a number of ways. First, it uses two counter-rotating rotors that spin around the same axis, one positioned above the other. So in forward flight each rotor can produce an equal amount of lift on each side, thus providing balance. The idea has been around for some time, but it proved difficult to make it work properly.

What has changed are technological advances in aircraft engineering and control systems. Now, vibrations can be reduced using "active control", which involves placing sensors around the helicopter to detect the onset of vibration and then using force generators on various parts of the frame to vibrate in such a way that they cancel out the original tremors. Advanced computer modelling has also made it possible to design more efficient rotors. A pusher propeller has been fitted at the rear of the X2 to provide extra oomph. According to the engineers, this propeller can also be used to slow the helicopter snappily. And computerised "fly-by-wire" controls allow the X2 to be flown relatively easily.

Sikorsky reckons that future helicopters built using the X2 technology would be extremely versatile machines. They would dash to and from a medical emergency a lot faster. They would also be very agile in flight, which would increase their capabilities in combat. Sikorsky has already produced a simulator so that potential customers can experience what these fast helicopters will be like to fly. Plenty of whirlybird pilots will be keen to get their hands on the real thing.

This article was first published in *The Economist* in September 2010.

V for victory

Copying birds may save aircraft fuel

BOTH BOEING AND AIRBUS have trumpeted the efficiency of their newest aircraft, the 787 and A350 respectively. Their clever designs and lightweight composites certainly make a difference. But a group of researchers at Stanford University, led by Ilan Kroo, has suggested that airlines could take a more naturalistic approach to cutting jet-fuel use, and it would not require them to buy new aircraft.

The answer, says Dr Kroo, lies with birds. Since 1914, and a seminal paper by a German researcher called Carl Wieselsberger, scientists have known that birds flying in formation – a V-shape, echelon or otherwise – expend less energy. The air flowing over a bird's wings curls upwards behind the wingtips, a phenomenon known as upwash. Other birds flying in the upwash experience reduced drag, and spend less energy propelling themselves. Peter Lissaman, an aeronautics expert who was formerly at Caltech and the University of Southern California, has suggested that a formation of 25 birds might enjoy a range increase of 71%.

When applied to aircraft, the principles are not substantially different. Dr Kroo and his team modelled what would happen if three passenger jets departing from Los Angeles, San Francisco and Las Vegas were to rendezvous over Utah, assume an inverted V-formation, occasionally swap places so all could have a turn in the most favourable positions, and proceed to London. They found that the aircraft consumed as much as 15% less fuel (with a concomitant reduction in carbon-dioxide output). Nitrogen-oxide emissions during the cruising portions of the flight fell by around a quarter.

There are, of course, kinks to be worked out. One consideration is safety, or at least the perception of it. Would passengers feel comfortable travelling in convoy? Dr Kroo points out that the aircraft could be separated by several nautical miles, and would not be in the unnervingly cosy groupings favoured by display teams like the Red Arrows. A passenger peering out of the window might not even see the other planes. Whether the separation distances involved would satisfy air-traffic-control regulations is another matter, although a working group at the International Civil Aviation Organisation has included the possibility of formation flying in a blueprint for new operational guidelines.

It remains to be seen how weather conditions affect the air flows that make formation flight more efficient. In zones of increased turbulence, the planes' wakes will decay more quickly and the effect will diminish. Dr Kroo says this is one of the areas his team will investigate further. It might also be hard for airlines to co-ordinate the departure times and destinations of passenger aircraft in a way that would allow them to gain from formation flight. Cargo aircraft, in contrast, might be easier to reschedule, as might routine military flights.

As it happens, America's armed forces are on the case already. In 2009 the country's Defence Advanced Research Projects Agency announced plans to pay Boeing to investigate formation flight, though the programme has yet to begin. There are reports that some military aircraft flew in formation when they were low on fuel during the second world war, but Dr Lissaman says they are apocryphal. "My father was an RAF pilot and my cousin the skipper of a Lancaster lost over Berlin," he adds. So he should know.

This article was first published in *The Economist* in December 2009.

11 Militarising space

Space invaders

China admits shooting down a satellite

"ALL WARFARE IS BASED ON DECEPTION", wrote Sun Tzu, a Chinese military strategist who lived 2,500 years ago and remains influential in China today. The revelation by the Americans that China had destroyed an ageing weather satellite with a missile has certainly caused surprise and confusion. Why should a country so insistent that its rise threatens no one stage such an open display of its ability to challenge American power in space?

China had been fuelling the mystery by neither confirming nor denying America's assertion on January 18th 2007 that the Chinese satellite was blown up about 500 miles above earth by a medium-range ballistic missile a week earlier. Less than a week later, on January 23rd, a spokesman for China's foreign ministry confirmed the satellite had been shot down. It was the first experiment of its kind by any country in more than 20 years (though there have been vague rumours of others). America itself, as well as the former Soviet Union, are the only other countries to have tested anti-satellite weapons.

Only two days after the apparently successful test, China's prime minister Wen Jiabao arrived in the Philippine city of Cebu to attend a regional summit. While there he called on fellow leaders to help China build a "harmonious East Asia". The test, however, has created widespread unease. Some of Mr Wen's interlocutors in Cebu, including Australia, Japan and South Korea, have since joined a chorus of Western criticism.

The Americans, with their heavy dependence on military satellites and their commitment to help Taiwan defend itself from any attack by China, have the most to worry about. China has never admitted to having an anti-satellite weapons programme. But since the 1990s, Western experts believe China has become increasingly alarmed by the military advantage enjoyed by America thanks to its satellites. China is also worried that its strategic nuclear arsenal could be rendered useless by American efforts to build a missile defence system that includes space-based components.

America has long suspected China of developing anti-satellite technology. In September 2006 reports emerged that China had been pointing high-powered lasers at American spy satellites passing over its territory. The apparent aim was to test an ability to blind them. A Pentagon report in May 2006 noted China's "rapid and relatively smooth rise as an emerging space power", with plans for its own manned space station by 2020. China's intention, it seems, is to show that American supremacy in space is not unassailable.

It also has a more immediate goal. In 2002, China and Russia proposed a treaty banning the deployment of weapons in space or attacks against space-based objects. China's concern was that the American missile defence system would lead to increasing use of space for military purposes and fuel an arms race. The Americans have refused to negotiate, saying such a treaty would be unenforceable and would only give an advantage to countries (for which read, China) that are trying hide their efforts to develop weapons for use in space.

By destroying one of its own weather satellites, China might have been trying to force the Americans to the table. If so, it was a risky strategy. The test is likely to reinforce perceptions in America of China as an emerging threat. Japan and Taiwan will also be rattled. On January 22nd 2007 Taiwan – apparently trying to reinforce international opprobrium directed at its rival – said China had deployed some 900 missiles on the coast facing the island in recent years. In August 2006 it had put the figure at 820.

The test is unlikely to foster closer co-operation between the American and Chinese civilian space programmes. In September 2006, in a sign of tentative warming between the two sides, Michael Griffin of NASA made the first trip to China by a head of the American government's space agency. But China will have made no friends in NASA by littering space with fragments from the explosion that could threaten other spacecraft. "If your opponent is of choleric temper, seek to irritate him", said Sun Tzu. China has certainly succeeded in that.

This article was first published in *The Economist* in January 2007.

Disharmony in the spheres

Modern American warfare relies on satellites. They make America powerful but also vulnerable, particularly in light of China's new celestial assertiveness

A HUSHED, DIMMED HALL in the nerve centre that controls America's air operations from Somalia to Afghanistan is dominated by giant video screens tracking coalition aircraft. Blue dots show the location of ground forces, with "troops in contact" highlighted for priority air support. Smaller screens show live black-and-white footage, relayed by satellite from unmanned drones which, in their turn, are remotely controlled by pilots in America.

The Combined Air Operations Centre's exact location in "southwest Asia" cannot be disclosed. But from here commanders supervise tens of thousands of sorties a year. Through aircraft surveillance pods they get a god's eye view of operations that range from old-fashioned strafing to the targeted killing of insurgent leaders with bombs guided by global positioning system (GPS) satellites, and emergency air drops to isolated soldiers using parachutes that steer themselves automatically to the chosen spot.

These days America fights not in a fog of war but, as one senior air-force officer puts it, in a "huge cloud of electrons". Large amounts of information, particularly surveillance videos, can be beamed to soldiers on the ground or leaders in America. The officer says this kind of "network centric" warfare is "as revolutionary as when the air force went from open cockpits to jet aeroplanes."

If Napoleon's armies marched on their stomachs, American ones march on bandwidth. Smaller Western allies struggle to keep up. Much of this electronic data is transmitted by satellites, most of them unprotected commercial systems. The revolution in military technology is, at heart, a revolution in the use of space. America's supremacy in the air is made possible by its mastery of space.

During the cold war space was largely thought of as part of the rarefied but terrifying domain of nuclear warfare. Satellites were

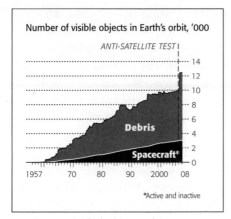

Number of visible objects in Earth's orbit, '000

ANTI-SATELLITE TEST

Debris

Spacecraft*

*Active and inactive

Source: NASA's *Orbital Debris Quarterly News*, January 2008

FIG 11.1 China launches its junk

used principally to monitor nuclear-missile facilities, provide early warning should they be fired and maintain secure communications between commanders and nuclear-strike forces. Now, by contrast, the use of space assets is ubiquitous; even the lowliest platoon makes use of satellites, if only to know its position.

Space wizardry has made possible unprecedented accuracy. As recently as the Vietnam war, destroying a bridge or building could take dozens if not hundreds of bombing runs. These days a plane with "smart" bombs can blast several targets in a single sortie, day or night, in good weather or bad. Needless to say, precise intelligence and sound judgment are as important to military success as fancy kit.

But might this growing reliance on space and cyberspace become a dangerous dependence, a fatal weakness? Air-force officers talk of space being America's Achilles heel. Satellites move in predictable orbits and anybody who can reach space can in theory destroy a satellite, even if only by releasing a cloud of "dumb" pellets in its path – using a shotgun rather than a hunter's rifle to kill the orbiting "bird".

The Taliban or al-Qaeda can do little about America's space power except hide themselves from its intelligence-gathering satellites. But the Pentagon worries about what would happen if America came up against a major power, a "near-peer" rival (as it calls China and Russia), able to intercept space assets with missiles and "space mines", or to disable them with lasers and electronic jammers. "There are a lot of vulnerabilities," admits an American general, "There are backups, but our space architecture is very fragile."

The precise nature of these weaknesses is a well-guarded secret.

But wargames simulating a future conflict over Taiwan often end up with the "Red Force" (China) either defeating the "Blue Force" (America) or inflicting grievous losses on it by launching an early attack in space, perhaps by setting off one or more nuclear explosions above the atmosphere. "I have played Red and had a wonderful time," says the general, "It is pretty easy to disrupt Blue. We should not expect an enemy to play by established norms in space. They will play dirty pool."

One shot China has been practising became clear on January 11th 2007. In a nuclear-proof air-force command centre, built on giant shock-absorbing springs within Cheyenne Mountain, outside Colorado Springs, officers tracked a missile fired from a mobile launcher deep inside China. It followed what one American official said was a "strange" trajectory, designed neither to land a warhead nor to put a payload into orbit. Instead it intercepted one of China's ageing weather satellites. The impact about 850km (530 miles) above Earth created a huge field of space debris, contributing about 28% of the junk now floating around in space (see Figure 11.1).

Litter louts do their worst

Creating all this rubbish seems a bit irresponsible for a country seeking to be a great space-faring nation. It is true that both America and Russia carried out scores of similar anti-satellite (ASAT) tests during the cold war. Then they stopped, not least because the celestial shrapnel was endangering their hugely expensive satellites. They also accepted that spy satellites provided a degree of mutual reassurance in nuclear arms control. The last piece of American ASAT debris fell back to Earth in 2006, say Pentagon officials. China's shrapnel, created in a higher orbit, could be around for a century to come.

The missile shot put America on notice that it can be challenged in space. The Chinese routinely turn powerful lasers skywards, demonstrating their potential to dazzle or permanently blind spy satellites. "They let us see their lasers. It is as if they are trying to intimidate us," says Gary Payton, a senior Pentagon official dealing with space programmes. The only conclusion, he argues, is that "space is no longer a sanctuary; it is a contested domain."

In a report to Congress in November 2008, a commission examining America's relations with China gave warning that "the pace and success of China's military modernisation continue to exceed US government estimates." China's principal aim, the report said, is to develop the wherewithal to delay or deter American military intervention in any war over Taiwan.

The ASAT test intensifies the concern of those who already find plenty to worry about in Chinese military literature. A study for the American Enterprise Institute, a think-tank, cites a Chinese theorist who argues that China should adopt a policy of overt deterrence in space. Other Chinese argue that their country's territorial sovereignty extends to space. This kind of thing reinforces the hawkishness of American hardliners.

Ashley Tellis, a senior associate at the Carnegie Endowment, another think-tank, believes China ultimately seeks to build a "Sino-centric order in Asia and perhaps globally." Any attempt to negotiate arms-control agreements in space would be futile, he argues, and America "has no choice but to run the offence-defence space race, and win."

Other experts, such as Michael Krepon, co-founder of the Henry L. Stimson Centre, a security think-tank, play down the Chinese peril. Mr Krepon says that though similarly alarming conclusions could have been drawn from American or Soviet military literature in the cold war, a space war never took place. What is more, the greater China's economic reliance on satellites, the keener it will be to protect them.

Even those who doubt that America would really go to war against China for the sake of Taiwan worry about the dangers posed by the growing number of countries that have access to outer space. Ten countries (or groups of countries) and two commercial consortia can launch satellites into orbit. A further 18 have ballistic missiles powerful enough to cross space briefly. By the end of 2006, 47 countries and other groups had placed satellites in orbit, either on their own or with help from others. In its crudest form, any object can become a space weapon if directed into the path of a satellite.

In testimony to Congress last year, General James Cartwright, a former head of America's Strategic Command, said that "intentional

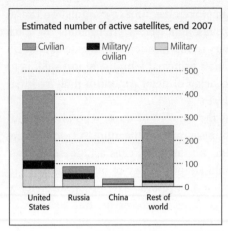

Source: Union of Concerned Scientists

FIG 11.2 Battle for space

interference" with all types of satellites, "while not routine, now occurs with some regularity". GPS signals are relatively weak and easy to jam. For several months in 2006 electronic jammers in Libya interfered with the Thuraya satellite telephone system, apparently because the Libyan government wanted to make life difficult for smugglers in the Sahara desert.

Satellites are not just military tools; they have also become a vital part of globalised civilian life. It is hard to disentangle military from civilian uses of space. Military GPS satellites support a myriad of civilian uses, including road directions for taxi drivers, navigation for commercial airliners, tracking goods in transit and time signals for cash dispensers. But the armed services' hunger for electronic data means that four-fifths of America's military data is transmitted through commercial satellites. A single Global Hawk unmanned surveillance aircraft flying over Afghanistan can eat up several times more satellite bandwidth than was used for the whole of the 1991 war against Iraq.

Star wars delayed

Space provides the high ground from which to watch, listen and direct military forces. But the idea that countries would fight it out in space has so far been confined to science fiction. International law treats outer space as a global common, akin to the high seas. Countries are free to use space for "peaceful purposes" but may not stake territorial claims to celestial bodies or place nuclear weapons in space. "Peaceful" has been interpreted to mean "non-aggressive" rather than non-military. Space is highly militarised but for the moment nobody has placed weapons there, not openly at least.

During the cold war, under Ronald Reagan's presidency, America worked on plans for space-based weapons designed to shoot down ballistic missiles. But this "star wars" programme faded with the collapse of Soviet communism. Before being appointed defence secretary in 2001, Donald Rumsfeld chaired a special commission to review America's space policy. It issued a stark warning that America could suffer a crippling surprise attack on its space systems – a "space Pearl Harbour" – and argued that America "must develop the means both to deter and to defend against hostile acts in and from space."

America then broke out of the Anti-Ballistic Missile Treaty, freeing itself to pursue a slimmed-down version of missile defence. The latest official statement on America's space policy, issued in 2006, affirms the country's freedom of action in space, the right of self-defence and the right to "deny, if necessary, its adversaries the use of space." At the UN General Assembly, America has stood alone in voting against a resolution supporting negotiations on a treaty to prevent a space arms race, an idea pushed by China and Russia.

Yet the Bush administration has stopped short of taking the fateful step of "weaponisation" in space. Perhaps it is too preoccupied with Iraq, and certainly the downfall of Mr Rumsfeld removed a powerful champion of space weapons. A year after China's ASAT shot, the defence budget passed by the Democrat-controlled Congress did not provide any money for a missile defence "space test-bed".

One of the big disincentives to placing weapons in space has been the technical difficulty and cost of such an enterprise. A study by the Centre for Strategic and Budgetary Assessments (CSBA), a defence think-tank, concluded that ground-based systems were almost always more cost effective and reliable than space-based weapons, whether used to attack missiles, enemy satellites or targets on land.

America is still hedging its bets. With some tweaking, say experts, the ground-based interceptors for shooting down ballistic missiles could be used against satellites. A host of technologies under research, such as high-powered lasers to destroy missiles rising through the air, could be applied to anti-satellite warfare.

A game of celestial dodgems

The core fear is that any conflict in space would cause the most injury to America since America has the most to lose. Damaged planes crash to the ground and destroyed ships sink to the bottom of the sea. But the weightlessness of space means that debris keeps spinning around the Earth for years, if not centuries. Each destruction of a satellite creates, in effect, thousands of missiles zipping round randomly; each subsequent impact provides yet more high-speed debris. At some point, given enough litter, there would be a chain reaction of impacts that would render parts of low-Earth orbit – the location of about half the active satellites – unusable.

As matters stand, ground controllers periodically have to shift the position of satellites to avoid other objects. In January 2008, NASA was tracking about 3,100 active and inactive satellites, and some 9,300 bits of junk larger than 5cm, about 2,600 of them from the Chinese ASAT test. Given their speed, even particles as small as 1cm (of which there may be hundreds of thousands) are enough to cripple a satellite.

For America, then, avoiding a space war may be a matter of self-preservation. The air force has adopted a doctrine of "counterspace operations" that envisages either destroying enemy satellites in a future war or temporarily disabling them. But for the most part, America's space security relies on passive measures: sidestepping an attacker by moving out of the way of possible strikes; protecting the vital organs of satellites by "hardening" them against laser or electromagnetic attack; replacing any damaged satellites; or finding alternative means to do the job, for example with blimps or unmanned aircraft.

More esoteric space research has ideas such as sending small satellites to act as "guardian angels", detecting possible attacks against the big birds. It also includes plans for breaking up satellites into smaller components that communicate wirelessly, or deploying "space tugs" that would repair and refuel existing satellites.

Few of these options are cost-free. More manoeuvrable satellites are heavier, as they have to carry more fuel; protective equipment makes satellites cumbrous and more expensive; placing a satellite farther away from Earth, where it is more difficult to attack, means it will broadcast a weaker signal or require more costly sensors and antennae. The promise of cheap, reuseable launch vehicles has yet to materialise. All this makes it hard for America to achieve its goal of "operationally responsive space": the ability to place satellites in orbit quickly and inexpensively.

The essential prerequisite for better space security is to improve "situational awareness": that is, to know what is in space, who it belongs to and whether it is acting in a threatening manner. America already has the world's most developed space monitoring system with a network of radars and telescopes. But its surveillance is patchy. Objects in orbit are catalogued periodically rather than tracked continuously. Space surveillance is not really like air-traffic control: it is more akin to trying to track ships at sea with the naked eye, watching them leave port and predicting when they will next come in sight of land. There are gaps in coverage, particularly over the southern hemisphere, and much of the antiquated surveillance system cannot fuse the data to create an overall picture.

Space surveillance would seem to be ideally suited to international co-operation. Yet the Americans, Chinese, Russians and Europeans all seem intent on doing their own monitoring. They are frightened of giving away their space secrets to rivals. Accurate and timely information on space objects is vital for defending a satellite, but also necessary for attacking one.

Coming back down to Earth

Many strategists argue that the most vulnerable parts of the American space system are closer to home. Ground stations and control centres, particularly those of commercial operations, are exposed to conventional bombing, whether by armies or terrorists. Communication links to and from satellites are open to interference. In cyber-warfare, critical parts of the space system could be attacked from distant computers. Even without external meddling, notes Tom Ehrhard, a senior fellow at the CSBA, American forces struggle to find enough bandwidth and to prevent the myriad of electronic systems from jamming each other.

Some remedial action is being taken. Backup ground stations are being set up in case the main GPS control centre outside Colorado

Springs is disabled. New satellites will have a more powerful GPS signal that is harder to block. America is experimenting with satellite-to-satellite communication by laser, which can carry more data and is less prone to interference than radio waves.

And the armed forces are starting to train for warfare with few or no data links. Simulated attacks by both space and cyberspace "aggressors" are being incorporated into events such as the regular "Red Flag" air-combat exercises over the Nevada desert. But, said an officer at one recent wargame, there are other ways of doing things. "If you really want to take us down, why go to space? You could just try to take out the control tower or bring down the electricity supply to the base."

This article was first published in *The Economist* in January 2008.

Anything you can do

As China's army flexes its muscles, a missile is intercepted in space

AFTER STARTLING THE WORLD in 2007 with the blizzard of hazardous space debris scattered by a secretive test of an anti-satellite missile, China recently tried a more upfront approach. Instead of waiting for the Pentagon to tell the world, the official news agency, Xinhua, on January 11th 2010 tersely announced China's successful test of a land-based missile-defence system. It was not, it said, directed at any other country.

For an army that rarely flaunts its technological achievements, this marked a cautious openness. But that will hardly reassure the Americans. The test apparently made China the only country after America to use a missile to destroy another in space. A Pentagon official confirmed that two missiles had been detected and that they had collided outside the earth's atmosphere. The Pentagon was not informed in advance.

The timing of the test suggested it was intended as a show of strength following the Pentagon's announcement four days earlier that it had cleared the long-expected sale of advanced Patriot missile-defence systems to Taiwan. China has been conducting on-and-off research into missile-defence systems since the 1960s. But the technology it appears now to be mastering could just as well be used for attacking satellites. This unsettles America, with an army that depends on space-based technologies.

China always reacts angrily to American arms sales to Taiwan, an island it considers its own. In this case it had reason to be somewhat relieved that the Americans did not agree to Taiwan's request for F-16 fighter jets and Black Hawk helicopters. But the Chinese government is in a muscle-flexing mood, encouraged by a sense that America increasingly needs China's help to solve its own, and the world's, problems.

In the past China's response has been limited to suspending

military dialogue with America. The government is still anxious to avoid serious disruption to ties to a vital trading partner with military capabilities that still far outstrip China's. But the official press has recently published unusually open calls on the government to boycott American companies that sell arms to Taiwan, applauded by China's notoriously nationalistic internet-users. *Global Times*, a Beijing newspaper, called for public discussion of possible retaliation. "Hold an open forum, and let the Chinese people have the last word," it said. Such a prospect, though hardly likely, would be truly chilling for America.

This article was first published in *The Economist* in January 2010.

Endangered birds

Space technology: Concern over anti-satellite weapons is changing the way satellites are designed, built and launched

IN JUNE 2010 THE US STRATEGIC COMMAND, an arm of America's Department of Defence, began operating a spy satellite called TacSat-3. It can see objects on the ground as small as four metres across, and its "hyperspectral" imaging system (which combines visible with infra-red light) can distinguish between various types of metal, rock and other materials. The results can then be beamed directly to soldiers on the ground, providing detailed information about the terrain and nearby targets. Being able to get precise, timely information from a satellite (or "bird") in this way is of great military value, and not just to ground troops. America's forthcoming "Prompt Global Strike" non-nuclear hypersonic missiles will be able to hit almost any spot on earth in less than an hour – provided excellent satellite data is available.

Even as satellites become more capable, however, they are also increasingly vulnerable to attack, says Lieut-Colonel Ryan Pendleton, who is in charge of TacSat-3 at the US Air Force Space Command. China and the United States have both shot down satellites using missiles in recent years, and the old Soviet Union tested several anti-satellite weapons. The other handful of countries able to place space-craft in orbit, including India and Iran, will probably be able to shoot down a satellite soon, reckons Uzi Rubin, a former head of Israel's Arrow missile-defence programme. This has led to what Colonel Pendleton calls a "revolutionary transition", as concern over anti-satellite weapons is changing the way satellites are designed, built and launched.

One way to protect a satellite would be to equip it with sensors and rockets to enable it to dodge an incoming missile. But this would not protect it against a sufficiently large detonation nearby, or a cloud of pellets shot into its path. A simpler approach is to build smaller satellites that can be assembled quickly and cheaply. These are harder to track and hit, and quicker and less expensive to replace. Today's biggest satellites, larger than a bus and nearly a decade in the making, can cost $10 billion. TacSat-3, roughly the size of two fridges, was built in about 15 months for $65m. Its offspring will cost even less and get into orbit even more quickly.

In 2007 America's Congress ordered the Department of Defence to establish a body to lead the shift toward quick-build, quick-launch replacements. Later that year the Operationally Responsive Space Office (ORSO) opened at Kirtland Air Force Base in New Mexico, staffed with experts from America's air force, army, marines and navy, a handful of intelligence agencies, and NASA, the space agency. The result, says the office's director, Peter Wegner, has been an "explosion in innovation".

For starters, ORSO is standardising satellite components so they can be quickly combined and assembled to meet the requirements for a particular military campaign. When possible, parts are linked with standard USB plugs like those found on personal computers. Shunning made-to-order satellite frames, ORSO's technologists use time-saving pegboard boxes perforated with screw-holes five centimetres apart. In one trial a satellite was assembled in less than four hours. ORSO also trains technologists in allied countries and then challenges them to beat its record. An air-force satellite engineer calls the method "Eli Whitney meets spacecraft", referring to the American inventor who promoted the use of interchangeable parts to speed up the manufacturing of muskets.

Software is also being simplified. In the past entirely new software was developed for each satellite. But a team led by James Lyke, a senior satellite engineer at the Kirtland base, together with Sweden's ministry of defence, is developing a "universal, standard, plug-and-play" operating system so that satellites, like personal computers, can easily recognise and accommodate new hardware as it is plugged in. The software will be distributed to America's allies in Europe and elsewhere.

As satellites shrink, launch costs can drop dramatically too, because new launch methods become feasible. Launching a payload to low-earth orbit can cost $20,000 or more per kilogram. But small satellites, including shoebox-sized "cubesats", are often used in place of the ballast carried by rockets to improve their weight distribution. This "almost free ride to orbit" is fuelling entrepreneurship and innovation, says Aaron Rogers, a designer of intelligence and military satellites at John Hopkins University's Applied Physics Lab in Maryland. Worldwide, more than 120 organisations, many of them student groups, are now designing cubesats, he reckons.

Fire when ready

Although TacSat-3 and its successors are still too large to take advantage of this approach, there is plenty of scope for other innovations in launching military satellites. Integrating a satellite with a launch rocket can take six months or more, but the US Air Force hopes to reduce this to days or even hours. Its new software will help; another improvement involves designing satellites to fit, alone or with others, inside a standardised "dispenser" that can be fastened to more than one rocket model.

Being able to build satellites quickly in a conflict is no good if your launch pads have been destroyed, however. Several countries have developed alternative ways to launch satellites. The Pegasus launcher operated by Orbital Sciences Corporation, an American firm, is a rocket that attaches to the underbelly of a modified jumbo jet and is capable of placing small payloads into orbit. China appears to be designing a spacecraft-launcher that attaches to the undercarriage of a large warplane. And France is going one step further. In 2013 its space agency, CNES, together with Dassault Aviation, a French firm, and German and Spanish partners, will test a satellite-launching rocket that attaches to the Rafale fighter jet. Unlike the American and Chinese planes, the Rafale, built by Dassault, can fly from aircraft carriers. This would allow naval fleets, which depend heavily on satellites for communications and intelligence, to launch their own satellites if needed.

With this launcher, called Aldebaran, France is pushing technological limits "perhaps more aggressively" than the United States, says a US Air Force space official and former defence attaché to Paris. He and others note that the Aldebaran rocket could be used to destroy satellites as well as launch them. But French officials deny such intentions: blowing up a satellite can litter orbits for decades with shrapnel that endangers all spacecraft, so "kinetic" anti-satellite weaponry is greatly stigmatised. Mr Rubin, a former head of Israel's Arrow missile-defence programme, reckons that the project gives France an edge in developing anti-satellite missiles, however, while avoiding the international criticism that would accompany an explicit anti-satellite programme.

Shooting at birds

In 2007 China was criticised when it used a missile to destroy an old Chinese weather satellite, spreading debris into other orbits. (A defence adviser to a west European head of state, requesting anonymity, says his government is still upset.) The following year America blew up a malfunctioning spy satellite, USA-193, using a ship-launched missile. The satellite was in a low orbit, which ensured that the resulting debris fell into the atmosphere within a few days. America said the satellite's hydrazine fuel might have caused injury if USA-193 had fallen to earth intact. But it was accused by Russia and China of using this as an excuse to demonstrate that it, too, could carry out a successful anti-satellite strike.

Yet there are other ways to disable or destroy a satellite. Dennis Göge of the German Aerospace Centre in Cologne, a government space-robotics lab, suggests that a spacecraft could spray a nearby enemy satellite with paint or goo to ruin its lenses, sensors, moving parts and solar panels. In an exercise in 2010, China appeared to demonstrate robotic technology for a "non-co-operative rendezvous" in orbit. A new Chinese satellite slowly approached, and possibly bumped into, an old Chinese satellite, which changed trajectory. The ability to nudge satellites has both peaceful and military uses. Roving "garbage man" robots might be a good way to clean up space debris, suggests Jeffrey Caton, a professor at the US Army War College, but they could also be used to knock enemy satellites out of orbit. As a result, concern over the militarisation of space threatens to hamper efforts to develop clean-up technology.

Satellites can be temporarily blinded with lasers fired from earth. Several countries, including America, Britain, China, France, Israel,

Japan and Russia, are thought to possess the necessary technology. (A US Air Force official would "neither confirm nor deny" America's development of anti-satellite lasers.) In the past few years French satellites have been hit several times with "dazzle" strikes from lasers in China, says Erwin Duhamel, head of security at the European Space Agency (ESA). An American general has complained of similar dazzle harassment from China's military. None of the satellites appeared to be permanently damaged, says Mr Duhamel. But a powerful laser could probably burn sensitive optical sensors on a satellite, doing permanent damage. Protective countermeasures are under development, including lens shutters and filters that block certain laser frequencies.

Only a few countries can carry out dazzle attacks, but dozens of countries can jam satellite signals using ground-based transmitters to overwhelm their signals. This does not damage satellites, but it worries governments because the technology is cheap, relatively easy to operate and widely available, says Rickard Nordenberg, an adviser at the Swedish Defence Materiel Administration, a military-procurement agency in Stockholm. The Hizbullah militia in Lebanon pulled off such an attack during its 2006 war with Israel, "significantly" scrambling signals for days from a big French military satellite uninvolved in the conflict, according to an ESA official.

With increasingly sophisticated technologies designed to "blind and deafen" satellites, to use a phrase from a 2010 Pentagon report, space powers will step up research into countermeasures. Clouds of radar-reflective foil known as "chaff", ejected from a satellite, might fool an incoming missile's homing sensors. Satellite cases are being hardened to prevent circuitry from being fried by microwaves or other electronic weaponry. Systems being designed by the US Air Force simultaneously perform identical "backup" calculations in five parts of the satellite. The Royal Dutch Defence Academy is working out how a "constellation" of small satellites can operate more safely than a big satellite, distributing operations to protect against the loss of some individual units, says Roy Lindelauf, one of the researchers.

With the emphasis on defence rather than attack, it is not an arms race yet. But nine countries can launch spacecraft and more than a dozen others can launch rockets (and therefore weapons) to altitudes close to orbit, according to the Space Security Index, a report funded by Canada's foreign ministry. Big space powers, including America, China and Russia, have not categorically ruled out the use of anti-satellite weapons. Bans on anti-satellite research have been proposed at the United Nations, but verifying compliance with such a ban would be almost impossible, as America has pointed out. Short of a big political turnaround, it seems likely that space will be increasingly contested – with satellites on the front-line.

This article was first published in *The Economist* in December 2010.

Earthbound

Gravity is not the main obstacle for America's space business. Government is

IN THE SPRING OF 2006 Robert Bigelow needed to take a stand on a trip to Russia to keep a satellite off the floor. The stand was made of aluminium. It had a circular base and legs. It was, says the entrepreneur and head of Bigelow Aerospace in Nevada, "indistinguishable from a common coffee table". Nonetheless, the American authorities told Mr Bigelow that this coffee table was part of a satellite assembly and so counted as a munition. During the trip it would have to be guarded by two security officers at all times.

Exporting technology has always presented a dilemma for America. The country leads the world in most technologies and some of these give it a military advantage. If export rules are too lax, foreign powers will be able to put American technology in their systems, or copy it. But if the rules are too tight, then it will stifle the industries that depend upon sales to create the next generation of technology.

It is a difficult balance to strike and critics charge that America has erred on the side of stifling. They claim that overly strict export controls have so damaged the space industry that America's national security is now threatened by its dwindling leadership in space technology. The system, they complain, fails to distinguish between militarily sensitive hardware that should be controlled and widely available commercial technologies, such as lithium-ion batteries and solar cells. The zealous application of the export rules is the American space industry's biggest handicap.

Egocentric orbit

The controls governing America's export of satellites are part of the International Traffic in Arms Regulation (ITAR) and they are handled in the Department of State. At one time the Department of Commerce had the job. But in the mid-1990s a great controversy arose when information was shared between American satellite makers and the Chinese. Politicians reacted to fears that secrets had been passed to China by moving control of space exports to the State Department.

Michael Beavin, a programme analyst at the Office of Space Commercialisation in America's Commerce Department, says that the wording of the legislation is open to broader interpretation than Congress intended. An international GPS ground station may have to get export approval to buy a new screen for its Dell laptop, because it is part of a system that is controlled. Pierre Chao, a senior associate at the Centre for Strategic and International Studies (CSIS), a think-tank in Washington, DC, says that as soon as satellites were put on the munitions list "the little screw and the commodity wiring became a munition". Furthermore, anything modified for a munition is a munition. This clause, he says, captures all the little "doodads". In fact, he explains, it's the extremely sophisticated "part X" that you want to keep out of the enemy's hands, not the whole box. "You are using an extremely blunt instrument for sophisticated policy needs."

You may think that is the price of security, but Lon Rains, the editor of *Space News*, says that ITAR has "sped up the inevitable proliferation of advanced technology, by forcing other countries to find other means of obtaining satellite components that had previously been manufactured only in the United States." Joe Rouge, the director of the National Space Security Office at the Pentagon, thinks that ITAR probably made sense a decade ago but agrees that it is now a blunt instrument. "The problem is that today you can buy international equivalents that are as good as what American industry is producing."

The result is a system that is too successful in keeping American technology out of foreign hands. Before 1999, when the State Department took over the export regulation of satellites, America dominated commercial satellite-making with an average market share of 83%. Since then, this share has declined to 50%, according to *Space Review*. ITAR's critics blame the change in export controls. As bidding opened in July 2008 for the €3.4 billion ($5 billion) of contracts for Galileo, a constellation of 30 positioning satellites being built by the European Union and the European Space Agency, European officials cited export controls as a reason for avoiding anything to do with America wherever possible.

At the start of the decade, Alcatel Alenia Space (now Thales Alenia) announced that it would create an "ITAR-free" spacecraft, purged of all American components. Between 1998 and 2004 the company doubled its market share to over 20%, becoming perhaps the greatest beneficiary of export policies. Export controls also prompted the European Space Agency to pay to develop a European supplier of solenoid valves, so that European space-propulsion systems do not depend on this American part. Similarly, Telesat, Canada's satellite-fleet operator, has said that ITAR is one of the reasons it has selected European satellite builders in recent competitions. And in 2005 EADS Sodern, a French maker of satellites' control and positioning systems and subsidiary of the Franco-German company EADS, said it would start to phase out its American supplier base.

Meanwhile, American components and satellites are suffering because of the cost and delays in doing business with the firms that make them. International companies cannot access an inventory of vital American satellite components and place orders as the need develops because each component must run the gauntlet of export controls. Whether the component is a motor, a control valve, a star tracker, an antenna or a chip, it is simpler to look for non-American alternatives.

For years, critics have grumbled about the export controls at meetings. Until recently, the State Department ignored such complaints. Mr Chao, of CSIS, reckons this attitude is changing. The marketing of the ITAR-free satellite woke people up. More than that, though, he says that data have started to accumulate.

In 2006 a survey of American industry executives found that ITAR's licensing requirements were hard to understand and took an unpredictable amount of time to negotiate; this hindered strategic decisions. And in 2007 a survey of around 200 space companies by the Air Force Research Laboratory cited export controls as the highest barrier to foreign markets.

Just across the border, in Canada, the effects were just as profound. A study in 2006 of Canadian space companies found that 70% faced delays of three to 12 months because of ITAR. All of them could find non-American suppliers for the technologies they were looking for. And after 1999 in Canada, there was also a big dip in the number of American-Canadian projects.

Reducing the revenue and profit of the space industry might be a reasonable thing to do if such constraints supported military objectives. But critics accuse ITAR of imposing such a burden on smaller companies that it is harming the entire industry, and thus national security.

Prime contractors, such as Boeing and Lockheed Martin, can absorb ITAR's costs as part of doing business. But the second-tier contractors that support them and the third-tier component suppliers are having much more trouble. The burden of compliance on the component-makers was nearly 8% of foreign sales in 2006. For prime contractors this was 1%. A spokesman for the State Department says that it would be wrong to assume export controls directly caused the weakness of third-tier component suppliers. He added that they could be suffering from any number of difficulties, including "offsets, globalisation, foreign industrial priorities and policy, even the domestic corporate-tax structure."

Whatever its cause, a CSIS study published in February 2008 concluded that America was being harmed. Second- and third-tier companies are important innovators. Moreover, in fields like solar cells, travelling-wave tubes and read-out integrated circuits, there is either only one domestic supplier or a financially weak supplier. The situation is so bad, say some, that the Pentagon fears it may have to start buying satellite components overseas – rather as NASA, America's space agency, is scrabbling around to find transport to carry its astronauts to the international space station. Mr Rouge thinks the health of the industry should be a matter of military concern.

It is not only private companies that are suffering. In 2005 the European Space Agency concluded that ITAR made its co-operation with NASA's Mars rover "too complicated to be feasible" and that it had to become more autonomous. Others have warned that delays in agreements allowing Americans to speak with foreigners (known as technical-assistance agreements) are a threat to the safe operation of the International Space Station.

Mr Beavin explains that ITAR may define technology "exports" as any disclosure to foreign nationals, such as web posts, international scientific meetings and exchanges, conferences and technical data. "The academic world is used to sharing and it really makes it hard for scientific exchange. Nobody wants to be slapped with a gigantic fee or go to jail. It is scaring everyone into not talking, and that's crippling for science."

Around the world, space-faring nations such as China and India are making great progress, whether they have access to American technology or not. Mike Gold, director of Bigelow Aerospace's office in Washington, DC, has nothing good to say about the country's export policy: "if the purpose of ITAR is to lose billions of dollars of business, ship jobs overseas, and the Iranians and the Chinese get the same technology anyway, then mission accomplished." The regime, he says, is obsolete and counterproductive.

Mr Gold believes that the State Department has failed to take the time and effort to distinguish between space technologies, as the law allows. Instead, he charges, the bureaucracy has taken the "safe and easy" option and declared everything to be a munition until proven otherwise. Given the fuss over the way the Commerce Department administered the legislation, perhaps that should come as no surprise.

Escape velocity

In December 2007 Bigelow Aerospace filed a commodity-jurisdiction request which would oblige the Directorate of Defence Trade Controls to rule whether one of its products, a set of inflatable space habitats, should be on the State Department's munitions list. Although it is unclear how far the request will get, it may be the first direct challenge to the department's implementation of ITAR for space technology.

There are signs of change. In late January 2007 the White House made some small adjustments to the way the ITAR regulations would be administered. The most important was a promise that licensing decisions would be taken within 60 days of an application. Mr Rouge says that work is also afoot to update the munitions list, which contains the set of military technologies that must be protected. The idea is to make sure the right technologies are controlled. "We are in the process of setting up to do that. We now understand the problem and its ramifications."

And Mr Rouge says that Congress and the White House are weighing whether to change the ITAR legislation itself. When might this happen? "It's a pre-decisional situation," he says obliquely. Mr Chao thinks that such a reform would represent a sea-change in export legislation.

Such change is overdue. There can be a trade-off between trade and security, but America's regime is so badly designed that it can have more of both. This means spending less time on schemes to control the movement of coffee tables, and more on what really matters.

This article was first published in *The Economist* in August 2008.

PART 3

The computer factor

MOST CYBER-ATTACKS are akin to rowdy football hooligans looking for trouble, says David Lindahl, an expert in computer warfare at the Swedish Defence Research Agency, a defence-ministry body in Stockholm. "If they come to a locked door, they stumble along and move to the next one," he says. In June 2010, however, a very different sort of cyber-weapon came to light.

The computer worm, dubbed Stuxnet, behaved more like a guided "cyber-missile" than opportunistic hooligans. It zeroed in on software that controls uranium-enrichment centrifuges in Iranian nuclear facilities, but left similar equipment elsewhere essentially unharmed. (Stuxnet was designed to spin centrifuges out of control while displaying normal readings to plant operators.) Iranian authorities acknowledged in September 2010 that equipment had been infected, and the International Atomic Energy Agency (IAEA) later reported that roughly half of Iran's centrifuges that still worked were producing little.

Part 3 examines the diverse ways computers are changing warfare. They range from facilitating the spread of propaganda to enabling a form of cyberwar in which computerised weaponry conceals "kill switches" that an exporting country could remotely flip. Cyberwar, in its various forms, is central to many of the articles in this section. Stuxnet reveals much about the future of such warfare.

To begin with, cyber-attackers often remain anonymous, as did those behind Stuxnet. Consequently, efforts to deter or control cyber-war are bound to fail. (Victims may not even know that they have been cyber-attacked.) But Stuxnet, like some other cyber-attacks, also raised hopes that such "logic bombs" might reduce the use of real ordnance in war.

That optimism soon faded. In a May 2011 report on Iran's nuclear programme, the IAEA stated that the main production site at Natanz was producing enriched uranium faster than before the attack. Stuxnet is thought to have been developed not by rogue hackers, but by America and Israel with help from European allies. The computer virus widely considered to be the world's most sophisticated has apparently failed. This suggests that computer attacks will not replace real bombs any time soon.

If cyber-attackers find nuclear or military targets hard to crack, they might concentrate efforts on less-protected civil infrastructure (electrical grids, say, or mass-transit systems). It is not even always clear who should be responsible for protecting what, says Peter Pry, a former electronics-systems analyst at America's Central Intelligence Agency. Unhelpfully, the Department of Defence and the Department of Homeland Security have wrangled over who should be responsible for protecting certain infrastructures, says Mr Pry, also a former member of a commission formed by Congress to study vulnerabilities in electronics-dependent infrastructure.

Caveat emptor

To activate a secret kill switch, a command could be transmitted from an aircraft, satellite, or mobile-phone tower to an antenna disguised as a metal component in an exported weapon system. At least three countries that export missiles could transmit such override instructions to disrupt the trajectories of those fired by certain customers "in the wrong context", says Jacques Quisquater, a Belgian microchip expert who has advised a foreign European defence ministry on weapons security.

Efforts to reliably detect kill switches in microchips have essentially failed. As a result, arms importers increasingly "try to buy from someone who hopefully will remain neutral", says Mr Lindahl of the

Swedish Defence Research Agency, which works out ways to defeat foreign weaponry. This fear of treachery will make it harder for American defence firms to clinch some international sales. America is more suspect than other arms-exporting countries because it has traditionally used arms deals as "a foreign-policy tool", in the words of an official at a large French defence contractor.

Defence contractors in Europe stand to benefit because their governments are considered less willing than America's to meddle with exported weaponry. Russian firms will probably profit even more. Russia's permissive policies on arms exports will reassure many potential buyers. Iran may be an exception, says David Kay, formerly the top UN arms inspector in post-Saddam Iraq. He reckons that Iran's difficulties in obtaining new anti-aircraft batteries from Russia are probably partly due to fears that Russian authorities might wish to affect their operation with a secret override capability.

As well as shuffling the cards in the arms business, computer technologies are providing new options for arms control. Weapons with kill switches could be shut down if stolen, notes a retired American army general who worked on technology transfer with Iraqi security officials in Baghdad. If a government armed by the West is toppled (as were Egypt's and Tunisia's in early 2011), kill switches could prevent a new and less-friendly regime from taking over certain weapons. The upshot is that computer technology, cleverly applied, can be used for arms control without relying on international agreements and inspections.

Put the word out

Terrorists, it seems, have either been unable to pull off big cyber-attacks or have preferred to seek the grim theatre of physical attacks. But terror groups have found computers invaluable in recruiting extremists and spreading propaganda. The ubiquity of computers (including mobile phones) has so raised the potential of "informational warfare" that foreign support for revolutionaries protesting or fighting a repressive government often involves keeping the dissidents online.

America's State Department has provided a $2m grant for the design of a wireless suitcase kit that could be smuggled across a border to connect a wide area to the web. At a June 2011 press conference, a State Department official said that the reforming potential of this sort of edgy and "sexy tech stuff" places it on the "cutting edge of history" in repressive countries. Used skilfully, "liberation technology" for communications can keep a revolution alive. But it may also lead to arrest or worse.

When Egypt's regime shut down the web in late January 2011, some protesters fashioned makeshift range-extension antennae to get back online and build international support. In Libya some anti-regime rebels have sidestepped communications blackouts by hacking cellular towers and improvising satellite web access for computers, often with foreign help. Revolutionaries in both countries have paid a price for their efforts to get online. In Egypt, security forces patrolling restive areas with signal-detection equipment rounded up many users. In Libya, similar gear has been used to find and target rebels, notes Rafal Rohozinski of the Information Warfare Monitor, a University of Toronto think-tank.

For decades, computers have enabled increasingly precise "surgical strikes" with bombs and missiles. This trend will continue. A new type of computerised bomb can self-destruct in the air if its laser or infrared sensors do not detect a given target on the ground below. Computers may be poised to revolutionise warfare once again – but this time providing a very different capability. Computer systems are being developed to instil weaponry with a sort of artificial conscience. The result could be fewer and less-damaging attacks.

Drone software in development, called Ethical Architecture, analyses Pentagon data about a potential target before a missile is fired. The software takes into account what a target is made of, what is nearby, and what the political or cultural repercussions of its destruction might be. With help from data on previous strikes, the system would warn its human operator if counterproductive collateral damage were expected. The operator might then choose a less-destructive weapon or angle of attack, or forgo the strike altogether.

Software that forecasts the outcome of a battle, campaign or entire war can also caution against unwise attacks. That is another reason, as the following articles make clear, that the role of computers in waging or preventing war will only grow.

12 The new realm of cyberwar

War in the fifth domain

Are the mouse and keyboard the new weapons of conflict?

AT THE HEIGHT OF THE COLD WAR, in June 1982, an American early-warning satellite detected a large blast in Siberia. A missile being fired? A nuclear test? It was, it seems, an explosion on a Soviet gas pipeline. The cause was a malfunction in the computer-control system that Soviet spies had stolen from a firm in Canada. They did not know that the CIA had tampered with the software so that it would "go haywire, after a decent interval, to reset pump speeds and valve settings to produce pressures far beyond those acceptable to pipeline joints and welds," according to the memoirs of Thomas Reed, a former air-force secretary. The result, he said, "was the most monumental non-nuclear explosion and fire ever seen from space."

This was one of the earliest demonstrations of the power of a "logic bomb". Three decades later, with more and more vital computer systems linked up to the internet, could enemies use logic bombs to, say, turn off the electricity from the other side of the world? Could terrorists or hackers cause financial chaos by tampering with Wall Street's computerised trading systems? And given that computer chips and software are produced globally, could a foreign power infect high-tech military equipment with computer bugs? "It scares me to death," says one senior military source. "The destructive potential is so great."

After land, sea, air and space, warfare has entered the fifth domain: cyberspace. President Barack Obama has declared America's digital infrastructure to be a "strategic national asset" and appointed Howard Schmidt, the former head of security at Microsoft, as his cyber-security tsar. In May 2010 the Pentagon set up its new Cyber Command (Cybercom) headed by General Keith Alexander, director of the National Security Agency (NSA). His mandate is to conduct "full spectrum" operations – to defend American military networks and attack other countries' systems. Precisely how, and by what rules, is secret.

Britain, too, has set up a cyber-security policy outfit, and an "operations centre" based in GCHQ, the British equivalent of the NSA. China talks of "winning informationised wars by the mid-21st century". Many other countries are organising for cyberwar, among them Russia, Israel and North Korea. Iran boasts of having the world's second-largest cyber-army.

What will cyberwar look like? In a book published in April 2010, Richard Clarke, a former White House staffer in charge of counter-terrorism and cyber-security, envisages a catastrophic breakdown within 15 minutes. Computer bugs bring down military e-mail systems; oil refineries and pipelines explode; air-traffic-control systems collapse; freight and metro trains derail; financial data are scrambled; the electrical grid goes down in the eastern United States; orbiting satellites spin out of control. Society soon breaks down as food becomes scarce and money runs out. Worst of all, the identity of the attacker may remain a mystery.

In the view of Mike McConnell, a former spy chief, the effects of full-blown cyberwar are much like nuclear attack. Cyberwar has already started, he says, "and we are losing it." Not so, retorts Mr Schmidt. There is no cyberwar. Bruce Schneier, an IT industry security guru, accuses securocrats like Mr Clarke of scaremongering. Cyberspace will certainly be part of any future war, he says, but an apocalyptic attack on America is both difficult to achieve technically ("movie-script stuff") and implausible except in the context of a real war, in which case the perpetrator is likely to be obvious.

For the top brass, computer technology is both a blessing and a curse. Bombs are guided by GPS satellites; drones are piloted remotely from across the world; fighter planes and warships are now huge data-processing centres; even the ordinary foot-soldier is being wired up. Yet growing connectivity over an insecure internet multiplies the avenues for e-attack; and growing dependence on computers increases the harm they can cause.

By breaking up data and sending it over multiple routes, the

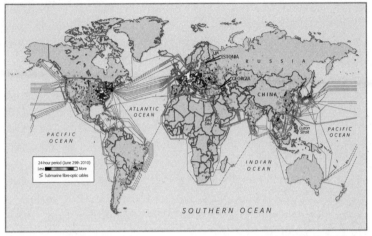

Source: team-cymru.org; telegeography.com

FIG 12.1 Infected IP addresses

internet can survive the loss of large parts of the network. Yet some of the global digital infrastructure is more fragile. More than nine-tenths of internet traffic travels through undersea fibre-optic cables, and these are dangerously bunched up in a few choke-points, for instance around New York, the Red Sea or the Luzon Strait in the Philippines (see Figure 12.1). Internet traffic is directed by just 13 clusters of potentially vulnerable domain-name servers. Other dangers are coming: weakly governed swathes of Africa are being connected up to fibre-optic cables, potentially creating new havens for cyber-criminals. And the spread of mobile internet will bring new means of attack.

The internet was designed for convenience and reliability, not security. Yet in wiring together the globe, it has merged the garden and the wilderness. No passport is required in cyberspace. And although police are constrained by national borders, criminals roam freely. Enemy states are no longer on the other side of the ocean, but just behind the firewall. The ill-intentioned can mask their identity and location, impersonate others and con their way into the buildings that hold the digitised wealth of the electronic age: money, personal data and intellectual property.

Mr Obama has quoted a figure of $1 trillion lost last year to

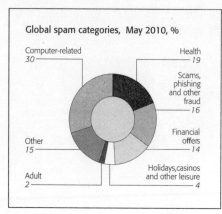

Global spam categories, May 2010, %

Computer-related 30

Health 19

Scams, phishing and other fraud 16

Financial offers 14

Other 15

Holidays, casinos and other leisure 4

Adult 2

Source: Symantec

FIG 12.2 Spamalot

cybercrime – a bigger underworld than the drugs trade, though such figures are disputed. Banks and other companies do not like to admit how much data they lose. In 2008 alone Verizon, a telecoms company, recorded the loss of 285m personal-data records, including credit-card and bank-account details, in investigations conducted for clients.

About nine-tenths of the 140 billion e-mails sent daily are spam; of these about 16% contain moneymaking scams (see Figure 12.2), including "phishing" attacks that seek to dupe recipients into giving out passwords or bank details, according to Symantec, a security-software vendor. The amount of information now available online about individuals makes it ever easier to attack a computer by crafting a personalised e-mail that is more likely to be trusted and opened. This is known as "spear-phishing".

The ostentatious hackers and virus-writers who once wrecked computers for fun are all but gone, replaced by criminal gangs seeking to harvest data. "Hacking used to be about making noise. Now it's about staying silent," says Greg Day of McAfee, a vendor of IT security products. Hackers have become wholesale providers of malware – viruses, worms and Trojans that infect computers – for others to use. Websites are now the favoured means of spreading malware, partly because the unwary are directed to them through spam or links posted on social-networking sites. And poorly designed websites often provide a window into valuable databases.

Malware is exploding (see Figure 12.3). It is typically used to steal passwords and other data, or to open a "back door" to a computer so that it can be taken over by outsiders. Such "zombie" machines can be

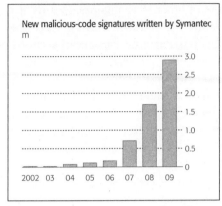

New malicious-code signatures written by Symantec
m

Source: Symantec

FIG 12.3 Beware of malware

linked up to thousands, if not millions, of others around the world to create a "botnet". Estimates for the number of infected machines range up to 100m (see Figure 12.1 for global distribution of infections). Botnets are used to send spam, spread malware or launch distributed denial-of-service (DDoS) attacks, which seek to bring down a targeted computer by overloading it with countless bogus requests.

The spy who spammed me

Criminals usually look for easy prey. But states can combine the criminal hacker's tricks, such as spear-phishing, with the intelligence apparatus to reconnoitre a target, the computing power to break codes and passwords, and the patience to probe a system until it finds a weakness – usually a fallible human being. Steven Chabinsky, a senior FBI official responsible for cyber-security, says that "given enough time, motivation and funding, a determined adversary will always – always – be able to penetrate a targeted system."

Traditional human spies risk arrest or execution by trying to smuggle out copies of documents. But those in the cyberworld face no such risks. "A spy might once have been able to take out a few books' worth of material," says one senior American military source, "Now they take the whole library. And if you restock the shelves, they will steal it again."

China, in particular, is accused of wholesale espionage, attacking the computers of major Western defence contractors and reputedly taking classified details of the F-35 fighter, the mainstay of future American air power. At the end of 2009 it appears to have targeted

Google and more than a score of other IT companies. Experts at a cyber-test-range built in Maryland by Lockheed Martin, a defence contractor (which denies losing the F-35 data), say "advanced persistent threats" are hard to fend off amid the countless minor probing of its networks. Sometimes attackers try to slip information out slowly, hidden in ordinary internet traffic. At other times they have tried to break in by leaving infected memory-sticks in the car park, hoping somebody would plug them into the network. Even unclassified e-mails can contain a wealth of useful information about projects under development.

"Cyber-espionage is the biggest intelligence disaster since the loss of the nuclear secrets [in the late 1940s]," says Jim Lewis of the Centre for Strategic and International Studies, a think-tank in Washington, DC. Spying probably presents the most immediate danger to the West: the loss of high-tech know-how that could erode its economic lead or, if it ever came to a shooting war, blunt its military edge.

Western spooks think China deploys the most assiduous, and most shameless, cyberspies, but Russian ones are probably more skilled and subtle. Top of the league, say the spooks, are still America's NSA and Britain's GCHQ, which may explain why Western countries have until recently been reluctant to complain too loudly about computer snooping.

The next step after penetrating networks to steal data is to disrupt or manipulate them. If military targeting information could be attacked, for example, ballistic missiles would be useless. Those who play war games speak of being able to "change the red and blue dots": make friendly (blue) forces appear to be the enemy (red), and vice versa.

General Alexander says the Pentagon and NSA started co-operating on cyberwarfare in late 2008 after "a serious intrusion into our classified networks". Mr Lewis says this refers to the penetration of Central Command, which oversees the wars in Iraq and Afghanistan, through an infected thumb-drive. It took a week to winkle out the intruder. Nobody knows what, if any, damage was caused. But the thought of an enemy lurking in battle-fighting systems alarms the top brass.

That said, an attacker might prefer to go after unclassified military logistics supply systems, or even the civilian infrastructure. A loss of confidence in financial data and electronic transfers could cause economic upheaval. An even bigger worry is an attack on the power grid. Power companies tend not to keep many spares of expensive generator parts, which can take months to replace. Emergency diesel generators cannot make up for the loss of the grid, and cannot operate indefinitely. Without electricity and other critical services, communications systems and cash-dispensers cease to work. A loss of power lasting just a few days, reckon some, starts to cause a cascade of economic damage.

Experts disagree about the vulnerability of systems that run industrial plants, known as supervisory control and data acquisition (SCADA). But more and more of these are being connected to the internet, raising the risk of remote attack. "Smart" grids", which relay information about energy use to the utilities, are promoted as ways of reducing energy waste. But they also increase security worries about both crime (eg, allowing bills to be falsified) and exposing SCADA networks to attack.

General Alexander has spoken of "hints that some penetrations are targeting systems for remote sabotage". But precisely what is happening is unclear: are outsiders probing SCADA systems only for reconnaissance, or to open "back doors" for future use? One senior American military source said that if any country were found to be planting logic bombs on the grid, it would provoke the equivalent of the Cuban missile crisis.

Estonia, Georgia and WWI

Important thinking about the tactical and legal concepts of cyber-warfare is taking place in a former Soviet barracks in Estonia, now home to NATO's "centre of excellence" for cyber-defence. It was established in response to what has become known as "Web War 1", a concerted denial-of-service attack on Estonian government, media and bank web servers that was precipitated by the decision to move a Soviet-era war memorial in central Tallinn in 2007. This was more a cyber-riot than a war, but it forced Estonia more or less to cut itself off from the internet.

Similar attacks during Russia's war with Georgia the next year looked more ominous, because they seemed to be co-ordinated with the advance of Russian military columns. Government and media websites went down and telephone lines were jammed, crippling Georgia's ability to present its case abroad. President Mikheil Saakashvili's website had to be moved to an American server better able to fight off the attack. Estonian experts were dispatched to Georgia to help out.

Many assume that both these attacks were instigated by the Kremlin. But investigations traced them only to Russian "hacktivists" and criminal botnets; many of the attacking computers were in Western countries. There are wider issues: did the cyber-attack on Estonia, a member of NATO, count as an armed attack, and should the alliance have defended it? And did Estonia's assistance to Georgia, which is not in NATO, risk drawing Estonia into the war, and NATO along with it?

Such questions permeate discussions of NATO's new "strategic concept", to be adopted in 2010. A panel of experts headed by Madeleine Albright, a former American secretary of state, reported in May 2010 that cyber-attacks are among the three most likely threats to the alliance. The next significant attack, it said, "may well come down a fibre-optic cable" and may be serious enough to merit a response under the mutual-defence provisions of Article 5.

During his confirmation hearing, senators sent General Alexander several questions. Would he have "significant" offensive cyber-weapons? Might these encourage others to follow suit? How sure would he need to be about the identity of an attacker to "fire back"? Answers to these were restricted to a classified supplement. In public the general said that the president would be the judge of what constituted cyber-war; if America responded with force in cyberspace it would be in keeping with the rules of war and the "principles of military necessity, discrimination, and proportionality".

General Alexander's seven-month confirmation process is a sign of the qualms senators felt at the merging of military and espionage functions, the militarisation of cyberspace and the fear that it may undermine Americans' right to privacy. Cybercommand will protect only the military ".mil" domain. The government domain, ".gov", and the corporate infrastructure, ".com" will be the responsibility respectively of the Department of Homeland Security and private companies, with support from Cybercom.

One senior military official says General Alexander's priority will be to improve the defences of military networks. Another bigwig casts some doubt on cyber-offence. "It's hard to do it at a specific time," he says. "If a cyber-attack is used as a military weapon, you want a predictable time and effect. If you are using it for espionage it does not matter; you can wait." He implies that cyber-weapons would be used mainly as an adjunct to conventional operations in a narrow theatre.

The Chinese may be thinking the same way. A report on China's cyber-warfare doctrine, written for the congressionally mandated US-China Economic and Security Review Commission, envisages China using cyber-weapons not to defeat America, but to disrupt and slow down its forces long enough for China to seize Taiwan without having to fight a shooting war.

Apocalypse or asymmetry?

Deterrence in cyber-warfare is more uncertain than, say, in nuclear strategy: there is no mutually assured destruction, the dividing line between criminality and war is blurred and identifying attacking computers, let alone the fingers on the keyboards, is difficult. Retaliation need not be confined to cyberspace; the one system that is certainly not linked to the public internet is America's nuclear firing chain. Still, the more likely use of cyber-weapons is probably not to bring about electronic apocalypse, but as tools of limited warfare.

Cyber-weapons are most effective in the hands of big states. But because they are cheap, they may be most useful to the comparatively weak. They may well suit terrorists. Fortunately, perhaps, the likes of al-Qaeda have mostly used the internet for propaganda and communication. It may be that jihadists lack the ability to, say, induce a refinery to blow itself up. Or it may be that they prefer the gory theatre of suicide-bombings to the anonymity of computer sabotage – for now.

This article was first published in *The Economist* in July 2010.

The meaning of Stuxnet

A sophisticated "cyber-missile" highlights the potential – and limitations – of cyberwar

IT HAS BEEN DESCRIBED as "amazing", "groundbreaking" and "impressive" by computer-security specialists. The Stuxnet worm, a piece of software that infects industrial-control systems, is remarkable in many ways. Its unusual complexity suggests that it is the work of a team of well-funded experts, probably with the backing of a national government, rather than rogue hackers or cyber-criminals. It is designed to infect a particular configuration of a particular type of industrial-control system – in other words, to disrupt the operation of a specific process or plant. The Stuxnet outbreak has been concentrated in Iran, which suggests that a nuclear facility in that country was the intended target.

This is, in short, a new kind of cyber-attack. Unlike the efforts to disrupt internet access in Estonia or Georgia (blamed on Russia), or the attacks to break into American systems to steal secrets (blamed on China), this was a weapon aimed at a specific target – it has been called a "cyber-missile". One or more governments (the prime suspects are Israel and America) were probably behind it. After years of speculation about the potential for this sort of attack, Stuxnet is a worked example of cyberwar's potential – and its limitations.

Much of the discussion of cyberwar has focused on the potential for a "digital Pearl Harbour", in which a country's power grids and other critical infrastructure are disabled by attackers. Many such systems are isolated from the internet for security reasons. Stuxnet, which exploits flaws in Microsoft Windows to spread on to stand-alone systems via USB memory sticks, shows they are more vulnerable than most people thought. The outbreak emphasises the importance of securing industrial-control systems properly, with both software (open-source code can be more easily checked for security holes) and appropriate policies (banning the use of memory sticks).

"Smart" electricity grids, which couple critical infrastructure to the internet, must be secured carefully.

Stuxnet is also illuminating in another way: it reveals the potential for cyber-weapons that target specific systems, rather than simply trying to cause as much mayhem as possible. It infected several plants in Germany, for example, but did no harm because they were not the target it was looking for. Such specificity, along with the deniability and difficulty of tracing a cyber-weapon, has obvious appeal to governments that would like to disable a particular target while avoiding a direct military attack – and firms interested in sabotaging their rivals.

Cyberwar is not declared

But the worm also highlights the limitations of cyber-attacks. Iran admits that some computers at its Bushehr nuclear plant were infected, but says no damage was done. The target may have been the centrifuges at its nuclear refinery at Natanz. Last year the number of working centrifuges at Natanz dropped, though it is unclear whether this was the result of Stuxnet. Even if it was, the attack will only have delayed Iran's nuclear programme: it will not have shut it down altogether. Whoever is behind Stuxnet may feel that a delay is better than nothing. But a cyber-attack is no substitute for a physical attack. The former would take weeks to recover from; the latter, years.

Stuxnet may have failed to do the damage its designers intended, but it has succeeded in undermining the widespread assumption that the West would be the victim rather than the progenitor of a cyber-attack. It has also illustrated the murkiness of this sort of warfare. It is rarely clear who is attacking whom. It is hard to tell whether a strike has been successful, or indeed has happened at all. This, it seems, is what cyberwar looks like. Get used to it.

This article was first published in *The Economist* in September 2010.

A worm in the centrifuge

An unusually sophisticated cyber-weapon is mysterious but important

IT SOUNDS LIKE THE PLOT OF AN AIRPORT THRILLER or a James Bond film. A crack team of experts, assembled by a shadowy government agency, develops a cyber-weapon designed to shut down a rogue country's nuclear programme. The software uses previously unknown tricks to worm its way into industrial control systems undetected, searching for a particular configuration that matches its target – at which point it wreaks havoc by reprogramming the system, closing valves and shutting down pipelines.

This is not fiction, but fact. A new software "worm" called Stuxnet (its name is derived from keywords buried in the code) seems to have been developed to attack a specific nuclear facility in Iran. Its sophistication suggests that it is the work of a well-financed team working for a government, rather than a group of rogue hackers trying to steal secrets or cause trouble. America and Israel are the obvious suspects. But Stuxnet's origins and effects are unknown.

Stuxnet first came to light in June 2010, when it was identified by VirusBlokAda, a security firm in Belarus. The next month Siemens, a German industrial giant, warned customers that their "supervisory control and data acquisition" (SCADA) management systems, which control valves, pipelines and industrial equipment, were vulnerable to the worm. It targets a piece of Siemens software, called WinCC, which runs on Microsoft Windows.

For security reasons SCADA systems are not usually connected to the internet. But Stuxnet can spread via infected memory sticks plugged into a computer's USB port. Stuxnet checks to see if WinCC is running. If it is, it tries to log in, to install a clandestine "back door" to the internet, and then to contact a server in Denmark or Malaysia for instructions. (Analysis of traffic to these servers is continuing, and may offer the best chance of casting light on Stuxnet's purpose and origins.) If it cannot find WinCC, it tries to copy itself on to other USB devices. It can also spread across local networks via shared folders and print spoolers.

Initially, Stuxnet seemed to be designed for industrial espionage or to allow hackers to blackmail companies by threatening to shut down vital systems. But its unusual characteristics suggest another explanation. WinCC is a rather obscure SCADA system. Hackers hoping to target as many companies as possible would have focused on more popular systems. And Stuxnet searches for a particular configuration of industrial equipment as it spreads. It launches an attack only when it finds a match. "The bad news is that the virus is targeting a specific process or plant," says Wieland Simon of Siemens. "The good news is that most industrial processes are not the target of the virus." (Siemens says it knows of 15 plants around the world that were infected by Stuxnet, but their operations were unaffected as they were not the intended target.)

Another odd feature is that Stuxnet uses two compromised security certificates (stolen from firms in Taiwan) and a previously unknown security hole in Windows to launch itself automatically from a memory stick. The use of such "zero-day vulnerabilities" by viruses is not unusual. But Stuxnet can exploit four entirely different ones in order to worm its way into a system. These holes are so valuable that hackers would not normally use four of them in a single attack. Whoever created Stuxnet did just that to boost its chances. They also had detailed knowledge of Siemens's industrial-production processes and control systems, and access to the target plant's blueprints. In short, Stuxnet was the work neither of amateur hackers nor of cybercriminals, but of a well-financed team. "Behind this virus there are experts," says Mr Simon. "They need money and know-how."

So what was the target? Microsoft said in August 2010 that Stuxnet had infected more than 45,000 computers. Symantec, a computer-security firm, found that 60% of the infected machines were in Iran, 18% in Indonesia and 8% in India. That could be a coincidence. But if Stuxnet was aimed at Iran, one possible target is the Bushehr nuclear reactor. In September 2010 Iranian officials confirmed that Stuxnet had infected computers at Bushehr, but said that no damage to major systems had been done. Bushehr has been dogged by problems for years and its opening has been delayed once again. Given that history, the latest hitch may not have been Stuxnet's work.

A more plausible target is Iran's uranium-enrichment plant at Natanz. Inspections by the International Atomic Energy Agency, the UN's watchdog, have found that about half Iran's centrifuges are idle and those that work are yielding little. Some say a fall in the number of working centrifuges at Natanz in early 2009 is evidence of a successful Stuxnet attack.

In 2009 Scott Borg of the United States Cyber-Consequences Unit, a think-tank, said that Israel might prefer to mount a cyber-attack rather than a military strike on Iran's nuclear facilities. That could involve disrupting sensitive equipment such as centrifuges, he said, using malware introduced via infected memory sticks.

His observation now looks astonishingly prescient. "Since the autumn of 2002, I have regularly predicted that this sort of cyber-attack tool would eventually be developed," he says. Israel certainly has the ability to create Stuxnet, he adds, and there is little downside to such an attack, because it would be virtually impossible to prove who did it. So a tool like Stuxnet is "Israel's obvious weapon of choice". Some have even noted keywords in Stuxnet's code drawn from the Bible's Book of Esther – in which the Jews fight back to foil a plot to exterminate them.

This article was first published in *The Economist* in September 2010.

Something wrong with our **** chips today

Kill switches are changing the conduct and politics of war

IN THE 1991 GULF WAR Iraq's armed forces used American-made colour photocopiers to produce their battle plans. That was a mistake. The circuitry in some of them contained concealed transmitters that revealed their position to American electronic-warfare aircraft, making bomb and missile strikes more precise. The operation, described by David Lindahl, a specialist at the Swedish Defence Research Agency, a government think-tank, highlights a secret front in high-tech warfare: turning enemy assets into liabilities.

The internet and the growing complexity of electronic circuitry have made it much easier to install what are known as "kill switches" and "back doors", which may disable, betray or blow up the devices in which they are installed. Chips can easily contain 2 billion transistors, leaving plenty of scope to design a few that operate secretly. Testing even a handful of them for anomalies requires weeks of work.

Kill switches and other remote controls are on the minds of Western governments pondering whether to send weapons such as sophisticated anti-tank missiles, normally tightly policed, to rebels in Libya. Keeping tabs on when and where they are fired will allay fears that they could end up in terrorist hands. Such efforts would not even need to be kept secret. A former CIA official says the rebels could be told: "Look, we're going to give you this, but we want to be able to control it."

That lesson was first learned in Afghanistan in the 1980s, when America supplied Stinger missiles to help Afghan fighters against Soviet helicopter gunships, only to have to comb the region's arms bazaars in later years to buy them back (some were then booby-trapped and sold again, to deter anyone tempted to use them).

America worries about becoming the victim of kill switches itself. Six years ago a report by America's Defence Science Board, an official advisory body, said "unauthorised design inclusions" in foreign-made chips could help an outside power gain a measure of control over critical American hardware.

Chips off the home block

In response, America has launched schemes such as the Trusted Foundry Programme, which certifies "secure, domestic" facilities for the manufacture of the most critical microchips. The Defence Advanced Research Projects Agency (DARPA), a Pentagon outfit devoted to expanding the military's technological abilities, will spend at least $20m in 2011 on ways to identify rogue microchips. The Army Research Office is holding a closed conference on kill switches in mid-April.

Farinaz Koushanfar, a DARPA-funded expert at Texas's Rice University, says microchip designers would like to be able to switch off their products "in the wild", in case the contractors that make the chips produce some extra ones to sell on the sly. She designs "active hardware metering" chips that, in devices connected to the internet, can remotely identify them and if necessary switch them off.

An obvious countermeasure is to keep critical defence equipment off the net. But that is only a partial solution. Chips can be designed to break down at a certain date. An innocent-looking component or even a bit of soldering can be a disguised antenna. When it receives the right radio signal, from, say, a mobile-phone network, aircraft or satellite, the device may blow up, shut down, or work differently.

Old-fashioned spying can reveal technological weaknesses too. Mr Lindahl says Sweden obtained detailed information on circuitry in a heat-seeking missile that at least one potential adversary might, in wartime, shoot at one of its eight C-130 Hercules military-transport planes. A slight but precise change in the ejection tempo of the decoy flares would direct those missiles towards the flame, not the aircraft.

Such tricks may be handy in dealing with unreliable allies as well as foes, but they can also hamper Western efforts to contain risk in unstable countries. Pakistan has blocked American efforts to safeguard its nuclear facilities. The country's former ambassador to the United Nations, Munir Akram, cites fears that such measures will include secret remote controls to shut the nuclear programme down.

A European defence official says even video surveillance cameras can intercept or disrupt communications. To avoid such threats, Pakistani engineers laboriously disassemble foreign components and replicate them.

Wesley Clark, a retired general who once headed NATO's forces, says that "rampant" fears of kill switches make American-backed defence co-operation agreements a harder sell. David Kay, a notable United Nations weapons inspector in Iraq, bemoans "scepticism and paranoia". You just can't trust anybody these days, even in the weapons business.

This article first appeared in *The Economist* in April 2011.

Marching off to cyberwar

The internet: Attacks launched over the internet on Estonia and Georgia highlight the difficulty of defining and dealing with "cyberwar"

AS RUSSIAN TANKS rolled into Georgia in August 2008, another force was also mobilising – not in the physical world, but online. Russian nationalists (or indeed anyone else) who wished to take part in the attack on Georgia could do so from anywhere with an internet connection, simply by visiting one of several pro-Russia websites and downloading the software and instructions needed to perform a "distributed denial of service" (DDoS) attack. This involves sending a flood of bogus requests to an internet server, so that it is overwhelmed by the demand and becomes unusable.

One website, called StopGeorgia, provided a utility called DoSHTTP, plus a handy list of target websites, including those of Georgian government agencies and the British and American embassies in the capital, Tbilisi. Launching an attack was as simple as entering the address and clicking a button labelled "Start Flood". The Stop-Georgia website helpfully indicated which target sites were still active and which had collapsed under the weight of bogus requests. Other websites explained how to write simple programs to send a flood of requests, or offered specially formatted webpages that could be set to reload themselves continuously, deluging particular Georgian websites with traffic.

The actual damage done was minimal: some e-mail was disrupted and some target sites were rendered unavailable to the public. The cyber-attacks on Estonia in 2007, also launched from Russia, were more effective because Estonia's government relies far more heavily on the internet (its parliament declared internet access a human right in 2000). They briefly upset the operations of some government organisations, including telephone access to the emergency services.

There is no conclusive evidence that either set of attacks was executed or sanctioned by the Russian government – though there is no evidence that it tried to stop them, either. Ethan Zuckerman, an internet expert at Harvard, has described the plethora of competing theories as "the fog of cyberwar". And in the Georgian case volunteer cyberwarriors – dubbed "a citizen DDoS army" by Artem Dinaburg of Damballa, a cybersecurity start-up – were also involved. Does any of this really count as an act of war? The Estonian and Georgian cyber-attacks have put to the test a host of theories about cyberwarfare: how to define it; whether to engage in it; and how to defend against it.

A definition of war

The discussion of cyber-attacks and cyberwarfare is complicated by widespread disagreement over how to define these terms. Many cyber-attacks are really examples of vandalism or hooliganism, observes Bruce Schneier, a security guru who works for BT, a British telecoms operator. A cyber-attack on a power station or an emergency-services call centre could be an act of war or of terrorism, depending on who carries it out and what their motives are.

For a cyber-attack to qualify as "cyberwar", some observers argue, it must take place alongside actual military operations. Trying to disrupt enemy communications during conflict is, after all, a practice that goes back to the earliest telecommunications technology, the telegraph. In 1862, for example, during the American Civil War, a landing party from *Thomas Freeborn*, a Union navy steamer, went ashore to cut the telegraph lines between Fredericksburg and Richmond. The Russian navy pioneered the use of radio jamming in the Russo-Japanese war of 1905. On this view, cyber-attacks on infrastructure are the next logical step. The attacks on Georgia might qualify as cyberwarfare by this definition, but those on Estonia would not, since there was no accompanying military offensive in the real world. As Mr Schneier puts it: "For it to be cyberwar, it must first be war."

Not everyone agrees. For years there has been talk of a "digital Pearl Harbour" – an unexpected attack on a nation's infrastructure via the internet, in which power stations are shut down, air-traffic control is sabotaged and telecoms networks are disabled. There have even been suggestions that future wars could be waged in cyberspace, displacing conventional military operations altogether. Why bomb your enemy's power-stations or stockmarkets if you can disable them with software? So far there have been no successful attacks of this type, but that does not stop people worrying about them – or speculating about how to launch them.

The strongest definition of cyberwar requires that cyber-attacks cause widespread harm, rather than mere inconvenience. The Georgian attacks did not cause physical harm, unlike the military operations going on at the same time.

Such definitions matter because cyber-vandalism or cyber-hooliganism are forms of cybercrime, which (in theory at least) is dealt with by various national and international law-enforcement agencies according to existing legal conventions, such as the Council of Europe Convention on Cybercrime. A private individual in Russia who defaces an Estonian website ought to be treated in a similar fashion to his neighbour who travels to Tallinn, breaks a shop window and goes into hiding in Russia – though identifying a cyber-attacker is far from easy and after the attacks in 2007 the Russian authorities refused to co-operate with Estonian investigators.

Such was the intensity of the attacks on Estonian websites, however, that the country's defence minister, Jaak Aaviksoo, warned that the action "cannot be treated as hooliganism, but has to be treated as an attack against the state". But treating the attacks as acts of war would mean applying a different set of rules, presenting a new challenge to policymakers.

All sorts of "translation problems" arise when trying to apply existing international rules relating to terrorism and warfare to online attacks, says Duncan Hollis, a professor of law at Temple University in Pennsylvania. The United Nations Charter prohibits the use of force except when authorised by the Security Council, for example, but does not spell out what counts as "the use of force" in cyberspace. Do DDoS attacks count? Perhaps not if aimed at a newspaper website, but what about an air-traffic-control system?

Agreement on a definition is needed, says Mr Hollis, because under international law a country that considers itself the victim of an act of war has the right to self-defence – with conventional military (not merely electronic) means. And members of an alliance with mutual-defence obligations, such as NATO, may be duty-bound to respond to an attack on any of their members. So the cyber-attack on Estonia, a NATO member, could in theory have prompted a military response. To grapple with questions like these, and to bring together a group of experts in "cyber-defence", NATO has set up a research centre in Tallinn.

Mr Hollis points out that the debate about how best to classify cyber-attacks has much in common with the debate about terrorism. Should terrorism be treated as a crime, as an act of war, as both at once, or as something entirely different that requires new laws? He favours this last approach for cyber-attacks because it avoids the translation problems that arise when applying existing rules to such attacks, and because those rules are themselves somewhat outdated, given that attacks (in the real world and online) may come from non-state actors such as terrorist groups. Mr Hollis proposes a new "international law for information operations" to alleviate the uncertainty. He concedes that there is unlikely to be international consensus in this area soon, but argues that it would be a big step in the right direction if a group of states such as NATO, or the OECD club of industrialised nations, agreed to be bound by a clear set of rules.

What effect such co-operation would have on containing anonymous and unofficial cyberwarriors is hard to say; the fight against real-world terrorism does not offer much hope. And it is attacks from such groups that some researchers are most worried about. John Robb, a military futurist, calls the spontaneous, bottom-up mobilisation of volunteer cyber-attackers in the Georgian conflict an example of "open-source cyberwarfare".

This approach has several advantages over centralised, state-directed cyber-attacks, he says. Leaving the attacks to informal cyber-gangs (the extent of the Russian state's involvement remains unclear), rather than trying to organise a formal cyberarmy, is cheaper, for one thing. The most talented attackers, with the best tools, might not want to work for the state directly. Best of all, from the state's point of view, is that it can deny responsibility for the attacks. It is the online equivalent of the use, by some governments, of gangs and militias to carry out attacks on political opponents or maintain control in particular regions.

Send in the botnet

There is no consensus among conventional military types about how to deal with such cyber-attackers. Writing in *Armed Forces Journal* in May 2008, Colonel Charles Williamson, of the intelligence and surveillance division of America's air force, proposed that the United States should establish its own "botnet" – a network of machines "that can direct such massive amounts of traffic to target computers that they can no longer communicate and become no more useful to our adversaries than hunks of metal and plastic." America, he wrote, "needs the ability to carpet-bomb in cyberspace to create the deterrent we lack." The botnet could be built out of obsolete computers that would otherwise be discarded, he suggested. But he conceded that there would be legal and political difficulties associated with its use.

Mr Robb is sceptical of the ability of formal military organisations to wage cyberwarfare. "A few top people with the right tools can do the work of thousands of less capable people, so it's better not to waste the money on 40,000 uniformed personnel dedicated to a bureaucratic and lethargic cyber command," he says. And after an attack from an informal, self-organised group, there is no clear target to strike in any case. It may make more sense for existing military bodies to concentrate on defence, by identifying the most vulnerable parts and working out how to protect them. "Anything they can do to us, we should be able to counter faster – that's the appropriate deterrence paradigm for this cyberage," says Thomas Barnett, a military strategist at Enterra Solutions, a technology firm. "We should concentrate on making ourselves resilient."

One way for governments to do this, says Richard Bejtlich, a former digital-security officer with the United States Air Force who now works at GE, an American conglomerate, might be to make greater use of open-source software, the underlying source code of which is available to anyone to inspect and improve. To those outside the field of computer security, and particularly to government types, the idea that such software can be more secure than code that is kept under lock and key can be difficult to accept. But from web-browsers to operating systems to encryption algorithms, the more people can scrutinise a piece of code, the more likely it is that its weak spots will be found and fixed. It may be that open-source defence is the best preparation for open-source attack.

This article was first published in *The Economist* in December 2008.

A Chinese ghost in the machine?

Identifying the perpetrator of cyber-attacks can be impossible

CYBERSPACE IS IDEAL FOR SPIES. Digitally disguised and undeterred by borders or passports, they can pick locks anywhere in the world, pilfer secrets without trace and even leave toxic traps for the unwary.

Security chiefs are very worried; NATO's new cyberwarfare think-tank in Estonia gets requests for help from across the world. And for researchers outside the charmed circle of high-security clearance, establishing hard evidence of mischief on the net is even harder.

Still, two reports released on March 29th 2009 managed to give an intriguing glimpse of the electronic front line, chronicling a systematic surveillance effort, probably controlled by China-based computers, of the Dalai Lama, the Tibetan government-in-exile, and the Tibetan diaspora.

Labelled GhostNet this operation infiltrated 1,295 computers in 103 countries over 22 months, including the foreign ministries of Iran, Indonesia and the Philippines; German, Indian and Pakistani embassies; and organisations such as the Asian Development Bank and NATO.

One report, by two researchers at the University of Cambridge Computer Laboratory in Britain, blamed the Chinese government and drew a firm denial from the authorities in Beijing. The other report, prepared in Canada, was more nuanced. (Both lots of researchers had previously worked in the same research team.)

That China might be using the internet to spy on Tibetan activists' international contacts is less striking, perhaps, than the remarkable ease with which they snooped on victims. Attackers used what are known as Targeted Trojans, e-mails sent to specific individuals that contain malicious software or "malware" hidden in an attached document or photo, or a link to an internet site to which the recipient is directed. To fool the victim, the sender poses as someone the recipient knows.

To make that disguise plausible, the sender must find out the victims' trusted contacts, their style of writing and preferred topics. The case cited in the investigation involved someone posing as a member of the Free Tibet group who sent a translation of a book – to a Tibetan monk.

When the attachment is opened, the malware burrows deep into the computer where it ferrets around for useful information, sends it back to the controlling computer and asks for further instructions.

Targeted Trojans are increasingly popular with spies and criminals. MessageLabs Intelligence, a British firm that monitors security threats, detected one or two per week in 2005, but is now seeing an average of 50 per day, says Paul Woods, the firm's senior strategist. The software does not require the resources of a state intelligence agency; it can easily be found on the internet. This is one reason why the Canadian researchers (at the University of Toronto and SecDev Group, a think-tank) were reluctant to say firmly that China's government mounted the attack on the Tibetans.

Much of the available malware emanates from China, whose 300m internet users represent the largest national group in the world. "We have reached the age of do-it-yourself signals intelligence," concludes the Canadian report.

As amateurs join the professionals, it is hard to tell whether mischief in cyberspace is the work of patriotic hackers, groups of individuals, or a government. The 2007 assault that nearly shut down Estonia's digital infrastructure was blamed on Russian ire over the moving of a Soviet war memorial. But that attack came from a "botnet" – a network of infected machines round the world – including many in America. The sale and rent of botnets is an established criminal business on the internet. An activist with a pro-Kremlin group has said that he mounted the attack on his own initiative. Other cyberattacks have coincided with conflicts between Israel and Hamas, and Russia and Georgia.

Cyber-defence efforts so far have focused on making networks more resilient. Progress on a global legal framework to control internet crime has been minimal, says a NATO cyberwarrior in Tallinn. If a host government refuses to probe further, as is the case with China, little can be done. "You need the right to send someone to the other side of the world with a search warrant to look at someone's computer, when that person may have no idea that it is even infected," says the official.

But it is not only governments which may need to rethink their approach. Software designers could also do more to build security into products so that computers are harder to hijack, says Shishir Nagaraja, an academic at the University of Illinois who studied the Dalai Lama's computers.

Victims of cyber-attacks should perhaps worry less about humiliation and more about helping others to escape the same fate: a novel aspect of the Tibetan episode was that the Dalai Lama and his followers suspected their computers had been infiltrated, called in experts and then allowed the results of the probe to be published. Government and corporate leaders elsewhere might ponder his example.

Meanwhile, the furore is fuelling suspicion of Chinese motives. In Britain Huawei, a Chinese firm, is one of the main contractors in a £10 billion ($14 billion) effort to upgrade the telephone system. Huawei's boss, Ren Zhengfei, is a former Chinese army officer, and Britain's spies fret that network equipment that will be used by firms, households and government departments could come with hidden "backdoors" that would let Chinese snoopers evade easy detection. In 2008 America's Congress blocked Huawei's plans to buy 3com, another computer-equipment firm, citing similar security worries. Cyberwarfare is a business with a future.

This article was first published in *The Economist* in April 2009.

Cyberwar

It is time for countries to start talking about arms control on the internet

THROUGHOUT HISTORY NEW TECHNOLOGIES have revolutionised warfare, sometimes abruptly, sometimes only gradually: think of the chariot, gunpowder, aircraft, radar and nuclear fission. So it has been with information technology. Computers and the internet have transformed economies and given Western armies great advantages, such as the ability to send remotely piloted aircraft across the world to gather intelligence and attack targets. But the spread of digital technology comes at a cost: it exposes armies and societies to digital attack.

The threat is complex, multifaceted and potentially very dangerous. Modern societies are ever more reliant on computer systems linked to the internet, giving enemies more avenues of attack. If power stations, refineries, banks and air-traffic-control systems were brought down, people would lose their lives. Yet there are few, if any, rules in cyberspace of the kind that govern behaviour, even warfare, in other domains. As with nuclear- and conventional-arms control, big countries should start talking about how to reduce the threat from cyberwar, the aim being to restrict attacks before it is too late.

The army reboots

Cyberspace has become the fifth domain of warfare, after land, sea, air and space. Some scenarios imagine the almost instantaneous failure of the systems that keep the modern world turning. As computer networks collapse, factories and chemical plants explode, satellites spin out of control and the financial and power grids fail.

That seems alarmist to many experts. Yet most agree that infiltrating networks is pretty easy for those who have the will, means and the time to spare. Governments know this because they are such enthusiastic hackers themselves. Spies frequently break into computer systems to steal information by the warehouse load, whether it is from Google or defence contractors. Penetrating networks to damage them is not much harder. And, if you take enough care, nobody can prove you did it.

The cyber-attacks on Estonia in 2007 and on Georgia in 2008 (the latter strangely happened to coincide with the advance of Russian troops across the Caucasus) are widely assumed to have been directed by the Kremlin, but they could be traced only to Russian cyber-criminals. Many of the computers used in the attack belonged to innocent Americans whose PCs had been hijacked. Companies suspect China of organising mini-raids to ransack Western know-how: but it could just have easily been Western criminals, computer hackers showing off or disillusioned former employees. One reason why Western governments have until recently been reticent about cyber-espionage is surely because they are dab hands at it, too.

As with nuclear bombs, the existence of cyber-weapons does not in itself mean they are about to be used. Moreover, an attacker cannot be sure what effect an assault will have on another country, making their deployment highly risky. That is a drawback for sophisticated military machines, but not necessarily for terrorists or the armies of rogue states. And it leaves the dangers of online crime and espionage.

All this makes for dangerous instability. Cyber-weapons are being developed secretly, without discussion of how and when they might be used. Nobody knows their true power, so countries must prepare for the worst. Anonymity adds to the risk that mistakes, misattribution and miscalculation will lead to military escalation – with conventional weapons or cyberarms. The speed with which electronic attacks could be launched gives little time for cool-headed reflection and favours early, even pre-emptive, attack. Even as computerised weapons systems and wired infantry have blown away some of the fog of war from the battlefield, they have covered cyberspace in a thick, menacing blanket of uncertainty.

One response to this growing threat has been military. Iran claims to have the world's second-largest cyber-army. Russia, Israel and North Korea boast efforts of their own. America has set up its new Cyber Command both to defend its networks and devise attacks on its enemies. NATO is debating the extent to which it should count cyberwar as a form of "armed attack" that would oblige its members to come to the aid of an ally.

But the world needs cyberarms-control as well as cyber-deterrence. America has until recently resisted weapons treaties for cyberspace for fear that they could lead to rigid global regulation of the internet, undermining the dominance of American internet companies, stifling innovation and restricting the openness that underpins the net. Perhaps America also fears that its own cyberwar effort has the most to lose if its well-regarded cyberspies and cyber-warriors are reined in.

Such thinking at last shows signs of changing, and a good thing too. America, as the country most reliant on computers, is probably most vulnerable to cyber-attack. Its conventional military power means that foes will look for asymmetric lines of attack. And the wholesale loss of secrets through espionage risks eroding its economic and military lead.

Hardware and soft war

If cyberarms-control is to America's advantage, it would be wise to shape such accords while it still has the upper hand in cyberspace. General Keith Alexander, the four-star general who heads Cyber Command, is therefore right to welcome Russia's longstanding calls for a treaty as a "starting point for international debate". That said, a START-style treaty may prove impossible to negotiate. Nuclear warheads can be counted and missiles tracked. Cyber-weapons are more like biological agents; they can be made just about anywhere.

So in the meantime countries should agree on more modest accords, or even just informal "rules of the road" that would raise the political cost of cyber-attacks. Perhaps there could be a deal to prevent the crude "denial-of-service" assaults that brought down Estonian and Georgian websites with a mass of bogus requests for information; NATO and the European Union could make it clear that attacks in cyberspace, as in the real world, will provoke a response; the UN or signatories of the Geneva Conventions could declare that cyber-attacks on civilian facilities are, like physical attacks with bomb and bullet, out of bounds in war; rich countries could exert economic pressure on states that do not adopt measures to fight online criminals.

Countries should be encouraged to spell out their military policies in cyberspace, as America does for nuclear weapons, missile defence and space. And there could be an international centre to monitor cyber-attacks, or an international "duty to assist" countries under cyber-attack, regardless of the nationality or motive of the attacker – akin to the duty of ships to help mariners in distress.

The internet is not a "commons", but a network of networks that are mostly privately owned. A lot could also be achieved by greater co-operation between governments and the private sector. But in the end more of the burden for ensuring that ordinary people's computer systems are not co-opted by criminals or cyber-warriors will end up with the latter – especially the internet-service providers that run the network. They could take more responsibility for identifying infected computers and spotting attacks as they happen.

None of this will eradicate crime, espionage or wars in cyberspace. But it could make the world a little bit safer.

This article was first published in *The Economist* in July 2010.

13 Better equations, smarter machines

Cry havoc! And let slip the maths of war

Warfare seems to obey mathematical rules. Whether soldiers can make use of that fact remains to be seen

IN 1948 LEWIS FRY RICHARDSON, a British scientist, published what was probably the first rigorous analysis of the statistics of war. Richardson had spent seven years gathering data on the wars waged in the century or so prior to his study. There were almost 300 of them. The list runs from conflicts that claimed a thousand or so lives to the devastation of the two world wars. But when he plotted his results, he found that these diverse events fell into a regular pattern. It was as if the chaos of war seemed to comply with some hitherto unknown law of nature.

At first glance the pattern seems obvious. Richardson found that wars with low death tolls far outnumber high-fatality conflicts. But that obvious observation conceals a precise mathematical description: the link between the severity and frequency of conflicts follows a smooth curve, known as a power law. One consequence is that extreme events such as the world wars do not appear to be anomalies. They are simply what should be expected to occur occasionally, given the frequency with which conflicts take place.

The results have fascinated mathematicians and military strategists ever since. They have also been replicated many times. But they have not had much impact on the conduct of actual wars. As a result, there is a certain "so what" quality to Richardson's results. It is one thing to show that a pattern exists, another to do something useful with it.

In a paper under review in early 2011 at *Science*, however, Neil

Johnson of the University of Miami in Coral Gables, Florida, and his colleagues hint at what that something useful might be. Dr Johnson's team is one of several groups who, in previous papers, have shown that Richardson's power law also applies to attacks by terrorists and insurgents. They and others have broadened Richardson's scope of inquiry to include the timing of attacks, as well as the severity. This prepared the ground for the new paper, which outlines a method for forecasting the evolution of conflicts.

Progress, of a sort

Dr Johnson's proposal rests on a pattern he and his team found in data on insurgent attacks against American forces in Afghanistan and Iraq. After the initial attacks in any given province, subsequent fatal incidents become more and more frequent. The intriguing point is that it is possible, using a formula Dr Johnson has derived, to predict the details of this pattern from the interval between the first two attacks.

The formula in question ($T_n = T_1 n^{-b}$) is one of a familiar type, known as a progress curve, that describes how productivity improves in a range of human activities from manufacturing to cancer surgery. T_n is the number of days between the nth attack and its successor. (T_1 is therefore the number of days between the first and second attacks.) The other element of the equation, b, turns out to be directly related to T_1. It is calculated from the relationship between the logarithms of the attack number, n, and the attack interval, T_n. The upshot is that knowing T_1 should be enough to predict the future course of a local insurgency. Conversely, changing b would change both T_1 and T_n, and thus change that future course.

Though the fit between the data and the prediction is not perfect (an example is illustrated in Figure 13.1), the match is close enough that Dr Johnson thinks he is onto something. Progress curves are a consequence of people adapting to circumstances and learning to do things better. And warfare is just as capable of productivity improvements as any other activity.

The twist in warfare is that two antagonistic groups of people are doing the adapting. Borrowing a term used by evolutionary biologists (who, in turn, stole it from Lewis Carroll's book, "Through

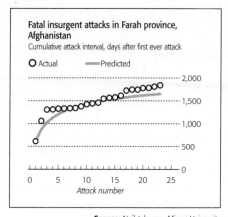

Fatal insurgent attacks in Farah province, Afghanistan
Cumulative attack interval, days after first ever attack

O Actual ──── Predicted

Source: Neil Johnson, Miami University

FIG 13.1 A lethal formula

the Looking-Glass"), Dr Johnson likens what is going on to the mad dash made by Alice and the Red Queen, after which they find themselves exactly where they started.

In biology, the Red Queen hypothesis is that predators and prey (or, more often, parasites and hosts) are in a constant competition that leads to stasis, as each adaptation by one is countered by an adaptation by the other. In the case Dr Johnson is examining the co-evolution is between the insurgents and the occupiers, each constantly adjusting to each other's tactics. The data come from 23 different provinces, each of which is, in effect, a separate theatre of war. In each case, the gap between fatal attacks shrinks, more or less according to Dr Johnson's model. Eventually, an equilibrium is reached, and the intervals become fairly regular.

The mathematics do not reveal anything about what the adaptations made by each side actually are, beyond the obvious observation that practice makes perfect. Nor do they illuminate why the value of b varies so much from place to place. Dr Johnson has already ruled out geography, density of displaced people, the identity of local warlords and even poppy production. If he does find the crucial link, though, military strategists will be all over him. But then such knowledge might perhaps be countered by the other side, in yet another lap of the Red Queen race.

This article was first published in *The Economist* in March 2011.

And now, the war forecast

Software: Can software really predict the outcome of an armed conflict, just as it can predict the course of the weather?

IN DECEMBER 1990, 35 days before the outbreak of the Gulf war, an unassuming retired colonel appeared before the Armed Services Committee of America's House of Representatives and made a startling prediction. The Pentagon's casualty projections – that 20,000 to 30,000 coalition soldiers would be killed in the first two weeks of combat against the Iraqi army – were, he declared, completely wrong. Casualties would, he said, still be less than 6,000 after a month of hostilities. Military officials had also projected that the war would take at least six months, including several months of fighting on the ground. That estimate was also wide of the mark, said the former colonel. The conflict would last less than two months, with the ground war taking just 10 to 14 days.

Operation Desert Storm began on January 17th 1991 with an aerial bombardment. President George Bush senior declared victory 43 days later. Fewer than 1,400 coalition troops had been killed or wounded, and the ground-war phase had lasted five days. The forecaster, a military historian called Trevor Dupuy, had been strikingly accurate. How had he managed to outperform the Pentagon itself in predicting the outcome of the conflict?

His secret weapon was a piece of software called the Tactical Numerical Deterministic Model, or TNDM, designed by the Dupuy Institute, an unusual military think-tank based near Washington, DC. It was the result of collaboration between computer programmers, mathematicians, weapons experts, military historians, retired generals and combat veterans. But was the result a fluke, or was the TNDM always so accurate?

Bosnia was its next big test. In November 1995, General Wesley Clark asked the Dupuy Institute to project casualty scenarios for NATO's impending peacekeeping mission, Operation Joint Endeavour. The resulting "Bosnia Casualty Estimate Study", prepared using results from the TNDM, stated that there was a 50% chance that no more than 17 peacekeepers would be killed in the first year. A year later, six had died – and the Dupuy Institute's reputation had been established.

The TNDM's predictive power is due in large part to the mountain of data on which it draws, thought to be the largest historical combat database in the world. The Dupuy Institute's researchers comb military archives worldwide, painstakingly assembling statistics which reveal cause-and-effect relationships, such as the influence of rainfall on the rate of rifle breakdowns during the Battle of the Ardennes, or the percentage of Iraqi soldiers killed in a unit before the survivors in that unit surrendered during the Gulf war.

Analysts then take a real battle or campaign and write equations linking causes (say, appropriateness of uniform camouflage) to effects (sniper kill ratios). These equations are then tested against the historical figures in the database, making it possible to identify relationships between the circumstances of an engagement and its outcome, says Chris Lawrence, the Dupuy Institute's director since its founder's death in 1995.

All of this is akin to working out the physical laws that govern the behaviour of the atmosphere, which can then be used in weather forecasting. But understanding the general behaviour of weather systems is not enough: weather forecasting also depends on detailed meteorological measurements that describe the initial conditions. The same is true of the TNDM. To model a specific conflict, analysts enter a vast number of combat factors, including data on such disparate variables as foliage, muzzle velocities, dimensions of fordable and unfordable rivers, armour resistance, length and vulnerabilities of supply lines, tank positions, reliability of weapons and density of targets. These initial conditions are then fed into the mathematical model, and the result is a three-page report containing predictions of personnel and equipment losses, prisoner-of-war capture rates, and gains and losses of terrain.

What is perhaps even more surprising than the TNDM's predictive accuracy is the fact that it is for sale. The $93,000 purchase price includes instruction classes, a year of technical support and a subscription to the TNDM newsletter, although subsequent updates to the software cost extra. Organisations that have acknowledged buying the software include the defence ministries of Sweden, South Africa, Finland, Switzerland and South Korea, along with the aerospace giant Boeing. Such customers rarely divulge the uses to which they put the software. But Niklas Zetterling, formerly a senior researcher at the Swedish National Defence Research Institute in Stockholm and now an academic at the Swedish War College, says his country uses the software to improve its arsenal. Mr Zetterling toyed with the software's technical variables "to create hypothetical weapons" that could then be proposed to engineers.

Rather than simply buying the TNDM, most clients contract the Dupuy Institute to produce studies that combine the software's predictions with human analysis. American clients have included the Joint Chiefs of Staff, the Army Medical Department, the Department of Defence, the Vietnam Veterans of America Foundation and the Sandia National Laboratories (a government-owned weapons-research centre run by Lockheed Martin). The institute is currently preparing a secret forecast of the duration and intensity of the Iraqi insurgency for the Centre for Army Analysis, a Pentagon agency.

Leader of the pack

The TNDM is not the only war-forecasting system. Many other systems have been developed, primarily by armed forces, government agencies and defence contractors in America, Australia, Britain, France and Germany. Some are glorified spreadsheets, but many are far more complex, including the American navy's GCAM software, the OneSAF model used by the army and Marine Corps, the air force's BRAWLER system and the Australian Department of Defence's JICM. With all these systems, younger officers tend to have more faith in the technology than their older counterparts. (According to a joke among technophiles, old-school military planners refuse to upgrade from BOGSAT, or "Bunch of Guys Sitting Around a Table".)

A survey of American war-forecasting systems by the Dupuy Institute found that very few are for sale or hire, and officials in charge of government models are often unwilling to share them with rival agencies. The simple availability of the TNDM has favoured its growth, although technology-transfer laws not surprisingly restrict its sale to certain countries.

Another attraction of the TNDM over rival models is the Dupuy Institute's independence: it has no weapons to sell, is not involved in internecine competition for budgetary funding, and has no political stake in military outcomes. Software developed primarily for, or by, a contractor or a branch of the armed forces often favours certain hardware or strategies, says Manfred Braitinger, head of forecasting software at IABG, a Munich-based firm that is Germany's leading developer of war-forecasting systems. The air-force and army models differ widely, for example, in their estimates of how easy it is to shoot down planes. "If you run both models you will see a remarkable difference in attrition rates simulating the same scenario," Mr Braitinger says. Systems with a wide customer base, like the TNDM, are regarded as more credible, since they do not have such biases.

The TNDM's reliance on real combat data, rather than results from war games or exercises, also gives it an edge. Another forecasting system, TACWAR, was used by America's Joint Chiefs of Staff to plan the overthrow of Saddam Hussein. Like many models, it was largely developed with data from war games. As a result, says Richard Anderson, a tank specialist at the Dupuy Institute, TACWAR and other programs based on "laser tag" exercises tend to "run hot", or over-estimate casualties. Real-bullet data is more reliable, because fear of death makes soldiers more conservative in actual combat than they are in exercises, resulting in fewer losses. The discipline is only just beginning to recognise the "tremendous value of real-world verification", says Andreas Tolk, an eminent modelling scientist at Virginia's Old Dominion University.

Yet another factor that distinguishes the TNDM from other war-forecasting systems is its unusual ability to take intangible factors into account. During NATO's air campaign above Serbia and Kosovo in 1999, for example, the Serbs built decoy tanks out of wood and tarpaulins and painted *trompe l'œil* bomb-holes on to bridges. Microwave ovens, modified to operate with their doors open and emit radiation, were used as decoys to attract HARM missiles that home in on the radar emissions of anti-aircraft batteries.

Such cunning is one of the many intangible variables that are taken into account by the TNDM's number-crunching equations. Mr Lawrence says incorporating human factors into equations is controversial: most models favour "harder" numbers such as weapons data. But Robert Alexander, an expert on war simulations at SAIC, an American defence contractor, says these are "almost secondary" to human factors.

The Concepts Evaluation Model (CEM) developed at the Pentagon's Centre for Army Analysis, provides an instructive example. While testing the model, programmers entered historical data from the Battle of the Bulge, the German offensive in 1944 against American forces in Belgium. The CEM predicted heavy German losses in the initial attack, yet German casualties were in fact light. The probable error? The model overlooked the shock value of launching a surprise attack. Analysts duly recalibrated the CEM – using an early version of the TNDM.

The Dupuy Institute is renowned for its ability to take into account such non-material factors: the effect of air support on morale, fear engendered by attack with unexpected weaponry, courage boosted by adequate field hospitals. The mother of all intangibles, within the TNDM model, is initiative, or the ability of lower-ranking soldiers to improvise on the battlefield. Armies from democratic countries – where people are empowered to make decisions – benefit by giving their soldiers some scope to change tactics in the midst of a firefight. Soldiers fighting for authoritarian regimes may not have the reflexes, or the permission, to seize opportunities when they arise in battle.

Maintaining the accuracy of the TNDM means feeding it with a constant stream of new information. The Dupuy Institute's analysts visit past battlefields to augment their statistical data, follow the arms industry closely and cultivate contacts with government defence procurers. In countries where access to military archives is limited, the Institute surreptitiously pays a handful of clerks to provide photocopies.

The next challenge will be to expand the TNDM's ability to forecast the outcomes of "asymmetric" conflicts, such as the Iraqi insurgency. To this end, the Dupuy Institute is hoping to get its hands on the Vietcong archives, as Vietnam opens up. Insurgencies rarely leave much of a paper trail, but the Vietnamese kept detailed records of their struggle against the French and Americans. The resulting papers provide the world's most extensive documentation of guerrilla fighting. "That's where warfare seems to be heading," says retired Major General Nicholas Krawciw, who is the president of the Dupuy Institute. And wherever warfare leads, war-forecasting systems must follow.

This article was first published in *The Economist* in September 2005.

No command, and control

Chaos fills battlefields and disaster zones. Artificial intelligence may be better than the natural sort at coping with it

ARMIES HAVE ALWAYS BEEN DIVIDED into officers and grunts. The officers give the orders. The grunts carry them out. But what if the grunts took over and tried to decide among themselves on the best course of action? The limits of human psychology, battlefield communications and (cynics might suggest) the brainpower of the average grunt mean this probably would not work in an army of people. It might, though, work in an army of robots.

Handing battlefield decisions to the collective intelligence of robot soldiers sounds risky, but it is the essence of a research project called ALADDIN. Autonomous Learning Agents for Decentralised Data and Information Networks, to give its full name, is a five-year-old collaboration between BAE Systems, a British defence contractor, the universities of Bristol, Oxford and Southampton, and Imperial College, London. In it, the grunts act as agents, collecting and exchanging information. They then bargain with each other over the best course of action, make a decision and carry it out.

So far, ALADDIN's researchers have limited themselves to tests that simulate disasters such as earthquakes rather than warfare; saving life, then, rather than taking it. That may make the technology seem less sinister. But disasters are similar to battlefields in their degree of confusion and complexity, and in the consequent unreliability and incompleteness of the information available. What works for disaster relief should therefore also work for conflict. BAE Systems has said that it plans to use some of the results from ALADDIN to improve military logistics, communications and combat-management systems.

War and peace

ALADDIN's agents – which might include fire alarms in burning buildings, devices carried by emergency services and drones flying over enemy territory – collect and process data using a range of algorithms that form the core of the project. To develop these algorithms the 60 researchers involved used techniques that include game theory (in which agents have to overcome barriers to collaboration in order to get the best outcome), probabilistic modelling (which is employed to predict missing data and reduce uncertainty) and optimisation techniques (which can provide means of making decisions when communications between agents are limited). A number of the algorithms also employ auctions to allocate resources among competing users.

In the case of an earthquake, for instance, the agents bid among themselves to allocate ambulances. This may seem callous, but the bids are based on data about how ill the casualties are at different places. In essence, what is going on is a sophisticated form of triage designed to make best use of the ambulances available. No human egos get in the way. Instead, the groups operating the ambulances loan them to each other on the basis of the bids. The result does seem to be a better allocation of resources than people would make by themselves. In simulations run without the auction, some of the ambulances were left standing idle.

The bidding algorithms can be tweaked to account for changing behaviour and circumstance. Proportional bidding, for instance, allows resources to be shared. If one agent bids twice as much as another for the use of a piece of equipment, the first agent will be given two-thirds of its capability and the second one-third. And, a bit like eBay, deadlines placed on making bids speed the process up.

All of which is very life-affirming when ambulances are being sent to help earthquake victims. The real prize, though, is processing battlefield information. Some 7,000 unmanned aerial vehicles, from small hand-launched devices to big robotic aircraft fitted with laser-guided bombs, are now deployed in Iraq and Afghanistan. Their combined video output in 2010 will be so great that it would take one person four decades to watch it. In 2011 things will be worse. America is about to deploy drones equipped with a surveillance system called Gorgon Stare. This stitches together images from lots of cameras to provide live video of an area as big as a town. Users will be able to zoom in for a closer look at whatever takes their interest: a particular house, say, or a car.

Data are also streaming in from other sources: remote sensors operating as fixed sentries, sensors on ground vehicles and sensors on the equipment that soldiers carry around with them (some have cameras on their helmets). On top of this is all the information from radars, satellites, radios and the monitoring of communications. The result, as an American general has put it, is that the armed forces could soon be "swimming in sensors and drowning in data".

ALADDIN, and systems like it, should help them keep afloat by automating some of the data analysis and the management of robots. Among BAE Systems' plans, for example, is the co-operative control of drones, which would allow a pilot in a jet to fly with a squadron of the robot aircraft on surveillance or combat missions.

The university researchers, meanwhile, are continuing to look at civilian applications. The next step, according to Nick Jennings of the University of Southampton, who is one of the project's leaders, is to examine more closely the interaction between people and agents. The earthquake in Haiti in 2010, he says, showed there is a lot of valuable information about things such as water, power supplies and blocked roads that can be gathered by "crowdsourcing" data using software agents monitoring social-networking websites. The group will also look at applying their algorithms to electricity grids, to make them work better with environmentally friendly but unreliable sources of power.

And for those worried about machines taking over, more research will be carried out into what Dr Jennings calls flexible autonomy. This involves limiting the agents' newfound freedom by handing some decisions back to people. In a military setting this could mean passing pictures recognised as a convoy of moving vehicles to a person for confirmation before, say, calling down an airstrike.

Whether that is a good idea is at least open to question. Given the propensity for human error in such circumstances, mechanised grunts might make such calls better than flesh-and-blood officers. The day of the people's – or, rather, the robots' – army, then, may soon be at hand.

This article was first published in *The Economist* in November 2010.

Droning on

How to build ethical understanding into pilotless war planes

WHAT THE HELICOPTER was to the Vietnam war, the drone is becoming to the Afghan conflict: both a crucial weapon in the American armoury and a symbol of technological might pitted against stubborn resistance. Pilotless aircraft such as the Predator and the Reaper, armed with Hellfire missiles, can hit targets without placing a pilot in harm's way. They have proved particularly useful for assassinations. On February 17th 2010, for example, Sheikh Mansoor, an al-Qaeda leader in the Pakistani district of North Waziristan, was killed by a drone-borne Hellfire. In consequence of this and actions like it, America wants to increase drone operations.

Assassinating "high-value targets", such as Mr Mansoor, often involves a moral quandary. A certain amount of collateral damage has always been accepted in the rough-and-tumble of the battlefield, but direct attacks on civilian sites, even if they have been commandeered for military use, causes queasiness in thoughtful soldiers. If they have not been so commandeered, attacks on such sites may constitute war crimes. And drone attacks often kill civilians. On June 23rd 2009, for example, an attack on a funeral in South Waziristan killed 80 non-combatants.

Such errors are not only tragic, but also counterproductive. Sympathetic local politicians will be embarrassed and previously neutral non-combatants may take the enemy's side. Moreover, the operators of drones, often on the other side of the world, are far removed from the sight, sound and smell of the battlefield. They may make decisions to attack that a commander on the ground might not, treating warfare as a video game.

Ronald Arkin of the Georgia Institute of Technology's School of Interactive Computing has a suggestion that might ease some of these concerns. He proposes involving the drone itself – or, rather, the software that is used to operate it – in the decision to attack. In effect, he plans to give the machine a conscience.

The software conscience that Dr Arkin and his colleagues have developed is called the Ethical Architecture. Its judgment may be better than a human's because it operates so fast and knows so much. And – like a human but unlike most machines – it can learn.

The drone would initially be programmed to understand the effects of the blast of the weapon it is armed with. It would also be linked to both the Global Positioning System (which tells it where on the Earth's surface the target is) and the Pentagon's Global Information Grid, a vast database that contains, among many other things, the locations of buildings in military theatres and what is known about their current use.

After each strike the drone would be updated with information about the actual destruction caused. It would note any damage to nearby buildings and would subsequently receive information from other sources, such as soldiers in the area, fixed cameras on the ground and other aircraft. Using this information, it could compare the level of destruction it expected with what actually happened. If it did more damage than expected – for example, if a nearby cemetery or mosque was harmed by an attack on a suspected terrorist safe house – then it could use this information to restrict its choice of weapon in future engagements. It could also pass the information to other drones.

No commander is going to give a machine a veto, of course, so the Ethical Architecture's decisions could be overridden. That, however, would take two humans – both the drone's operator and his commanding officer. That might not save a target from destruction but it would, at least, provide room for a pause for reflection before the pressing of the "fire" button.

This article was first published in *The Economist* in March 2010.

14 Propaganda ops, online

A world wide web of terror

Al-Qaeda's most famous web propagandist is jailed, but the internet remains its best friend

BY HIS OWN ADMISSION, he never fired a single bullet or "stood for a second in a trench" in the great *jihad* against America. Yet the man who called himself "Irhabi007" – a play on the Arabic word for terrorist and the code-name for James Bond – was far more important than any foot soldier or suicide-bomber in Iraq. He led the charge of *jihad* on the internet.

In doing so, Irhabi007 was a central figure in enabling al-Qaeda to reconstitute itself after the fall of the Taliban and its eviction from Afghanistan. Al-Qaeda ("the base") and its followers moved to cyberspace, the ultimate ungoverned territory, where jihadists have set up virtual schools for ideological and military training and active propaganda arms.

Irhabi007 pioneered many of the techniques required to make all this happen. He was a tireless "webmaster" for several extremist websites, especially those issuing the statements of the late Abu Musab al-Zarqawi, the leader of al-Qaeda in Iraq. Intelligence agencies watched powerlessly as Irhabi007 hacked into computers, for instance appropriating that of the Arkansas Highway and Transportation Department to distribute large video files, and taught his fellow cyber-jihadists how to protect their anonymity online.

Despite his celebrity, this was not good enough for Irhabi007. "Dude," he complained to a fellow cyber-jihadist (who called himself "Abuthaabit") during one encrypted web chat, "my heart is in Iraq."

Abuthaabit: How are you going to have enough to go there?

Irhabioo7: I suppose someone gotta be here!
Abuthaabit: This media work, I am telling you, is very important. Very, very, very, very.
Irhabioo7: I know, I know.
Abuthaabit: Because a lot of the funds brothers are getting is because they are seeing stuff like this coming out. Imagine how many people have gone [to Iraq] after seeing the situation because of the videos. Imagine how many of them could have been shaheed [martyrs] as well.

Irhabioo7's desire for real action may have led to his downfall. He was not only involved in a dispersed network of *jihadi* propaganda, but also, it seems, in a decentralised web of terrorist plots. In October 2005 police in Bosnia arrested a cyber-jihadist who called himself "Maximus", a Swedish teenager of Bosnian extraction called Mirsad Bektasevic. He and three others were later sentenced to jail terms of up to 15 years for plotting attacks that were to take place either in Bosnia or in other European countries.

Among the material recovered from Mr Bektasevic's flat, police found 19kg of explosives, weapons, a video with instructions for making a suicide vest and a video recording of masked men proclaiming their membership of "al-Qaeda in northern Europe". On his computer they found evidence of contacts with other jihadists across Europe. Among them was Irhabioo7.

Two days later, British police raided a flat in a terraced house in west London next to one of the rougher pubs in Shepherd's Bush. After an altercation, they arrested Younis Tsouli. The elusive Irhabioo7 turned out to be the 22-year-old son of a Moroccan tourism-board official and a student of information technology. Two other men, also students, were arrested at the same time, although Mr Tsouli had never met them except on the internet.

The trial of Mr Tsouli and his co-defendants – Waseem Mughal, a British-born graduate in biochemistry (aka Abuthaabit), and Tariq al-Daour, a law student born in the United Arab Emirates – came to an end in July 2007 when they belatedly pleaded guilty to charges of incitement to murder and conspiracy to murder. The court also heard that Mr al-Daour ran a £1.8m credit-card fraud and used the funds to buy equipment for *jihadi* groups. Mr Tsouli and Mr Mughal used stolen credit-card numbers to set up *jihadi* websites. Mr Tsouli was sent to jail for ten years; the others received shorter sentences.

There have been several arrests in Denmark, where a 17-year-old man of Palestinian origin was convicted in February 2007 for his involvement in Mr Bektasevic's plot. Three others were found guilty, but the jury's verdict was overturned. Irhabi007 has also been reported to be linked to plots in America, where two men living in Atlanta, Georgia, have been charged with planning attacks against civilian and military targets in and around Washington, DC, including the Capitol, the World Bank, the George Washington Masonic Memorial and a fuel depot. According to the indictment, the two men – Syed Ahmed, 21, and Ehsanul Sadequee, 19 – sent Irhabi007 photographs of the proposed targets, and also travelled to Canada to meet fellow plotters and discuss attacks.

Many of the details are still subject to court restrictions. But these interlinked investigations underline the words of Peter Clarke, the head of the counter-terrorism branch of London's Metropolitan Police, who said in April 2007 that his officers were contending with "networks within networks, connections within connections and links between individuals that cross local, national and international boundaries".

In light of failed attempts in July 2007 to set off car bombs in London and at Glasgow airport, allegedly by a group of foreign doctors and other medical staff, one exchange of messages found on Irhabi007's computer, in a folder marked "*jihad*", makes intriguing reading. "We are 45 doctors and we are determined to undertake *jihad* for Allah's sake and to take the battle inside damaged America, Allah willing," ran part of it.

The message purported to set out a plot to attack a naval base, apparently Mayport in Jacksonville, Florida, with the aim of achieving the "complete destruction" of the *USS John F. Kennedy*, an aircraft carrier, and 12 escort vessels, as well as blowing up "clubs for naked women" around the base. "The anticipated number of pig casualties is 200–300," said the author, unidentified except for the boast that he had been discharged from the Jordanian army. He claimed to have the support of a pilot who would provide air cover for the operation, but he lacked one essential piece of information that he asked Irhabioo7 to provide: a guide for making car bombs. The FBI said it had investigated the plot at the time and found it to be "not credible".

Nevertheless, the capability of the internet to promote terrorism is worrying intelligence agencies. According to America's National Intelligence Estimate in April 2006, "The radicalisation process is occurring more quickly, more widely and more anonymously in the internet age, raising the likelihood of surprise attacks by unknown groups whose members and supporters may be difficult to pinpoint."

Bomb.com

Past technological innovations, such as telephones or fax machines, have quickly been exploited by terrorists. But the information revolution is particularly useful to them. To begin with, encrypted communications, whether in the form of e-mail messages or, better still, voice-over-internet audio, make it much harder for investigators to monitor their activity. Messages can be hidden, for instance, within innocuous-looking pictures.

More important, the internet gives jihadists an ideal vehicle for propaganda, providing access to large audiences free of government censorship or media filters, while carefully preserving their anonymity. Its ability to connect disparate *jihadi* groups creates a sense of a global Islamic movement fighting to defend the global *ummah*, or community, from a common enemy. It provides a low-risk means of taking part in *jihad* for sympathisers across the world.

The ease and cheapness of processing words, pictures, sound and video has brought the era not only of the citizen-journalist but also the terrorist-journalist. Al-Qaeda now sends out regular "news bulletins" with a masked man in a studio recounting events from the many fronts of *jihad*, whether in Iraq, Afghanistan, Chechnya or Palestine. *Jihadi* ticker-tape feeds provide running updates on the number of Americans killed (about ten times more than the Pentagon's death toll).

Battlefield footage of American Humvees being blown up to shouts of "Allahu Akbar!" (God is Great) appear on the internet within minutes of the attacks taking place. The most popular scenes are often compiled into films with musical soundtracks of male choirs performing songs such as "Caravans of Martyrs". Jihadists have even released a computer video game, "Night of Bush Capturing", in which participants play at shooting American soldiers and President George Bush. Inevitably, experts say, jihadists have also started to create "residents" in the virtual world of Second Life.

As well as war fantasies, there is sometimes also a dose of sexual wish-fulfilment. A video recording by a Kuwaiti ideologue, Hamid al-Ali, declares that a martyr in the cause of *jihad* goes to paradise to enjoy delicious food, drink and a wife who will "astonish your mind" and much else besides; her vagina, apparently, "never complains about how much sex she had", and she reverts back to being a virgin.

The internet is awash with communiqués from insurgent groups extolling their own success or denouncing rivals. Even the most hunted figures, such as Ayman al-Zawahiri, the second-most-senior figure in al-Qaeda, regularly put out video statements commenting on political developments within just a few days.

In short, the hand-held video camera has become as important a tool of insurgency as the AK-47 or the RPG rocket-launcher. As Mr Zawahiri himself once put it in an intercepted letter to Zarqawi, "More than half of this battle is taking place in the battlefield of the media." Or as one *jihadi* magazine found on Irhabi007's computer explained: "Film everything; this is good advice for all mujahideen [holy warriors]. Brothers, don't disdain photography. You should be aware that every frame you take is as good as a missile fired at the Crusader enemy and his puppets." Just before his arrest, Irhabi007 had set up a website that, he hoped, would rival YouTube, to share *jihadi* videos. He called it Youbombit.com.

Of jihad and camels

The internet's decentralised structure, with its origins in military networks designed to survive nuclear strikes, now gives *jihadi* networks tremendousresilience. *Jihadi* websites constantly come and go, sometimes taken down by service providers only to reappear elsewhere, sometimes shifted deliberately to stay ahead of investigators. As one expert put it: "It's like the old game of Space Invaders. When you clear one screen of potential attackers, another simply appears to take its place."

The number of extremist websites is increasing exponentially, from a handful in 2000 to several thousand today. Some are overtly militant, while others give *jihad* second place to promoting a puritanical brand of piety known as "salafism", that is modelled on the earliest followers of the Prophet Muhammad and regards later developments as degenerate. Most are in Arabic, but some have started to translate their material into English, French and other languages to reach a wider audience.

The most headline-grabbing material on the internet is the military manuals – whether as books, films or PowerPoint slides – giving instruction on a myriad of subjects, not least weapons, assassination techniques, the manufacture of poisons and how to make explosives. But intelligence agencies say there is nothing like having hands-on experience in a place like Iraq, or at least a training camp. In the latest attempted attacks in London and Glasgow, for example, the attackers clearly botched the manufacture of their car bombs even though many of the alleged plotters were well educated.

Still, internet-based compilations such as the vast and constantly updated "Encyclopedia of Preparation", as well as militant e-magazines such as the *Tip of the Camel's Hump* (used to mean "the pinnacle") found on Irhabi007's computer, make it easier for self-starting groups around the world to try their hand at terrorism. The Dutch counter-terrorism office, which publishes many of its studies on extremism, concludes that the existence of virtual training camps "has the effect of lowering the threshold against the commission of attacks".

Many *jihadi* websites put their most inflammatory information and discussions in password-protected areas. Here participants can be gradually groomed, invited to take part in more confidential discussions, drawn into one-on-one chats, indoctrinated and at last recruited to the cause.

But the very anonymity that the internet affords jihadists can also work against them; it lets police and intelligence agencies enter the jihadists' world without being identified. Many postings to web forums are filled with (rightly) paranoid postings about who is watching. A lengthy posting on a Syrian *jihadi* site in 2005, entitled "Advice to Brothers Seeking *Jihad* in Iraq", said raw recruits offering only "enthusiasm or impetuousness or love of martyrdom" were no longer wanted. Instead, the mujahideen needed money and experienced fighters, but they should not assume that the smuggling routes through Syria were safe. It advocated communicating in secret through trusted sources in mosques rather than on the internet, noting that "this forum, like the others, is under ... surveillance; any information is obviously not secret, so any individuals you meet and correspond with on the forums cannot be trusted at all."

Contributors to *jihadi* websites are regularly told not to divulge secrets. When news of Irhabi007's arrest emerged last year, some of the postings stressed the need for greater caution online. One of these, signed by "Badr17", gave the warning "Trust in Allah, but tie your camel."

Open university of jihad

One of the most prolific al-Qaeda strategists is Abu Musab al-Suri. He is now in American custody, but his 1,600-page opus, "The Global Islamic Call to Resistance", survives. It advocates the creation in the West of self-starting, independent terrorist cells, not directly affiliated to existing groups, to stage spectacular attacks.

For many who study the *jihadi* websites, however, the bigger danger is indoctrination. The Dutch domestic intelligence service, the AIVD, regards the internet as the "turbocharger" of *jihadi* radicalisation. Stephen Ulph, a senior fellow at the Jamestown Foundation, an American research institute that monitors terrorism, says the internet provides an open university for jihadists. At least 60% of the material on *jihadi* websites deals not with current events or with war videos, but instead concerns ideological and cultural questions. Jihadists, Mr Ulph says, are fighting less a war against the West than "a civil war for the minds of Muslim youth". In this process of radicalisation, "the mujahideen attract the uncommitted armchair sympathiser, detach him from his social and intellectual environment, undermine his self-image as an observant Muslim, introduce what they claim is 'real Islam', re-script history in terms of a perennial conflict, centralise *jihad* as his Islamic identity, train him not only militarily but also socially and psychologically."

A key text is the ever-expanding e-book, "Questions and

Uncertainties Concerning the Mujahideen and their Operations", which seeks to arm jihadists with responses to questions and doubts about their actions, ranging from the admissibility of killing Muslims, the use of weapons of mass destruction and the acceptability of shaving one's beard for the sake of *jihad*. "It is important we do not get distracted by focusing on organisations rather than against ideology," argues Mr Ulph.

The point is underlined in a study by the Combating Terrorism Centre at America's military academy at West Point, which has tried to "map" the most important ideological influences by searching citations in *jihadi* online documents. Top of the list is Ibn Taymiyya, a scholar who lived at the time of the medieval Mongol invasions. He strove to return Islam to the pure faith of Muhammad's followers, advocated *jihad* to repel foreign invaders and taught that Mongol leaders who converted to Islam were not really Muslims because they did not implement *sharia*. These ideas strike a chord with today's jihadists, who see Americans as the new Mongols.

Osama bin Laden does not make the top ten most-cited figures, even among modern authors. Abu Muhammad al-Maqdisi, the theorist jailed in Jordan (and who directly inspired Zarqawi), is regarded as a higher authority. And Mr Zawahiri, the ubiquitous internet propagandist who is often described as the real brains behind al-Qaeda, does not even figure in the jihadists' intellectual universe.

Western intelligence agencies trawl the internet to look for evidence of terrorist plots, but lack the resources or desire to challenge the wider ideology. In a global network, outside the control of any single government, attempts to close down extremist sites are little more than short-lived harassment. What is needed is a systematic campaign of counter-propaganda, not least in support of friendly Muslim governments and moderate Muslims, to try to reclaim the ground ceded to the jihadists.

"Intelligence agencies are dealing with the problem once people have manifested themselves as existing terrorists," says Professor Bruce Hoffman, an expert on terrorism at Georgetown University. "We have to find a way to stanch the flow. The internet creates a constant reservoir of radicalised people which terrorist groups and networks can draw upon."

So Irhabi007 may be off the internet, but others like him remain. Among the most prolific is a figure who roams the web by the name of, yes, Irhabi11.

This article was first published in *The Economist* in July 2007.

Signalling dissent

Savvy techies are finding ways to circumvent politically motivated shutdowns of the internet

WITH A TIN CAN, some copper wire and a few dollars' worth of nuts, bolts and other hardware, a do-it-yourselfer can build a make-shift directional antenna. A mobile phone, souped-up with such an antenna, can talk to a network tower that is dozens of kilometres beyond its normal range (about 5km, or 3 miles). As Gregory Rehm, the author of an online assembly guide for such things, puts it, home-made antennae are "as cool as the other side of the pillow on a hot night". Of late, however, such antennae have proved much more than simply cool.

According to Jeff Moss, a communications adviser to America's Department of Homeland Security, their existence has been valuable to the operation of several groups of revolutionaries in Egypt, Libya and elsewhere. To get round government shutdowns of internet and mobile-phone networks, resourceful dissidents have used such makeshift antennae to link their computers and handsets to more orthodox transmission equipment in neighbouring countries.

Technologies that transmit data under the noses of repressive authorities in this way are spreading like wildfire among pro-democracy groups, says Mr Moss. For example, after Egypt switched off its internet in January 2011 some activists brought laptops to places like Tahrir Square in Cairo to collect, via short-range wireless links, demonstrators' video recordings and other electronic messages. These activists then broadcast the material to the outside world using range-extending antennae.

According to Bobby Soriano, an instructor at the Philippine branch of Tactical Tech, a British organisation that teaches communication techniques to dissidents in five countries, such antennae can even foil government eavesdropping and jamming efforts. Directional antennae, unlike the omnidirectional sort, transmit on a narrow beam. This makes it hard for eavesdroppers to notice a signal is there.

Citizens banned?

Another way of confounding the authorities is to build portable FM radio stations. One broadcasting expert, who prefers not to be named but is currently based in Europe, is helping to develop a dozen such "backpack" radio stations for anti-government protesters in his native land in the Arabian peninsula. Though these stations have a range of only a few kilometres, that is enough for the leaders of a protest to use them to co-ordinate their followers. The stations' operators act as clearing houses for text messages, reading important ones over the air for everyone to hear.

Conventional radio of this sort cannot, unfortunately, transmit video or web pages. But a group called Access, based in New York, is trying to overcome that. To help democracy movements in the Middle East and North Africa get online, it is equipping a network of ham-radio operators with special modems that convert digital computer data into analogue radio signals that their equipment can cope with. These signals are then broadcast from operator to operator until they reach a network member in an area where the internet functions. This operator reconverts the signal into computer-readable data and then e-mails or posts the information online.

Satellites provide yet another way of getting online, though they are expensive to connect to. It is beyond the authorities in most places to shut down a satellite operated by a foreign company or country. The best they can do is try to locate live satellite links using radiation-detection kit similar to that supposedly employed in Britain to seek out unlicensed televisions. The result is a game of cat and mouse between the authorities and satellite-using dissidents. Tactical Tech, for example, has trained dissidents in five countries to rig satellite dishes to computers in order to get online. It advises some users to log on only for short sessions, and to do so from a moving vehicle.

Such dishes can also be repurposed for long-range internet connections that do not involve satellites. Yahel Ben-David, an electrical engineer at the University of California, Berkeley, who has designed secret cross-border links to the internet for people in several countries, does so by adding standard USB dongles designed for home Wi-Fi networks. Thus equipped, two properly aligned dishes as much as 100km apart can transmit enough data to carry high-quality video. Moreover, the beam is so tightly focused that equipment a mere dozen metres away from its line would struggle to detect it.

Creative ideas for circumventing cyber-attacks even extend to the redesign of apparently innocent domestic equipment. Kenneth Geers, an American naval-intelligence analyst at a NATO cyberwar unit in Tallinn, Estonia, describes a curious microwave oven. Though still able to cook food, its microwaves (essentially, short radio waves) are modulated to encode information as though it were a normal radio transmitter. Thus things turn full circle, for the original microwave oven was based on the magnetron from a military radar. From conflict to domesticity to conflict, then, in a mere six decades.

This article was first published in *The Economist* in March 2011.

PART 4

Intelligence and spycraft

IN THE HUNT FOR MEMBERS of al-Qaeda and other terror groups, Western intelligence agencies use special software that sifts through enormous quantities of diverse data to map "non-obvious relationships" among people, places, behaviour and ideas. If, for example, two Saudi men have phoned a radical Afghan cleric and twice stayed in the same Islamabad hotel when the cleric was also in the city, the three may be working together. This effort to sort out "who's who in the zoo", in the words of Bob Griffin, head of i2, a British developer of the software, identified a certain man in Pakistan whose atypical behaviour and social ties were particularly intriguing.

The man repeated certain behaviours in the days or hours before the release of Osama bin Laden's communiqués – perhaps, for example, travelling to meet a non-relative from an apparently different walk of life and with whom he neither communicated electronically nor interacted publicly. By looking for possible linkages in data from diverse intelligence sources, "network analysis" software, as it is known, had apparently helped identify one of bin Laden's couriers, says Mr Griffin, whose firm's software was used in the manhunt.

Part 4 explores technology's impact on intelligence and spycraft. The technologies are diverse. Spy drones will shrink to about the size of a large insect. At some American military checkpoints video technology analyses body movements to detect hostile intent. For cargo-scanning, a sort of X-ray vision can be obtained using a hydrogen isotope to bombard a heavier form of the gas. Yet the burgeoning field of network analysis best illustrates how technology is driving transformations in the intelligence world as a whole. To begin with, many of the technologies examined in this section, no matter what their stripe, will increasingly gather or process information to feed network-analysis systems.

Breakthroughs in radar instrumentation, for example, are making it easier to discover tunnels and bunkers. And American military software that analyses aerial video of traffic can detect suspicious vehicles (such as those that pause near a building that is later attacked or return to their starting point with no one having left or entered the vehicle). The information from both radar and video is useful. But it becomes far more valuable when woven together with network analysis. This might reveal that, say, a truck flagged as suspicious is parked close to a newly discovered smuggling tunnel near a border and that the driver appears linked (through phone calls or other means) to a member of an armed group.

A tangled web

Advances in network analysis underscore improvements in spycraft technologies as a whole. During the 2003 hunt for Saddam Hussein, it was difficult to integrate network-analysis data from different computer systems. So American army analysts partly resorted to using string to link photographs and notes tacked to the wall of an operations room in Iraq, says Ian McCulloh, an instructor at the West Point military academy who conducts network-analysis workshops for intelligence officials. Stephen Borgatti, a University of Kentucky expert who has helped the Department of Defence develop network-analysis software, says that not long ago intelligence analysts commonly covered walls with sticky notes and pictures and "just stared at it until something came to them".

Drones both produce and require copious intelligence. Accordingly, investment in spy technologies, including network analysis, has boomed along with the use of drones. In the five years before 2009, American drone strikes killed at least 215 militants in Pakistan. The death toll leapt to at least 1,012 militants in the following two and a half years, according to the conservative estimates in one tally. Network analysis helped identify many of those targets. The tool will become even more formidable as other spy technologies leave the lab. For example, devices that analyse the wavelengths of infrared light reflected by airborne particles may soon allow drones to sniff out explosives or clandestine bomb-making facilities.

Intelligence technologies often fuel privacy worries, perhaps none more so than network analysis and its cousin data mining. Massive amounts of data are collected about people's whereabouts, purchases and activities. Is the loss of privacy worth it?

Many would say yes, at least to combat serious threats. World-wide, more than 25 agencies use network analysis to detect trafficking in nuclear materials and expertise, according to one estimate. The technology works well, notes a Frenchman who leads a firm that calibrated a model using data on the nuclear-smuggling network of Abdul Qadeer Khan, a Pakistani. Thanks to university and research-lab records, he says, most nuclear experts are known and accomplices generally share strong ties (needed to develop trust) that the software makes apparent.

By and large, the public has also accepted efforts to flush out lesser wrongdoers by analysing all manner of legal but potentially suspect behaviour (including web browsing). To detect fraud, software developed by an American firm, SAS, can link Internal Revenue Service tax records to credit-card data, property deeds and much more. The police department of Richmond, Virginia, uses network analysis with data from Facebook, MySpace and Twitter to better dispatch police officers to the parties most likely to become rowdy. A computer scientist at Britain's Cambridge University likens the general acceptance of reduced privacy to a "boiled frog" that did not jump out of a saucepan because it was heated gradually.

Connecting the dots

Upcoming intelligence technologies will go well beyond Western efforts to "make every soldier a sensor", says Jared Freeman, the top technologist at Aptima, a Massachusetts company. With US Department of Defence funding, Aptima is developing a handheld network-analysis system called NETSTORM, which will rapidly convert raw information from the field into processed tactical intelligence. A soldier or police officer might, for example, upload the name, occupation and phone number of a young villager being questioned. Quickly returned intelligence might reveal that, say, the villager had received a phone call from a wealthy and unrelated foreigner who had exchanged e-mails with a teenager who became a suicide bomber.

In matters of war and peace, intelligence has been enormously valuable for millennia. But the electronic age is making intelligence far easier to gather, process and use. Electronics have also made it easier to defeat some sophisticated weaponry with intelligence alone.

In the run-up to the first Gulf war, America obtained intelligence on the technical specifications of Iraqi air-defence systems imported from the Soviet Union, says David Kay, formerly the top UN weapons inspector in Iraq. Based on the information, adjustments were made to coalition electronic-warfare systems that rendered Iraq's anti-aircraft missiles "extremely ineffective", says Siemon Wezeman, an arms-trade expert at the Stockholm International Peace Research Institute, a Swedish think-tank.

The trick is known as "delinking" a missile. Efforts to obtain this sort of intelligence in the electronic age have spawned a booming underground trade, says an official at the Swedish Defence Research Agency, a defence-ministry body in Stockholm. The agency, he says, continuously gathers and shares this sort of technical information with allies. Rarely is it sold; instead, countries swap such secrets or pass them on to buy goodwill, the official says.

The use or development of spy and intelligence technologies is unlikely to grab as many headlines as the use or sale of weaponry. But, as the following articles show, the myriad technologies of modern spycraft are nonetheless dramatically reshaping efforts to keep the peace or prevail in conflict.

15 Identifying, and killing, the quarry

A tide turns

Technology used to help spies. Now it hinders them

DEPENDING ON WHAT KIND OF SPY YOU ARE, you either love technology or hate it. For intelligence-gatherers whose work is based on bugging and eavesdropping, life has never been better. Finicky miniature cameras and tape recorders have given way to pinhead-sized gadgets, powered remotely (a big problem in the old days used to be changing the batteries on bugs).

Encrypted electronic communications are a splendid target for the huge computers at places such as America's National Security Agency. Even a message that is impregnably encoded by today's standards may be cracked in the future. That gives security-conscious officials the shivers.

But the same advances are making life a lot harder for the kind of spy who deals with humans rather than bytes. The basis of spy-craft is breaking the rules without being noticed. As with the Russians arrested in June 2010 in America and now deported, that involves moving around inconspicuously, usually under false identities, and handing over and receiving money by undetectable means. For those who get caught, the consequences can be catastrophic.

The biggest headache is mobile phones. For spycatchers, these are ideal bugging and tracking devices, which the target kindly keeps powered up. But that makes them a menace for spies (and for terrorists, who often operate under the same constraints). Removing the battery and putting the bits in a fridge or other metal container disables any bug, but instantly arouses suspicion. If two people being followed both take this unusual precaution near the same location at the same time, even the most dull-witted watcher may infer that a clandestine meeting is afoot.

Creating false identities used to be easy: an intelligence officer setting off on a job would take a scuffed passport, a wallet with a couple of credit cards, a driving licence and some family snaps. In a world based on atoms, cracking that was hard.

Thanks to electrons, it is easy to see if a suspicious visitor's "shadow" checks out. Visa stamps from other countries can be verified against records in their immigration computers. A credit reference instantly reveals when the credit cards were issued and how much they have been used. A claimed employment history can be googled. Mobile-phone billing records reveal past contacts (or lack of them).

Missing links, in fact, are almost as bad as mistakes. A pristine mobile phone number is suspicious (especially when coupled with new credit cards and a new e-mail address, but no Facebook account). An investigation that would have once tied up a team of counter-espionage officers for weeks now takes a few mouse clicks.

With enough effort, a few convincing identities can be kept alive – a minor industry in the spy world involves keeping the credit cards for clandestine work credibly active. But for serious spies these legends wear out faster than they can be created.

Dead on arrival

Biometric passports are making matters worse. If you have once entered the United States as a foreigner, your fingerprints and that name are linked for ever in the government's computers. The data can be checked by any of several dozen close American allies. Obtaining a passport with a dead child's birth certificate is increasingly risky as population registers are computerised. Stealing a tourist's passport and changing the photo (a tactic favoured by Israel's Mossad) is no longer easy: in future the biometric data on the chip will need to check out too. Only the most determined and resourceful countries can do that – and the cost is spiralling.

Technology creates other problems. Take the dead-letter drop, where an item can be left inconspicuously and securely for someone else to pick up. Intelligence officers are trained to spot these, in places that are easy to visit and hard to observe (cisterns and waste bins in public lavatories, or under a heating grating in a church pew, for example). Time was when monitoring a suspected dead-letter box involved laborious work by humans. Now it can be done invisibly, remotely and automatically. Next time you bury a beer bottle stuffed with money in a park, you should ponder what cameras and sensors may be hidden in the trees nearby.

The days of the "illegal", living for many years in a foreign country under a near-foolproof false identity, are drawing to a close. Spymasters are increasingly using "real people" instead: globalisation makes it unremarkable for those such as Anna Chapman, one of the ten Russians deported from America (under her own, legally acquired, British name), to study, marry, work and live in a bunch of different countries. Like so many other once-solid professions, spying is becoming less of a career and more a job for freelancers.

This article was first published in *The Economist* in July 2010.

What's in a name?

Computing: Intelligence agencies are using new software to handle the arcane business of comparing lists of names

IN 1990 A PAKISTANI named Mir Aimal Kansi used an alternative transliteration of his Urdu family name, Kasi, to obtain a visa at the American consulate in Karachi. He entered America, overstayed his one-month visa and then went to the Pakistani embassy in Washington, DC, and obtained a new Pakistani passport, this time with the "n" reinserted in his surname. Using this new identity, he obtained working papers and a driving licence, bought a gun and went on to shoot five CIA employees, killing two, outside the agency's headquarters. (Kansi spent four years on the Federal Bureau of Investigation's Ten Most Wanted list before being captured, and was executed in 2002.)

This case shows how the apparently humdrum process of transliterating names from one language to another can be exploited by criminals. According to the FBI, Kansi also used the names Mir Aimal Kanci, Mir Aman Qazi, Amial Khan and Mohammed Alam Kasi. That last name introduces a further twist: there are more than 15 accepted ways to transliterate "Mohammed" from Arabic into English, and when you count the ways the name is written in the other 160-plus languages that use the Roman alphabet, the figure jumps to more than 200 correct spellings. Transposing words or names from one language or alphabet into another is evidently an inexact science.

In Indonesia, where single names are common, what appears to be just part of a name may in fact be the whole name. Chinese and Korean surnames are often mistakenly written last by Westerners, but some Chinese and Koreans are now adopting the Western convention. And then there is the problem of spelling variants. The Chinese family name Zhou, for example, may be written by English speakers as Jhou, Joe, Chou or Chow. Jafari, the common English transliteration of an Iranian family name, is rendered in German as Djafari or Dschafari. Shahram, the standard English spelling of an Iranian first name, becomes Scharam in German (and Chahram in French).

Such ambiguities cause huge problems for intelligence analysts trying to monitor and prevent terrorist activity. In an effort to avoid being picked out by computer watch-lists, many terrorists use alternative (but linguistically legitimate) transliterations of their names. "It's extremely commonplace, particularly with Islamic names," says Dennis Lormel, former director of the FBI's Terrorist Financing Operations Section, who is now an intelligence consultant at Corporate Risk International, near Washington, DC. "There are just so many variations of a name and they know that, so they can just flip-flop their name around," he says.

But companies in a fast-growing corner of the software industry have developed name-matching programs that can take into account the thousands of possible transliterations of a particular name – say, Mohammed bin Abdul Aziz bin Abdul Rahman Al-Khalifa – as they scan through watch-lists and databases looking for a match. The industry was flooded with investment in 2004 when the 9/11 Commission noted that the terrorists who attacked New York and Washington, DC, on September 11th 2001 defeated watch-lists by using different transliterations of their names. The commission urged the government "to close the long-standing holes in our border security that are caused by the US government's ineffective name-handling software." In-Q-Tel, the investment arm of the Central Intelligence Agency (CIA), began pouring money into name-matching software developers, according to a former official who chose which firms to finance. He says the technology is now becoming "pretty solid, robust stuff".

A name by any other name

"One of our biggest problems has always been variations of names," says Michael Scheuer, who was the head of the CIA's Osama bin Laden Unit from 1996 to 1999. Mr Scheuer says analysis was "backbreaking", especially for Arabic names, because it involved manually compiling lists of variations deemed worthy of tracing. This included positing names with or without titles such as bin ("son of", also written as ben or ibn), abu ("father of", also written as abou), sheikh (tribal leader, also written as sheik, shaikh, shaykh, cheik and cheikh) or haji (Mecca pilgrim, also written as hajj, hajji, hadj, haaji, haajj, haajji and haadj). The article al (also written as el) may be attached to surnames directly, separated from surnames with a hyphen or a space, or omitted altogether. Some variants do not even look similar. Sheikh can be written as jeque in Spanish. Wled, one English transliteration of an Arabic first (and last) name, is often written as Ould in French.

To make matters worse, many bureaucracies tolerate name abbreviations and short forms. The result is that intelligence analysts, no matter how expert, are often plagued by doubts. Has a Russian-speaking intelligence officer in Moscow transliterated into Cyrillic the name of a Nepalese suspect in exactly the same way as a Russian-speaking Uzbek field officer? Has an Italian analyst working with Russian intelligence caught and corrected the error, or passed it along?

Name-matching difficulties actually worsened when counterterrorism activity increased in late 2001. Analysts were granted greater access to databases kept by foreign agencies – but locating relevant files proved hard. A Portuguese case officer, for example, might have difficulty taking advantage of Dutch intelligence on, say, Nepalese Maoist extremists, if he is unfamiliar with Dutch conventions for the transliterations of Nepalese names. The number of people gathering and handling intelligence also increased suddenly, and many newcomers had little language training or were unsure how to transliterate names from spoken sources. Information on suspects increased, but spelling variations – due both to terrorist subterfuge and intelligence shortcomings – made it harder to interpret.

Mr Scheuer says that by late 2004, when he left the CIA, name-matching software was beginning to perform well, and American agencies were investing heavily in the latest technology – with one glaring exception. Computer systems at the State Department, according to Mr Scheuer, were "archaic compared to the rest of the intelligence community". That was a grave weakness, considering that the State Department issues passports and visas for travel to the United States.

If someone fears that the Romanised version of his name has been flagged, he can choose a new (but linguistically correct) transliteration, and then establish that spelling gradually by using it on low-level documents such as a gym-membership card or a lease agreement. These "feeder documents" are used to obtain progressively higher-level identity documents, such as a city-issued residence card, a driving licence or a certified birth-certificate translation. These documents, in turn, are presented at consulates to obtain the ultimate prize – passports and visas using the new variation of the name.

"It's a very tough set of problems," says Philip Zelikow, executive director of the now-dissolved 9/11 Commission. The group's research turned up numerous cases of transliteration fraud. Mr Zelikow notes, however, that the American government is now doing a better job handling names. Other experts affirm that the State Department has dramatically upgraded its name-matching software.

There are no firm estimates of how much name-matching software is being sold worldwide. Government agencies generally decline to release figures, and software firms shy from discussing hard numbers. Those in the industry, however, claim that growth is spectacular. Sam Kharoba of First Capital Technologies, based in Baton Rouge, Louisiana, says his firm's sales doubled in each of the three years 2004 through 2006. Its clients include America's Defence Department and over 20 other government agencies. Around 25 companies are working in the field in America, and a handful are in Europe.

As watch-lists multiply beyond the realms of intelligence and international travel, demand for such software is likely to grow. Increasingly, watch-lists are used to restrict access to training and education, and to stop people buying property, guns, chemicals and other things that can be made into weapons. Many postal services rely on name-matching software to pick out packages for inspection.

The financial services industry is also adopting the technology, which is often required by central banks and monetary authorities. In America, the Treasury's Office of Foreign Assets Control is one of the world's largest users of name-matching technology. It uses it to compile watch-lists that are sent to thousands of banks worldwide. Credit-card companies use the software to spot recidivists applying for new cards under modified names. (Names are cross-referenced with addresses, dates of birth and other data.) Developers and users are hesitant to discuss costs. But OMS Services, a British software firm, says government agencies pay a lot more than commercial users, who pay about $50,000 for its NameX programme.

Name-matching software is also becoming more sophisticated and performing other functions. The name-matching software made by Identity Systems, based in Old Greenwich, Connecticut, is used by more than 200 government agencies around the world. As well as flagging names on watch-lists, it also sifts historical records to reveal hidden relationships: if two men have entered a country several times on the same plane, sitting apart from each other, might one be a moneyrunner and the other his overseer?

Names and numbers

GNR, a software firm owned by IBM, makes software that "enriches" names by annotating them with inferred cultural information, scored according to probabilities derived from demographic data. Given a particular name it can, for example, say how likely someone is to have a particular place of birth. Names and titles can also provide clues as to birth order, occupation, deaths of spouses and immigration history. GNR also repairs names that are "damaged" by transliteration because the original non-Roman script is lost. The software generates possible original spellings and provides accuracy probabilities for each one. This helps spooks starting with the Romanised versions of, say, Pushtu names, to gather intelligence on those individuals in their native Afghanistan. GNR sells its software to law-enforcement and intelligence agencies – those in Australia, Israel and Singapore are particularly big spenders.

Name-matching software is just one small item in the counter-terrorism toolbox. But it can play a crucial role by enabling analysts to piece together snippets of intelligence. What's in a name? The answer, in some cases, is a surprising amount of valuable information.

This article was first published in *The Economist* in March 2007.

If looks could kill

Security experts reckon the latest technology can detect hostile intentions before something bad happens. Unless it is perfect, though, that may be bad in itself

MONITORING SURVEILLANCE CAMERAS is tedious work. Even if you are concentrating, identifying suspicious behaviour is hard. Suppose a nondescript man descends to a subway platform several times over the course of a few days without getting on a train. Is that suspicious? Possibly. Is the average security guard going to notice? Probably not. A good example, then – if a fictional one – of why many people would like to develop intelligent computerised surveillance systems.

The perceived need for such systems is stimulating the development of devices that can both recognise people and objects and detect suspicious behaviour. Much of this technology remains, for the moment, in laboratories. But Charles Cohen, the boss of Cybernet Systems, a firm based in Ann Arbor, Michigan, which is working for America's Army Research Laboratory, says behaviour-recognition systems are getting good, and are already deployed at some security checkpoints.

Human gaits, for example, can provide a lot of information about people's intentions. At the American Army's Aberdeen Proving Ground in Maryland, a team of gait analysts and psychologists led by Frank Morelli study video, much of it conveniently posted on the internet by insurgents in Afghanistan and Iraq. They use special object-recognition software to lock onto particular features of a video recording (a person's knees or elbow joints, for example) and follow them around. Correlating those movements with consequences, such as the throwing of a bomb, allows them to develop computer models that link posture and consequence reasonably reliably. The system can, for example, pick out a person in a crowd who is carrying a concealed package with the weight of a large explosives belt. According to Mr Morelli, the army plans to deploy the system at military checkpoints, on vehicles and at embassy perimeters.

Guilty

Some intelligent surveillance systems are able to go beyond even this. Instead of merely learning what a threat looks like, they can learn the context in which behaviour is probably threatening. That people linger in places such as bus stops, for example, is normal. Loitering in a stairwell, however, is a rarer occurrence that may warrant examination by human security staff (so impatient lovers beware). James Davis, a video-security expert at Ohio State University in Columbus, says such systems are already in use. Dr Davis is developing one for America's Air Force Research Laboratory. It uses a network of cameras to track people identified as suspicious – for example, pedestrians who have left a package on the ground – as they walk through town.

As object- and motion-recognition technology improves, researchers are starting to focus on facial expressions and what they can reveal. The Human Factors Division of America's Department of Homeland Security (DHS), for example, is running what it calls Project Hostile Intent. This boasts a system that scrutinises fleeting "micro-expressions", easily missed by human eyes. Many flash for less than a tenth of a second and involve just a small portion of the face.

Terrorists are often trained to conceal emotions; micro-expressions, however, are largely involuntary. Even better, from the researchers' point of view, conscious attempts to suppress facial expressions actually accentuate micro-expressions. Sharla Rausch, director of the Human Factors Division, refers to this somewhat disturbingly as "micro-facial leakage".

There are about 40 micro-expressions. The DHS's officials refuse to describe them in detail, which is a bit daft, as they have been studied for years by civilian researchers. But Paul Ekman, who was one of those researchers (he retired from the University of California, San Francisco, in 2004) and who now advises the DHS and other intelligence and law-enforcement agencies in the United States and elsewhere, points out that signals which seem to reveal hostile intent change with context. If many travellers in an airport-screening line are running late, telltales of anguish – raised cheeks and eyebrows, lowered lips and gaze – cause less concern.

Supporters of this sort of technology argue that it avoids controversial racial profiling: only behaviour is studied. This is a sticky issue, however, because cultures – and races – express themselves differently. Judee Burgoon, an expert on automated behaviour-recognition at the University of Arizona, Tucson, who conducts research for America's Department of Defence, says systems should be improved with cultural input. For example, passengers from repressive countries, who may already be under suspicion because of their origins, typically display extra anxiety (often revealed by rigid body movements) when near security officials. That could result in a lot of false positives and consequent ill-will. Dr Burgoon is upgrading her software, called Agent 99, by fine-tuning the interpretations of body movements of people from about 15 cultures.

Another programme run by the Human Factors Division, Future Attributable Screening Technology, or FAST, is being developed as a complement to Project Hostile Intent. An array of sensors, at a distance of a couple of metres, measures skin temperature, blood-flow patterns, perspiration, and heart and breathing rates. In a series of tests with role-playing volunteers, the system detected about 80% of those who had been asked to try to deceive it by being hostile or trying to smuggle a weapon through it.

A number of "innocents", though, were snagged too. The trial's organisers are unwilling to go into detail, and are now playing down the significance of the testing statistics. But FAST began just 16 months ago in June 2007. Bob Burns, the project's leader, says its accuracy will improve thanks to extra sensors that can detect eye movements and body odours, both of which can provide further clues to emotional states.

Until proved innocent

That alarms some civil-libertarians. FAST, they say, amounts to a forced medical examination, and hostile-intent systems in general smack of the "pre-crime" technology featured in Philip K. Dick's short story "The Minority Report" and the film based on it. An exaggeration, perhaps. But the result of using these devices, according to Barry Steinhardt, the head of technology and liberty at the American Civil Liberties Union in Washington, DC, will inevitably be that too many innocents are entangled in intrusive questioning or worse with "voodoo science" security measures.

To the historically minded it smacks of polygraphs, the so-called lie-detectors that rely on measuring physiological correlates of stress. Those have had a patchy and controversial history, fingering nervous innocents while acquitting practised liars. Supporters of hostile-intent systems argue that the computers will not be taking over completely, and human security agents will always remain the final arbiters. Try telling that, though, to an innocent traveller who was in too much of a hurry – or even a couple smooching in a stairwell.

This article was first published in *The Economist* in October 2008.

Worse than useless

An American government attempt to help Iranian dissidents backfires

FOR IRAN'S BELEAGUERED OPPOSITION, the internet is a potent weapon and a big hope. During the Green movement's protests in 2009, activists used Twitter and Facebook, often from mobile phones, to upload videos of police brutality and spread messages of support and news of new demonstrations. The authorities responded not only by cracking heads, but cracking computers: trying to trace users, block services and close websites.

Outsiders found the struggle inspirational. Austin Heap, a 26-year-old hacker born in Ohio, decided to develop anti-censorship software to foil the authorities' efforts. He named the product Haystack, and began in 2010 to distribute it to Iranian opposition leaders. The publicity was excellent: he was named "Innovator of the Year" by the *Guardian*, a British newspaper, and gained a plaudit from Hillary Clinton, America's secretary of state. The Treasury, State Department and Commerce Department hastened to grant Mr Heap a licence to export the software to Iran – not normally a favoured destination for American sales efforts, especially cryptographical ones.

But experts rapidly raised doubts. On investigation, Haystack looked dangerously insecure. Not only did it fail to encrypt secrets properly, but it could also reveal its users' identities and locations. Amid mounting criticism, Haystack's backers withdrew it on September 10th 2010.

Mr Heap's reaction heightened the worries. He admitted the project's faults but claimed only "a couple of dozen" people had been testing the product; all bar one had been alerted in writing that it was still being developed. How many of those people were in Iran, and why they had not been informed at the outset, was unclear. A disquieting message on the Haystack website reads "We have halted ongoing testing of Haystack in Iran pending a security review. If you have a copy of the test program, please refrain from using it." That suggests that the test was anything but controlled. Some reports suggest that up to 5,000 people had the software (though some say it did not work).

A tweet from Daniel Colascione, Haystack's lead developer, on September 13th 2010 added to the cringeworthy picture. "A whirlwind is coming straight for me...I flee". That option will not be available to Haystack's users in Iran, where the authorities have sometimes tortured and raped opposition activists. Ross Anderson, a professor of security engineering at Cambridge University, calls it "exceptionally stupid" to ship such a product in this way. The effect is to signal "I'm an important target, come get me," he says.

The news follows other rows involving American companies and totalitarian regimes, including Google's flirtation with Chinese censorship and Yahoo!'s failure to protect the identity of dissidents there who used its e-mail accounts. In September 2010 the *New York Times* accused Microsoft of colluding with the Russian authorities' attempts to harass opposition groups, by backing false charges that they used pirated software. Now the American government is open to the charge of recklessness.

While geeks unpick Haystack's technical failings, the political storm is growing. The unthinking praise for the project may have temporarily boosted Mr Heap's Censorship Research Center. But the wider effect was to violate a central principle of democracy-promotion: "first, do no harm".

This article was first published in *The Economist* in September 2010.

A time to kill

The professional and presumably state-directed killing of a leading Palestinian has been exposed in embarrassing detail. Perhaps such methods have had their day

USING SUBTERFUGE TO ENTRAP and kill adversaries, in locations far from any battlefield, has been a feature of conflict for the past 3,000 years or so – at least since Jael, one of the warrior heroines of ancient Israel, lured the enemy commander Sisera into her tent, lulled him to sleep with a refreshing drink of milk, and then used a tent peg to smash out his brains.

In modern times targeted killing is a more elaborate business, and many of the finer points – how the victim is stalked, how many people are involved – usually remain under wraps. But the plot to eliminate Mahmoud al-Mabhouh, a Hamas commander who was found dead in a Dubai hotel room on January 20th 2010, has been laid bare in stark detail by the police in that country, not normally regarded as a model of open government.

Hamas instantly blamed Mossad, the Israeli intelligence service, confirming that the dead man was a founder of the movement's military wing. Israel had fingered him in particular for the abduction and killing of two soldiers in 1989. Mr Mabhouh's brother claimed that he had been killed by an electrical appliance that was held to his head. The local police said he had been suffocated.

The gory details of his end were not made public in Dubai, but many of the events that led up to it were starkly exposed. Indeed any amateur student of espionage and its tradecraft can now consult YouTube, the video-sharing site, to see closed-circuit television footage of some of the 11 people (all travelling on European passports) who are said by the Dubai authorities to have joined in the plot. On February 15th 2010 the country's police chief offered a blow-by-blow account of the plotters' doings, elucidating the images.

The key agents were "Gail" and "Kevin" who supervised the hit, and "Peter" who was in charge of preparatory logistics. In the films their appearances changed frequently. Kevin acquires glasses and a full head of hair, after going to the loo. It is clear that the plotters were expecting Mr Mabhouh's arrival. One spotter waited at the airport; he duly tipped off a couple of colleagues, stout figures in tennis gear, who wait at the hotel and take note of the victim's room number, 230. The plotters book room 237, which they use as a base. In later footage Gail and Kevin are seen pacing the corridor nearby. Four men in baseball caps, one also wearing gloves, are seen getting into a lift to leave; they seem to be the ones who did the job.

In Israel the initial reaction to the killing was of telling smirks, plus leaks to the effect that the victim was buying arms from Iran. But this gave way to embarrassment as the Dubai authorities produced their evidence, and as protests came from countries – Britain, France, Germany and Ireland – whose passports had apparently been faked or abused; and from individuals whose identities were "borrowed".

The Israeli security services have never voiced any moral doubts about targeted assassinations (whether in the neighbourhood or farther afield) but there was a concern that the latest killing might go down on a list of plots that have misfired in unforeseen ways. In 1997, for instance, Mossad agents tried to eliminate Khaled Meshal, a senior Hamas official, in Jordan. Two agents posing as Canadians were caught trying to poison him and Israel, under threat that its agents would be executed, agreed to send an antidote. In 1973 Israeli agents murdered a Moroccan waiter in Lillehammer in Norway, mistaking him for the leader of Black September, the group blamed for a massacre of Israeli athletes at the Munich Olympics.

These bungles contrast with operations that Israeli spooks recall with defiant pride: the killing of Imad Mughniyeh, a top member of Hizbullah, in Damascus in 2008 (a particular coup since Syria is hostile territory for Israel); and the dispatch of Abu Jihad, a senior Palestinian official and founder of the Fatah movement, by a squad that swooped into Tunis in 1988.

The not-so-cold war

Israel has no monopoly on killing its foes far from home. European countries, including Britain (since the 1950s, anyway) claim to eschew such methods. But during the cold war both superpowers conspired eagerly to eliminate people they deemed undesirable. In America there was a rethink after a committee, under Senator Frank Church, disclosed that it was probing a web of plots to kill senior figures in countries like Congo, Cuba, the Dominican Republic and Vietnam. This led to a series of presidential decisions – most famously order number 12,333, signed by Ronald Reagan in 1981 – which barred assassinations.

The real force of such orders was to squelch rogue plots hatched in the lower levels of the security services; procedures still exist for the president, in consultation with congressional leaders, to authorise the killing of a perceived adversary. In 1998, three years before the 9/11 attacks, Bill Clinton mandated the capture or killing of Osama bin Laden, after bombs at American embassies in Kenya and Tanzania.

Since the start of the "war on terror", the boundaries in American thinking between legitimate military action and cold-blooded assassination have become fuzzier still. Among America's foreign-policy pundits there were serious discussions, back in 2003, as to whether simply killing Saddam Hussein would be a humane alternative to waging war against Iraq. As the fronts in the battle with al-Qaeda have broadened from Afghanistan and Pakistan to Somalia and Yemen, so too has the scope of American actions to eliminate perceived foes. In September 2009, for example, American helicopters fired on a convoy of trucks in Somalia and killed Saleh Ali Saleh Nabhan, who was blamed for an attack on an Israeli hotel in Kenya in 2002, and for the embassy bombs of 1998.

On February 3rd 2010 Dennis Blair, the director of national intelligence, told Congress that American forces might sometimes seek permission to kill a citizen of the United States, if he was a terrorist. This followed a report that Barack Obama had authorised an attack on Anwar al-Awlaki, a radical American imam, in Yemen.

The operation in Somalia earned Mr Obama a rebuke in the Harvard law faculty, where he first shone as a progressive young legal scholar. Such actions were counterproductive and of dubious legitimacy, a columnist in the *Harvard Law Record* argued. But defenders of the right to kill selectively cite the shooting down of Japan's Admiral Isoroku Yamamoto in the second world war, which was quite a cold-blooded business – though he was clearly an enemy combatant.

In truth, the factor that has changed the tactics of the American administration is less legal than mechanical: the advent of drones that can be directed with lethal accuracy (most of the time) from offices in Virginia. The best-known target was Baitullah Mehsud, leader of the Pakistani Taliban, who was blown up at his home in Waziristan in August 2009. A study by the New America Foundation, a think-thank, points out that CIA drone attacks have become far more frequent since Mr Obama took office, with more strikes being ordered in his first ten months than in George Bush's last three years.

In a world where Western voters demand maximum results for minimum expenditure of blood and treasure, assassination by machine has an obvious appeal to political leaders. Although they cost more "enemy" lives (including civilian ones) than old-time stabbing or poisoning, they also arouse less controversy. But for how long? Legal watchdogs say it makes unlawful killing more likely by dehumanising the process; and Pakistani officials, even those committed to fighting the Taliban, say the ruthless use of drones is alienating local people.

Whether death is by computer or by more old-fashioned methods, the antecedents and details of assassination are easier to hide in rough, remote locations than in rich, westernised ones. And even in wild places, awkward facts can come out – as they obviously did in Dubai.

This article was first published in *The Economist* in February 2010.

Hitmen old and new

Modern technology makes killing easier – but harder to get away with

ONLY A DECADE AGO the assassins who killed Mahmoud al-Mabhouh, a Palestinian Hamas commander found dead in a Dubai hotel room on January 20th 2010, would have disappeared into oblivion. Now that would be much harder, and not merely for the obvious reason that lenses are ubiquitous. Modern cameras capture more than blurred images: they record the precise bone structure of people's faces. Digitised and interpreted by an algorithm, this information is fed to police computers all over the world.

The net is closing around old-fashioned secret-service methods. Biometric passports are already the norm in most European countries. Their chips hold easily checkable data such as retina scans, which are both unique and unfakeable. The thought of an easily disproved false identity fills spymasters with horror. They remember the fate of western agents, in the Soviet Union after the second world war, whose painstakingly forged identity documents had a fatal flaw: they used stainless steel staples, rather than the soft iron fastenings found in authentic Soviet documents. The tell-tale absence of rust allowed Stalin's secret police to spot them.

The age of Facebook creates another problem. Creating a false identity used to be simply a matter of forging a few documents and finding a plausible life story. Nowadays, leaving an internet trail of convincing evidence for a fake identity is increasingly difficult – and a phoney detail is worse than none at all.

Even poisoning, for a long time the best way to hide a killing, may have become more difficult. The Soviet Union developed formidable expertise in the art of assassination, and (as a by-product of its germ-war and poison-gas efforts) in making toxins. A book published in Britain in 2009 and written by Boris Volodarsky, described as a former Russian military-intelligence officer, provided a glimpse into "The KGB's Poison Factory" from 1917 until the present day. Its "successes" included the killing of a Soviet defector in Frankfurt with thallium in 1957, and that of a Bulgarian dissident, Georgy Markov, in 1978, in London with a ricin-tipped umbrella.

Toxin analysis has improved but sometimes it is only luck that reveals ingeniously administered substances. Alexander Litvinenko, a renegade Russian security officer living in London, was killed by poisoning with polonium, a rare radioactive substance, in 2006. His assassins – said by British officials to have had help from Russia's security service – nearly got away with it. Had their victim died sooner, nobody would have tried the highly unusual test for that kind of radiation poisoning.

As another sign that sending hit squads to distant lands can go wrong, consider the tale of Zelimkhan Yandarbiyev, a Chechen ex-president killed in 2004 by a car-bomb in Qatar. The Qatari authorities, using well-honed surveillance, arrested three Russian officials; one had diplomatic immunity, but the other two were sentenced to jail. Only after a messy row between Russia and Qatar, and much damage to Russia's ties with Islam, did the pair return to Moscow – and a hero's welcome.

This article was first published in *The Economist* in February 2010.

16 Finding what's hidden

Looking beyond

A cheap way of using small radios to see inside buildings

SUPERMAN HAD X-RAY VISION, which was useful for looking through walls when rescuing heroines and collaring villains. But beyond Hollywood, the best that engineers have been able to come up with to see inside buildings are devices that use radar. Some are portable enough to be placed against an outside wall by, say, a police unit planning a raid – and sophisticated enough to show, with reasonable accuracy, the location of anyone inside. But the best models cost more than $100,000, so they are not widely deployed. Now a team led by Neal Patwari and Joey Wilson of the University of Utah has come up with a way to peer through the walls of a building using a network of little radios that cost only a few dollars each.

Radar works by recording radio waves that have been reflected from the object under observation. Dr Patwari's and Mr Wilson's insight was to look not for reflections but for shadows. Their device broadcasts a radio signal through a building and, when that signal comes out the other side, monitors variations in its strength. The need for variation means the system cannot see things that are stationary. When the signal is temporarily blocked by a moving object such as a person, however, it shows up loud and clear.

Using a network of small transmitters and receivers, the researchers have found it is possible to plot a person's position quite accurately and display it on the screen of a laptop. They call the process radio tomographic imaging, because constructing an image by measuring the strengths of radio signals along several pathways is similar to the computerised tomographic body-scanning used by hospitals – though medical machines employ X-rays, not radio waves, to do the scanning.

The radios used by Dr Patwari and Mr Wilson are low-cost types designed for use in what are known as ZigBee networks. In that application they transmit data between devices such as thermostats, fire detectors and some automated factory equipment. They are not even as powerful as the radios used in Wi-Fi networks to link computers together.

Small and inexpensive as these ZigBee radios are, though, there is strength in their numbers. Each is in contact with all of the others. A building under examination is thus penetrated by a dense web of links. In one experiment, for example, a network of 34 radios was able to keep track of Mr Wilson's position with an accuracy of less than a metre – a figure that Dr Patwari and Mr Wilson think could be improved greatly by using specially designed radios instead of off-the-shelf ones. Moreover, putting radios on the roof of a building as well as around its walls should make it possible to produce three-dimensional views of what is going on inside.

The ability to "see" people moving around in a building with such a cheap system has many plausible applications, and Mr Wilson has set up a company called Xandem to commercialise the idea. Besides military, police and private-security uses, radio networks might be employed to locate people trapped by fire or earthquake. More commercially, they might be used to measure what retailers call "footfall" – recording how people use stores and shopping centres. At the moment, this is done with cameras, or by triangulating the position of signals given off by mobile phones that customers are carrying. Radio tomography could be simpler, more accurate and, some might feel, less intrusive. Certainly less so than a man in tights with X-ray eyes.

This article was first published in *The Economist* in October 2009.

Tunnel vision

A sensitive mobile radar system will pinpoint illegal traffic

MOVING PEOPLE AND CONTRABAND unseen from one place to another is what smugglers do best. Governments, for their part, try to stop such traffic. The task is made more difficult when smugglers use deep underground tunnels linking, for example, Mexico and the United States. These are tricky to locate from the surface, but a new radar system should help.

Civilian engineers already use ground-penetrating radar to peer at what lies beneath building sites. These systems fire radio waves directly into the ground. When the waves strike a discontinuity – such as a layer of rock, a cavity or a foreign object – they bounce back and are detected by a small device on the surface next to the transmitter. The timing, strength and behaviour of the returned waves are used to identify what was struck and where it is.

This radar technique helps engineers look for cables and pipes that are just a few metres underground but, for security forces looking for tunnels that can be much deeper, it is ineffective. That is because such systems use high-frequency (and therefore short-wavelength) radio waves that readily bounce off small objects that they encounter. This makes them effective at forming sharp images at shallow depths, but useless beyond a few metres.

What is needed is a system that uses low-frequency radio waves. Researchers at the science and technology directorate of the American Department of Homeland Security and their counterparts at Lockheed Martin, a defence company, have now designed such a system.

Low-frequency radio waves, with their long wavelengths, are less susceptible to small-scale scattering and can thus travel deeper underground. The exact depth depends on the soil's composition and moisture content, but is enough to reach tunnel depths in most areas of interest. (The department will not reveal the exact figures in case such revelations prompt its quarry to dig deeper.)

The catch is that because low-frequency waves can travel great distances, when they do bounce off cavities or objects underground, they often end up far from the detection equipment at the surface. What is needed is antennae that are large enough to round up most of these errant waves, but small enough to keep the system relatively mobile.

The researchers are therefore experimenting with antennae that fit into trailers a few metres wide and which can be towed by patrol cars. These antennae are small enough to be mobile, but they are not quite big enough to catch all of the low-frequency radio waves. To overcome this limitation, an antenna is towed over the area of interest and signals recorded from different places are combined to form the final image.

The system also has software that helps it to avoid frequencies subject to interference, such as those used by local radio stations. In the wilderness such interference is rare, but in cities (where tunnels often start and finish) radio stations constantly blare out noise on many frequencies, making such filtering essential.

The researchers are confident that their more sensitive mobile radar system will soon be detecting tunnels that had previously been missed. Criminal underground beware.

This article was first published in *The Economist* in July 2009.

Bangers

An explosive cat-and-mouse game

CONFLICT CREATES ARMS RACES. As in the struggle against computer hacking or drug detection, stopping bomb-makers is a race between two kinds of innovation: creating the bad stuff and detecting it. Intelligence agencies regularly draw up lists of "substances of interest" and pass them on to firms that design and supply detection technology, says Kevin Riordan, of Smiths, an aviation-security firm. But once a substance can be routinely detected, terrorists will either attempt to conceal it better, or make something else.

A dog's nose is still a good detector for many explosives. Some have suggested bomb-sniffing bees as a further step. But technology is the basis of the explosive-detection business and it usually works either by examining the density of material using X-rays or by using spectroscopy to detect the mass and mobility of molecules. For more advanced machines, detecting a new explosive can be as simple as upgrading the software. First, the new target is characterised, then an algorithm (a series of rules programmed into a computer) is devised to detect it in scanned samples.

John Wyatt, a terrorism expert at SDS, a security company, says that only the most advanced X-ray machines can flag up the penta-erythritol tetranitrate (PETN) used in the Yemeni cargo bombs. Other X-ray machines may find it if the operators know what to look for (it should show up orange instead of blue). Swabs should pick up it up too (removing traces of most explosives requires thorough scrubbing) but poor training means that operators often use them incorrectly.

As military high-explosives have become harder to get hold of, terrorists have moved to commercially available materials. Counter-terrorism experts fret about home-made high explosives. But made in any useful quantity, these require large amounts of suspicious substances. They are tricky to concoct and more likely to kill their makers than their targets.

PETN, for example, is found in military devices such as landmines, and it is sold commercially as a heart drug. But making it yourself requires two nasty acids to be heated to 800°C. "If you don't know what you are doing," says Keith Plumb, of Britain's Institution of Chemical Engineers, "you have a 100% chance of death". PETN is also not particularly easy to detonate. That stymied the "underpants bomber" on a Detroit-bound plane at Christmas 2009.

Although American and British authorities have said the devices dispatched from Yemen were intended to blow up aeroplanes and were capable of doing so, experts in explosions and explosives are more cautious. Whether a bomb of this size could bring down a plane would depend on the size of the aircraft and where in the hold it was placed (next to the hull would be ideal). The bomb-maker has no control over either.

Hans Michels, a professor of safety engineering at London's Imperial College, estimates that about 1.5lb (0.7kg) of PETN could be packed into the kind of printer cartridges used in the bombs. That is around a tenth to a fifth of the power of the bomb that blew up a London bus in the bombing in July 2005. Something of this size, he reckons, would destroy two rooms in a suburban dwelling. Or a synagogue.

This article was first published in *The Economist* in November 2010.

Mr Neutron

Security technology: A new scanning technology, which can see things X-rays cannot, could help to beef up the inspection of air freight

AIRLINE PASSENGERS MIGHT BE FORGIVEN for thinking that security inspections are already quite tight enough, thank you. For accompanied luggage, they probably are. But accompanied luggage is only a fraction of what aircraft carry around. The rest is commercial freight, which is harder to examine with the rigour that is applied to passengers' baggage.

Part of the reason is that when an X-ray machine is faced with a containerful of cargo, the image it produces may be confused by the large number of objects packed inside. In addition, X-rays are poor at distinguishing between objects of identical shape but different composition. That is particularly true if the objects are made of material with a low density – as both explosives and drugs are. Moreover, something hidden in a container that is opaque to X-rays will not be noticed at all.

Of course, other security measures, such as explosive sniffers, can be employed, and often are. But the most reliable alternative to X-ray scanning, hand-searching everything, is slow and expensive. The upshot is that contraband is frequently smuggled in cargo and one day a bomb may be, too.

A joint venture just announced by Australia's Commonwealth Scientific and Industrial Research Organisation (CSIRO) and Nuctech Company, a security-equipment maker based in Beijing, is setting out to improve the situation by combining traditional X-ray scanning with a second scan using neutrons. In combination, the two techniques should be better at spotting threats than X-rays are alone.

The new system, adapted from mineral-analysis technology, exploits differences in the amount of X-ray and neutron energy absorbed by different types of material. By combining two sources of data it is easier to understand the nature of an object than if only one is employed.

The container to be examined passes on a conveyor belt into a tunnel shielded by steel and concrete to protect operators from radiation. The X-rays come from a standard X-ray machine. The neutrons are generated by bombarding a heavy form of hydrogen, called tritium, with a lighter isotope of the gas, called deuterium. The resulting collisions create helium atoms and a stream of neutrons.

The X-ray and neutron beams pass across the tunnel through the cargo and are detected on the other side. The detectors measure how much of each type of radiation got through. A computer then compares the results with the known absorption properties of different types of materials, to work out what the objects in the container are made from. It adds this information, suitably colour-coded, to the image. The whole process takes about a minute, and the scanner can be slotted into existing airport freight-handling systems. Security personnel can thus detect suspicious objects at a glance, and either clear the container for loading or redirect it for close inspection.

In trials conducted last year at Brisbane Airport, a prototype was able to detect a range of explosives, drugs and other contraband. The system can also distinguish nuclear materials, such as uranium, from other heavy metals, according to Nick Cutmore, a CSIRO researcher who is leading the project. And it can spot non-metallic materials, such as drugs and explosives, hidden inside large metal objects that are opaque to X-rays.

The CSIRO and Nuctech plan to conduct trials on the next version of the scanner in Beijing at the end of the year. If it works there, it will be offered for general sale, and a potential loophole in airport security will thus gradually be closed.

This article was first published in *The Economist* in July 2008.

17 Getting to know you better

The fly's a spy

A new type of flying machine is watching you

JUST BELOW A HALF-OPENED GARAGE DOOR a tiny device can be seen at the feet of someone lurking in the shadows. It looks like a blue dragonfly. Then its miniature wings begin to flap as it slips under the door and darts along the street. After rising through the air it stops to hover outside the window of a building several storeys high. There is an opening on the roof, and it slips inside. As it flits from room to room its video-camera "eye" transmits pictures to a screen on a remote-control unit strapped to the wrist of its clandestine operator.

This is not a scene from a James Bond film, in which 007 tests a new device from "Q", but an animated video produced by Onera, France's national aerospace centre, to explain REMANTA, a project to develop the technologies needed for miniature robotic aircraft. More bug-like flying devices are being developed in other research laboratories around the world. A few are already small enough to be carried in a briefcase; others are the size of a jet fighter and need a runway for take-off.

Having evolved from military use, drones, or unmanned aerial vehicles (UAVs), are taking to the air in increasing numbers for public-service and civilian roles. They are being operated by groups as diverse as police, surveyors and archaeologists. A UAV helped firemen track the blaze that ravaged southern California in October 2007. The most immediate advantage of a UAV is cost: operating even a small helicopter can cost $1,000 an hour or more, but the bill for a drone is a fraction of that. However, the growing use of UAVs is causing a number of concerns.

The first is safety. In October 2007 America's National Transportation Safety Board (NTSB) completed its first-ever investigation into an unmanned-aircraft accident. Pilot error was blamed for the crash in Arizona in April 2006 of a 4,500kg (10,000lb) Predator B, a type of UAV used by American forces in Iraq and Afghanistan. It was being operated by Customs and Border Protection when its engine was accidentally turned off by the team piloting it from a control room at an army base. No one was hurt, but the NTSB issued 22 recommendations to address what Mark Rosenker, its chairman, described as "a wide range of safety issues involving the civilian use of unmanned aircraft."

The second concern is privacy. UAVs can peek much more easily and cheaply than satellites and fixed cameras can. Although it is possible to peer into someone's back garden with Google Earth, the images are not "live" – some are years old. Live satellite images can be impaired by clouds and darkness. A UAV, however, is more flexible. It can get closer to its target, move to new locations faster and hover almost silently above a property or outside a window. And the tiny ones that are coming will be able to fly inside buildings. Before long paparazzi will put cameras in them to snatch pictures of celebrities.

Unmanned aircraft have been around almost as long as powered flight. In the first world war they were used as flying bombs and by the second as radio-controlled targets and for reconnaissance missions. In Afghanistan and Iraq they have also been fitted with missiles.

In more recent years the development of unmanned aircraft has become a process of technological democratisation. Lightweight construction materials, engines, microelectronics, signal-processing equipment and navigation by global-positioning satellites (GPS), are all getting more sophisticated, smaller and cheaper. As a result, so have UAVs.

Flown from afar

A Predator, including ground equipment, costs around $8m. It is capable of operating in harsh conditions for more than a day. Even though a Predator may be flying over a remote part of Iraq, it is more than likely being controlled by pilots working in shifts and sitting in front of a video screen thousands of miles away at an air-force base in America. Smaller, lighter and simpler UAV reconnaissance systems are being developed for troops in the field. These can be hand-launched, which reduces the need for remote-control piloting skills. Landings can be as simple as cutting the engine once the UAV has returned from its pre-programmed mission, at which point it flutters down to earth on a parachute.

Some hovering types can land automatically. One such device is made by Microdrones, a German company. Their flying machine looks like a small flying saucer with four rotor blades on stubby arms. It is not much bigger than the laptop computer used to program its flight and monitor what it is looking at. It can stooge around for about 20 minutes carrying video and infra-red cameras. Some police forces have started to try it out. In 2007 British bobbies used one to keep an eye on a music festival, busting people for drug offences and catching others breaking into cars.

The Los Angeles County Sheriff's Department, which operates more than a dozen helicopters, has experimented with a foldaway UAV. It has wings and an electric engine, and can be assembled in minutes for hand-launching. It has a flight time of around 70 minutes. At around $30,000 all in, it is a lot cheaper than another new helicopter at around $3m.

Scientists are using UAVs to help with experiments. The Scripps Institute of Oceanography in San Diego flew a fleet of them in stacked formation over the Maldives in the Indian Ocean last year. They were collecting air samples simultaneously from different altitudes for research into the effects of global warming.

In time, UAVs are likely to be employed for all sorts of jobs for which the use of an aircraft big enough to carry a pilot would be too dangerous, impractical or too expensive. Surveyors, for instance, could use a hovering UAV to inspect the walls of a tall building in a crowded city. A television station could use one to show traffic conditions. And as with all new technologies, unmanned vehicles will have uses that have not yet been imagined.

Already, the technology is so easily available that you can build a basic UAV for around $1,000 from model-aircraft parts, the innards of a GPS unit and a Lego Mindstorms robotics kit – just as Chris Anderson has done. Mr Anderson, the editor of *WIRED* magazine, has set up a website for other DIY-makers of low-cost UAVs.

Not surprisingly aviation officials are watching things closely. "We have just entered a new era, and we have got to be concerned about protecting persons and property," says Nicholas Sabatini, who is in charge of aviation safety at America's Federal Aviation Administration (FAA).

As the difference between sophisticated model aircraft equipped with auto-pilot systems and cameras and commercial UAVs blurs, the FAA is reconsidering its guidelines for model-flyers. At the moment these basically amount to keeping unmanned planes in sight at all times and away from people, buildings and other aircraft. Britain's Civil Aviation Authority is working with various industry groups to see what new rules may be needed. As a spokesman points out, UAVs will range from large jet-powered machines capable of flying across the Atlantic to tiny devices, so regulations will vary too depending on their size, weight and speed. Below a certain size, unmanned aircraft could be impossible to regulate. Nor would regulation do much to remove a chilling worry: that a UAV could be used as a weapon, to carry explosives or a biological agent.

Blown away

The smallest UAVS are the most intriguing because they will be able to fly in places where it was never thought aircraft could venture. Just how small might these machines be? The REMANTA bug has a total wingspan of less than 15cm (six inches). It flies by flapping its wings a bit like an insect. This means it needs less power than helicopter-type rotors and should be better able to withstand being blown off-course by wind, says Agnès Luc-Bouhali, a member of the project team.

Such a device can fly and be controlled remotely, but it could not yet conduct a mission like that portrayed in Onera's video. "Today, that is a dream," admits Ms Luc-Bouhali. But the team is working on it. Miniaturising power sources and sensors, and fitting REMANTA with systems to operate semi-autonomously in order to avoid obstacles such as walls are the main areas of future research and development.

Such concerns also occupy researchers at Harvard University. They are working on a fly-like robot which weighs only 60 milligrams (0.002 ounces) and has a wingspan of just three centimetres – not much bigger than a real fly and so most unlikely to be noticed. This means going beyond scaling down existing components, like electric motors, and trying entirely new manufacturing processes. The Harvard "fly-bot" has flown, but so far only on a tether from which it gets external power.

A different approach is being tried by a team at Britain's Portsmouth University working with a company called ANT Scientific. The university group is working on a UAV small enough to fit on a hand. Charlie Barker-Wyatt, a member of the university group, says all he can reveal about the device is that it contains sensors, can remain airborne for about 15 minutes, has a range of 500 metres and flies like a "hovering and spinning frisbee".

Such tiny devices are of less concern to safety officials than bigger UAVs that would cause damage if they hit an aeroplane or crashed to the ground. Until now UAVs have mostly been confined to conflict zones, no-go military areas or remote places. Some operate under the same guidelines as for model aircraft. But they are not welcome in "controlled" airspace, where manned aircraft fly under air-traffic control. The FAA's Mr Sabatini says his agency does not want to stifle their development, but insists it must at the same time maintain safety standards. This means larger UAVs could be considered "experimental" aircraft and allowed to operate in closely controlled circumstances. But until they have some ability reliably to detect and avoid other aircraft they will have to keep clear of controlled airspace.

Some bigger systems operate like manned aircraft even in remote areas. The "pilots" of the Predator that crashed in Arizona in 2006 were in contact with air-traffic controllers. But NTSB officials were still concerned about UAVs being flown too much like a computer game rather than as they would be if their pilots were on board.

Strict operating conditions for bigger UAVs might suit aviation firms, which are used to regulation and face competition from unmanned aircraft. Evergreen, a big aerospace group based in Oregon, has set up a UAV operation within its helicopter division. It offers relatively large and sophisticated systems for use in long-range operations, like checking on oil rigs, search and rescue, and wildlife monitoring.

Medium-sized systems might also have to be regulated, especially if used commercially. In the case of the smallest UAVs, the genie is already out of the bottle. When such devices are so small they might not even be noticed it would prove extremely difficult to regulate their use.

Unmanned aircraft will become more common, but how they swarm will depend on how safely they are used and how people react to the invasion of privacy. Some UAV missions may not be very welcome at all. "It smacks of Big Brother if every time you look up there's a bug looking at you," reckons the FAA's Mr Sabatini. Time to buy a good fly swat, perhaps.

This article was first published in *The Economist* in November 2007.

Learning to live with Big Brother

The new technologies for collecting personal information, and the dangers of abuse

IT USED TO BE EASY to tell whether you were in a free country or a dictatorship. In an old-time police state, the goons are everywhere, both in person and through a web of informers that penetrates every workplace, community and family. They glean whatever they can about your political views, if you are careless enough to express them in public, and your personal foibles. What they fail to pick up in the café or canteen, they learn by reading your letters or tapping your phone. The knowledge thus amassed is then stored on millions of yellowing pieces of paper, typed or handwritten; from an old-time dictator's viewpoint, exclusive access to these files is at least as powerful an instrument of fear as any torture chamber. Only when a regime falls will the files either be destroyed, or thrown open so people can see which of their friends was an informer.

These days, data about people's whereabouts, purchases, behaviour and personal lives are gathered, stored and shared on a scale that no dictator of the old school ever thought possible. Most of the time, there is nothing obviously malign about this. Governments say they need to gather data to ward off terrorism or protect public health; corporations say they do it to deliver goods and services more efficiently. But the ubiquity of electronic data-gathering and processing – and above all, its acceptance by the public – is still astonishing, even compared with a decade ago. Nor is it confined to one region or political system.

In China, even as economic freedom burgeons, millions of city-dwellers are being issued with obligatory high-tech "residency" cards. These hold details of their ethnicity, religion, educational background, police record and even reproductive history – a refinement of the identity papers used by communist regimes.

Britain used to pride itself on respecting privacy more than most other democracies do. But there is not much objection among

Britons as "talking" surveillance cameras, fitted with loudspeakers, are installed, enabling human monitors to shout rebukes at anyone spotted dropping litter, relieving themselves against a wall or engaging in other "anti-social" behaviour.

Even smarter technology than that – the sort that has been designed to fight 21st-century wars – is being used in the fight against crime, both petty and serious. In Britain, Italy and America, police are experimenting with the use of miniature remote-controlled drone aircraft, fitted with video cameras and infra-red night vision, to detect "suspicious" behaviour in crowds. Weighing no more than a bag of sugar and so quiet that it cannot be heard (or seen) when more than 50 metres (150 feet) from the ground, the battery-operated UAV (unmanned aerial vehicle) can be flown even when out of sight by virtue of the images beamed back to a field operator equipped with special goggles. MW Power, the firm that distributes the technology in Britain, has plans to add a "smart water" spray that would be squirted at suspects, infusing their skin and clothes with genetic tags, enabling police to identify them later.

Most of the time, the convenience of electronic technology, and the perceived need to fight the bad guys, seems to outweigh any worries about where it could lead. That is a recent development. On America's religious right, it was common in the late 1990s to hear dark warnings about the routine use of electronic barcodes in the retail trade: was this not reminiscent of the "mark of the beast" without which "no man might buy or sell", predicted in the final pages of the Bible? But today's technophobes, religious or otherwise, are having to get used to devices that they find even spookier.

Take radio-frequency identification (RFID) microchips, long used to track goods and identify family pets; increasingly they are being implanted in human beings. Such implants are used to help American carers keep track of old people; to give employees access to high-security areas (in Mexico and Ohio); and even to give willing night-club patrons the chance to jump entry queues and dispense with cash at the bar (in Spain and the Netherlands). Some people want everyone to be implanted with RFIDs, as the answer to identity theft.

Across the rich and not-so-rich world, electronic devices are already being used to keep tabs on ordinary citizens as never before.

Closed-circuit television cameras (CCTV) with infra-red night vision peer down at citizens from street corners, and in banks, airports and shopping malls. Every time someone clicks on a web page, makes a phone call, uses a credit card, or checks in with a microchipped pass at work, that person leaves a data trail that can later be tracked. Every day, billions of bits of such personal data are stored, sifted, analysed, cross-referenced with other information and, in many cases, used to build up profiles to predict possible future behaviour. Sometimes this information is collected by governments; mostly it is gathered by companies, though in many cases they are obliged to make it available to law-enforcement agencies and other state bodies when asked.

Follow the data

The more data are collected and stored, the greater the potential for "data mining" – using mathematical formulas to sift through large sets of data to discover patterns and predict future behaviour. If the public had any strong concerns about the legitimacy of this process, many of them evaporated on September 11th 2001 – when it became widely accepted that against a deadly and globally networked enemy, every stratagem was needed. Techniques for processing personal information, which might have raised eyebrows in the world before 2001, suddenly seemed indispensable.

Two days after the attacks on New York and Washington, Frank Asher, a drug dealer turned technology entrepreneur, decided to examine the data amassed on 450m people by his private data-service company, Seisint, to see if he could identify possible terrorists. After giving each person a risk score based on name, religion, travel history, reading preferences and so on, Mr Asher came up with a list of 1,200 "suspicious" individuals, which he handed to the FBI. Unknown to him, five of the terrorist hijackers were on his list.

The FBI was impressed. Rebranded the Multistate Anti-Terrorism Information Exchange, or Matrix, Mr Asher's programme, now taken over by the FBI, could soon access 20 billion pieces of information, all of them churned and sorted and analysed to predict who might one day turn into a terrorist. A new version, called the System to Assess Risk, or STAR, was launched in 2007 using information drawn from both private and public databases. As most of the data have already been disclosed to third parties – airline tickets, job records, car rentals and the like – they are not covered by the American constitution's Fourth Amendment, so no court warrant is required.

In an age of global terror, when governments are desperately trying to pre-empt future attacks, such profiling has become a favourite tool. But although it can predict the behaviour of large groups, this technique is "incredibly inaccurate" when it comes to individuals, says Simon Wessely, a professor of psychiatry at King's College London. Bruce Schneier, an American security guru, agrees. Mining vast amounts of data for well-established behaviour patterns, such as credit-card fraud, works very well, he says. But it is "extraordinarily unreliable" when sniffing out terrorist plots, which are uncommon and rarely have a well-defined profile.

By way of example, Mr Schneier points to the Automated Targeting System, operated by the American Customs and Border Protection, which assigns a terrorist risk-assessment score to anyone entering or leaving the United States. In 2005 some 431m people were processed. Assuming an unrealistically accurate model able to identify terrorists (and innocent people) with 99.9% accuracy, that means some 431,000 false alarms annually, all of which presumably need checking. Given the unreliability of passenger data, the real number is likely to be far higher, he says.

Those caught up in terrorist-profiling systems are not allowed to know their scores or challenge the data. Yet their profiles, which may be shared with federal, state and even foreign governments, could damage their chances of getting a state job, a student grant, a public contract or a visa. It could even prevent them from ever being able to fly again. Such mistakes are rife, as the unmistakable Senator "Ted" Kennedy found to his cost. In the space of a single month in 2004, he was prevented five times from getting on a flight because the name "T Kennedy" had been used by a suspected terrorist on a secret "no-fly" list.

Watching everybody

Another worry: whereas information on people used to be gathered selectively – following a suspect's car, for example – it is now gathered indiscriminately. The best example of such universal surveillance is the spread of CCTV cameras. With an estimated 5m CCTV cameras in public places, nearly one for every ten inhabitants, England and Wales are among the most closely scrutinised countries in the world – along with America which has an estimated 30m surveillance cameras, again one for every ten inhabitants. Every Briton can expect to be caught on camera on average some 300 times a day. Few seem to mind, despite research suggesting that CCTV does little to deter overall crime.

In any case, says Britain's "No2ID" movement, a lobby group that is resisting government plans to introduce identity cards, cameras are a less important issue than the emergence of a "database state" in which the personal records of every citizen are encoded and too easily accessible.

Alongside fingerprints, DNA has also become an increasingly popular tool to help detect terrorists and solve crime. Here again Britain (minus Scotland) is a world leader, with the DNA samples of 4.1m individuals, representing 7% of the population, on its national database, set up in 1995. (Most other EU countries have no more than 100,000 profiles on their DNA databases.) The British database includes samples from one in three black males and nearly 900,000 juveniles between ten and 17 – all tagged for life as possible criminals, since inclusion in the database indicates that someone has had a run-in with the law. This is because in Britain, DNA is taken from anyone arrested for a "recordable" offence – usually one carrying a custodial sentence, but including such peccadillos as begging or being drunk and disorderly. It is then stored for life, even if that person is never charged or is later acquitted. No other democracy does this.

In America, the federal DNA databank holds 4.6m profiles, representing 1.5% of the population. But nearly all are from convicted criminals. Since January 2006 the FBI has been permitted to take DNA samples on arrest, but these can be expunged, at the suspect's request, if no charges are brought or if he is later acquitted. Of some

40 states that have their own DNA databases, only California allows the permanent storage of samples of those charged, but later cleared. In Britain, where people cannot ask for samples to be removed from the database, it has been proposed that the best way to prevent discrimination is therefore to include the whole population in the DNA database, plus all visitors to the country. Although this approach is commendably fair, it would be extremely expensive as well as an administrative nightmare.

In popular culture, the use of DNA has become rather glamorous. Tabloids and television dramas tell stories of DNA being used by police to find kidnappers or exonerate convicts on death row. According to a poll carried out for a BBC "Panorama" programme in September 2007, two-thirds of Britons would favour a new law requiring that everyone's DNA be stored. But DNA is less reliable as a crime-detection tool than most people think. Although it almost never provides a false "negative" reading, it can produce false "positives". Professor Allan Jamieson, director of the Forensic Institute in Glasgow, believes too much faith is placed in it. As he points out, a person can transfer DNA to a place, or weapon, that he (or she) has never seen or touched.

Wiretapping is too easy

More disturbing for most Americans are the greatly expanded powers the government has given itself over the past six years to spy on its citizens. Under the Patriot Act, rushed through after the 2001 attacks, the intelligence services and the FBI can now oblige third parties – internet providers, libraries, phone companies, political parties and the like – to hand over an individual's personal data, without a court warrant or that person's knowledge, if they claim that the information is needed for "an authorised investigation" in connection with international terrorism. (In September 2007, a federal court in New York held this to be unconstitutional.)

Under the Patriot Act's "sneak and peek" provisions, a person's house or office can likewise now be searched without his knowledge or a prior court warrant. The act also expanded the administration's ability to intercept private e-mails and phone calls, though for this a court warrant was supposedly still needed. But in his capacity as wartime commander-in-chief, George Bush decided to ignore this requirement and set up his own secret "warrantless" eavesdropping programme.

The outcry when this was revealed was deafening, and the programme was dropped. But in August 2007 Mr Bush signed into law an amendment to the 1978 Foreign Intelligence Surveillance Act, allowing the warrantless intercept of phone calls and e-mails if at least one of the parties is "reasonably believed" to be outside America. So ordinary Americans will continue to be spied on without the need for warrants – but no one is protesting, because now it is legal.

Where's your warrant?

According to defenders of warrantless interception, requiring warrants for all government surveillance would dramatically limit the stream of foreign intelligence available. Privacy should not be elevated above all other concerns, they argue. But would it really impede law-enforcement that much if a judge was required to issue a warrant on each occasion? Technology makes wiretapping much easier than it used to be – too easy, perhaps – so requiring warrants would help to restore the balance, say privacy advocates.

Britain has long permitted the "warrantless" eavesdropping of its citizens (only the home secretary's authorisation is required), and few people appear to mind. What does seem to worry people is the sheer volume of information now being kept on them and the degree to which it is being made accessible to an ever wider group of individuals and agencies. The government is now developing the world's first national children's database for every child under 18. The National Health Service database, already the biggest of its kind in Europe, will eventually hold the medical records of all 53m people in England and Wales.

Companies are also amassing huge amounts of data about people. Most people do not think about what information they are handing over when they use their credit or shop "loyalty" card, buy something online or sign up for a loan. Nor do they usually have much idea of the use to which such data are subsequently put. Not only do companies "mine" them to target their advertising more effectively, for example, but also to give their more valued (ie, higher-spending) customers better service. They may also "share" their data with the police – without the individual's consent or knowledge.

Most democratic countries now have comprehensive data-protection and/or privacy laws, laying down strict rules for the collection, storage and use of personal data. There is also often a national information or privacy commissioner to police it all (though not in America). Intelligence agencies, and law-enforcement authorities often as well, are usually exempt from such data-protection laws whenever national security is involved. But such laws generally stipulate that the data be used only for a specific purpose, held no longer than necessary, kept accurate and up-to-date and protected from unauthorised prying.

That all sounds great. But as a series of leaks in the past few years has shown, no data are ever really secure. Laptops containing sensitive data are stolen from cars, backup tapes go missing in transit and hackers can break into databases, even the Pentagon's. Then there are "insider attacks", in which people abuse the access they enjoy through their jobs. National Health Service workers in Britain were reported to have peeked at the intimate medical details of an unnamed celebrity. All of this can lead to invasions of privacy and identity theft. As the Surveillance Studies Network concludes in its 2007 report on the "surveillance society", drawn up for Britain's information commissioner, Richard Thomas, "The jury is out on whether privacy regulation ... is not ineffective in the face of novel threats."

Boiling the frog

If the erosion of individual privacy began long before 2001, it has accelerated enormously since. And by no means always to bad effect: suicide-bombers, by their very nature, may not be deterred by a CCTV camera (even a talking one), but security wonks say many terrorist plots have been foiled, and lives saved, through increased eavesdropping, computer profiling and "sneak and peek" searches. But at what cost to civil liberties?

Privacy is a modern "right". It is not even mentioned in the 18th-century revolutionaries' list of demands. Indeed, it was not explicitly enshrined in international human-rights laws and treaties until after the second world war. Few people outside the civil-liberties community seem to be really worried about its loss now.

That may be because electronic surveillance has not yet had a big impact on most people's lives, other than (usually) making it easier to deal with officialdom. But with the collection and centralisation of such vast amounts of data, the potential for abuse is huge and the safeguards paltry.

Ross Anderson, a professor at Cambridge University in Britain, has compared the present situation to a "boiled frog" – which fails to jump out of the saucepan as the water gradually heats. If liberty is eroded slowly, people will get used to it. He added a caveat: it was possible the invasion of privacy would reach a critical mass and prompt a revolt.

If there is not much sign of that in Western democracies, this may be because most people rightly or wrongly trust their own authorities to fight the good fight against terrorism, and avoid abusing the data they possess. The prospect is much scarier in countries like Russia and China, which have embraced capitalist technology and the information revolution without entirely exorcising the ethos of an authoritarian state where dissent, however peaceful, is closely monitored.

On the face of things, the information age renders impossible an old-fashioned, file-collecting dictatorship, based on a state monopoly of communications. But imagine what sort of state may emerge as the best brains of a secret police force – a force whose house culture treats all dissent as dangerous – perfect the art of gathering and using information on massive computer banks, not yellowing paper.

This article was first published in *The Economist* in September 2007.

Know-alls

Electronic snooping by the state may safeguard liberty – and also threaten it

IF A MUSLIM CHEMISTRY GRADUATE takes an ill-paid job at a farm-supplies store what does it signify? Is he just earning extra cash, or getting close to a supply of potassium nitrate (used in fertiliser, and explosives)? What if apparent strangers with Arabic names have wired him money? What if he has taken air flights with one of those men, with separate reservations and different seats, paid in cash? What if his credit-card records show purchases of gadgets such as timing devices?

If the authorities can and do collect such bits of data, piecing them together offers the tantalising prospect of foiling terrorist conspiracies. It also raises the spectre of criminalising or constraining innocent people's eccentric but legal behaviour.

In November 2002 news reports revealed the existence of a big, secret Pentagon programme called Total Information Awareness. This aimed to identify suspicious patterns of behaviour by "data mining" (also known as "pattern recognition"): computer-driven searches of large quantities of electronic information. After a public outcry it was dubbed, perhaps more palatably, Terrorism Information Awareness. But protests continued, and in September 2003 Congress blocked its funding.

That, many people may have assumed, was that. But six of TIA's seven components survived as secret stand-alone projects with classified funding. A report in February 2008 by America's Department of Homeland Security named three programmes it operates to sniff out suspicious patterns in the transport of goods. Similar projects have mushroomed in, among other countries, Britain, China, France, Germany and Israel.

Civil-liberties defenders are trying hard to stop data mining becoming a routine tool for the FBI to spy on ordinary Americans. They say that the Bush administration is racing in its final months to formalise in law programmes that have run solely under authorisation from the White House that bypasses Congress. One pending change would authorise more intelligence sharing between federal and local officials. In a federal court filing made public on September 20th 2008, America's attorney-general, Michael Mukasey, sought legal immunity for telecoms firms which have provided details on international phone calls. What happens in practice, and what the law permits, is a hot and unresolved issue.

In August 2008, after a briefing by the Department of Justice about a secret data-mining plan for the FBI, a group of American lawmakers wrote to Mr Mukasey complaining that the plan would allow the FBI to spy on Americans "without any basis for suspicion". No similar pan-European data-mining programme is operating, at least to public knowledge.

Yet under an agreement signed in July 2007 airlines flying from the European Union to America have had to provide the authorities there with reservations data, as well as information obtained by airport-security screeners. This can include passengers' race, religion, occupation, relatives, hotel reservations and credit-card details. Internet service providers and telecoms firms in the EU must now keep for up to two years, though not automatically hand over, data on websites visited and phone calls made and received (but not the content of conversations).

Fast company

FAST, a Norwegian company bought by Microsoft in 2008 for $1.3 billion, collects data from more than 300 sources (including the web) for national data-mining programmes in a dozen countries in Asia, Europe and North America. In April 2008 British members of Parliament learned that almost a year earlier the home secretary, Jacqui Smith, had secretly authorised the transfer of licence-plate data recorded by roadside cameras to foreign intelligence agencies. In June the Swedish Parliament voted into law a data-mining programme strongly backed by the defence ministry. From January 1st 2009 it will provide sweeping powers to monitor international electronic messages and telephone traffic.

The staggering, and fast-growing, information-crunching capabilities of data-mining technology broaden the definition of what is considered suspicious. In June 2008 America's Departments of Justice and Homeland Security and a grouping of American police chiefs released the "Suspicious Activity Report – Support and Implementation Project". Inspired in part by the approach of the Los Angeles Police Department, it urges police to question people who, among other things, use binoculars, count footsteps, take notes, draw diagrams, change appearance, speak with security staff, and photograph objects "with no apparent aesthetic value".

Companies, and especially credit-reporting firms, generally enjoy more latitude than government bodies do in making personal information available to third parties. They find intelligence agencies are eager clients. Chris Westphal, head of Visual Analytics, a firm in Poolesville, Maryland that operates data-mining software for security and intelligence agencies, says the data provided by such firms is "very significant". Narayanan Kulathuramaiyer, an expert in data mining at UNIMAS, a Malaysian university, says companies are selling database access to intelligence and law-enforcement agencies "at a level you would not even imagine".

Legal challenges to governments' use of personal information held by companies have reached high courts in many countries, including America's Supreme Court. Rulings, however, have for the most part frustrated privacy advocates. Suzanne Spaulding, a former legal adviser to the Senate and House intelligence committees, says improvements in data-mining technology have enabled intelligence agencies to milk favourable court rulings in ways that exceed judicial intent. For example, such cases typically concern permission to use data from a single source, such as a phone company's billing records. When different databases are mined simultaneously, the value of information increases exponentially.

Spies are increasingly snooping on private internet use. Katharina von Knop, a data-mining expert at the University of German Federal Armed Forces in Munich, says many systems remotely analyse the content of web pages people visit. A man who has travelled to, say, Peshawar, a stronghold of Islamist extremism in Pakistan, is considered more dangerous if he also reads the blog of an extremist Muslim cleric. If the cleric lives in Peshawar, the man's suspicion score rises further. Data-mining software develops profiles by taking into account all web pages visited by a computer user; if a suspect visits a stamp-collecting website, the suspicion score is lowered.

Such profiling increasingly relies on "sentiment analysis". Hsinc-hun Chen, head of the Artificial Intelligence Lab at the University of Arizona says this technique, which he performs for American and international intelligence agencies, is an emerging and booming field. The goal is to identify changes in the behaviour and language of internet users that could indicate that angry young men are becoming potential suicide-bombers. For example, a person who exhibits curiosity by visiting many Islamist websites and asking numerous questions in online forums might be flagged by sentiment-analysis software if he shows signs of resentment and eventually turns to "radicalising" others by, say, justifying violence and providing links to militant videos. Mr Chen says intelligence agencies in the United States, Canada, China, Germany, Israel, Singapore and Taiwan are customers for this technique.

Does it work?

Donald Tighe, vice-president for public affairs at In-Q-Tel, a non-profit investment outfit that helps the CIA stay abreast of advances in computing, says that data mining is now so powerful it has become "essential to our national security". But campaigners for privacy have many worries. One fear, prevalent in Britain after incidents in which officials lost huge quantities of confidential personal information, is that the state may be even more careless with data than private firms are. Another is that innocents are flagged for further investigation or added to "watch-lists" that may impede air travel, banking and gaining jobs in places where radioactive materials are used, such as hospitals. The American Civil Liberties Union (ACLU), a lobby, says the list maintained by the Terrorist Screening Centre at the FBI now has more than 900,000 names, with 20,000 more every month. Being removed is tricky.

Data mining may be bad for national security as well as for civil liberties. The software is often modelled on the fraud-detection applications used by financial institutions. But terrorism is much rarer. So spotting conditions that may precede attacks is harder. Mike German, a former FBI agent who now advises the ACLU, says intelligence agencies too readily believe in the "snake oil" of total information awareness, which drains effort from more useful activities such as using informers and infiltrators.

Abdul Bakier, a former official in Jordan's General Intelligence Department, says that tips to foil data-mining systems are discussed at length on some extremist online forums. Tricks such as calling phone-sex hotlines can help make a profile less suspicious. "The new generation of al-Qaeda is practising all that," he says.

In 2007 two pattern-detection programmes, ADVISE and TALON, run respectively by America's Department of Homeland Security and the Pentagon, were shut down following privacy concerns and irregularities. Privacy advocates, however, say that other programmes continue – and many are operated, with minimal oversight, by the National Security Agency. The NSA insists that it does keep Congress informed. It also vigorously defends data mining, saying that if today's systems were in place before the terrorist attacks of September 11th 2001, some of the hijackers would have been identified.

In July 2008, after fierce debate, Congress imposed new limitations on government wiretapping when it renewed the expiring Foreign Intelligence Surveillance Act (FISA) sought by President George Bush after September 11th. The main law governing data mining, this has provided the administration with broad and unprecedented electronic-spying powers. But civil-liberties lobbies such as Amnesty International and Human Rights Watch say the renewed, restricted law leaves largely untouched far-reaching secret "black" programmes, run by the NSA, which crunch data on great numbers of people, including millions of Americans. Much of that is personal financial information collected by the Treasury.

Mr Bush has said that FISA helps protect citizens' liberties "while maintaining the vital flow of intelligence". Several hours after the president signed the bill into law, the ACLU filed a federal lawsuit, on the grounds that the executive branch's expanded wiretapping powers violated the constitution.

In 2001 American-led forces routed the Taliban in Afghanistan, destroying al-Qaeda training camps there. Berndt Thamm, who advises Germany's armed forces on terrorism, says that in retreat the Islamists left valuable clues about their online communications and electronic plotting. It is in following up these leads that data mining and pattern analysis can, and should, be used. Such techniques, says Mr Thamm, are "the only answer" to jihadist extremists. That is the argument which the strenuous objections of civil libertarians need to overcome.

This article was first published in *The Economist* in September 2008.

Untangling the social web

Software: From retailing to counterterrorism, the ability to analyse social connections is proving increasingly useful

TELECOMS OPERATORS NATURALLY PRIZE mobile-phone subscribers who spend a lot, but some thriftier customers, it turns out, are actually more valuable. Known as "influencers", these subscribers frequently persuade their friends, family and colleagues to follow them when they switch to a rival operator. The trick, then, is to identify such trendsetting subscribers and keep them on board with special discounts and promotions. People at the top of the office or social pecking order often receive quick callbacks, do not worry about calling other people late at night and tend to get more calls at times when social events are most often organised, such as Friday afternoons. Influential customers also reveal their clout by making long calls, while the calls they receive are generally short.

Companies can spot these influencers, and work out all sorts of other things about their customers, by crunching vast quantities of calling data with sophisticated "network analysis" software. Instead of looking at the call records of a single customer at a time, it looks at customers within the context of their social network. The ability to retain customers is particularly important in hyper-competitive markets, such as India. Bharti Airtel, India's biggest mobile operator, which handles over 3 billion calls a day, has greatly reduced customer defections by deploying the software, says Amrita Gangotra, the firm's director for information technology.

The market for such software is booming. By one estimate there are more than 100 programs for network analysis, also known as link analysis or predictive analysis. The raw data used may extend far beyond phone records to encompass information available from private and governmental entities, and internet sources such as Facebook. IBM, the supplier of the system used by Bharti Airtel, says its annual sales of such software, now growing at double-digit rates, will exceed $15 billion by 2015. In the past five years IBM has spent more than $11 billion buying makers of network-analysis software. Gartner, a market-research firm, ranked the technology at number two in its list of strategic business operations meriting significant investment in 2010.

Adoption is being driven by the availability of more sources of information, and by the fact that network-analysis software is becoming easier to use. A decade ago IBM employed experts with PhDs in mathematics to study social networks, according to Mark Ramsey, the firm's head of business analytics for eastern Europe, the Middle East and Africa. Today, college graduates can operate analysis software handling enormous quantities of data. Bharti Airtel employs only about 100 analysts to keep tabs on its 135m subscribers.

Take me to your leaders

Of course, companies have long mined their data to improve sales and productivity. But broadening data mining to include analysis of social networks makes new things possible. Modelling social relationships is akin to creating an "index of power", says Stephen Borgatti, a network-analysis expert at the University of Kentucky in Lexington. In some companies, e-mails are analysed automatically to help bosses manage their workers. Employees who are often asked for advice may be good candidates for promotion, for example.

Ellen Joyner of SAS, an analytics firm based in Cary, North Carolina, notes that more and more financial firms are using the software to uncover fraud. The latest version of SAS's software identifies risky borrowers by examining their social networks and Internal Revenue Service records, she says. For example, an applicant may be a bad risk, or even a fraudster, if he plans to launch a type of business which has no links to his social network, education, previous business dealings or travel history, which can be pieced together with credit-card records. Ms Joyner says the software can also determine if an applicant has associated with known criminals – perhaps his fiancée has shared an address with a parolee. Some insurers reduce premiums for banks that protect themselves with such software.

In 2009 an American government body called the Recovery Accountability and Transparency Board (RATB) began using network-analysis software to look for fraud within $780 billion of financial-stimulus spending. In addition to the internet, RATB combs Treasury and law-enforcement databases to uncover "non-obvious relationships", says Earl Devaney, its chairman. The software works very well, he says. It has triggered about 250 ongoing criminal investigations and 400 audits.

Joe Biden, America's vice-president, said in June 2010 that such software would be used to prevent fraud within the government's Medicaid and Medicare health-care schemes. The Army Criminal Investigation Command already sniffs out procurement fraud by scanning text in e-mails. The software, developed by SRA, an American firm, can correlate numbers and phrases written in nine languages with financial databases. If a person discusses a particular Department of Defence payment with an individual not officially linked to the deal, SRA's software may notice it.

The police department of Richmond, Virginia, has pioneered the use of network-analysis software to predict crimes. Police officers know that crime increases at certain times, such as on paydays and when there is a full moon. But the software lets them analyse the social networks around suspects, such as dealings with employers, collection agencies and the Department of Motor Vehicles. The goal, according to Stephen Hollifield, the department's technology chief, is to "pull together a complete picture" of suspects and their social circle.

Party plans turn out to be a particularly useful part of this picture. Richmond's police have started monitoring Facebook, MySpace and Twitter messages to determine where the rowdiest festivities will be. On big party nights, the department now saves about $15,000 on overtime pay, because officers are deployed to areas that the software deems ripe for criminal activity. Crime has "dramatically" declined as a result, says Mr Hollifield. Colin Shearer, vice-president of predictive analytics at SPSS, a division of IBM that makes the software in question, says it can largely replace police officers' reliance on "gut feel".

Network analysis also has a useful role to play in counter-terrorism. Terror groups are often decentralised, so mapping their social networks is akin to deciphering "a big spaghetti picture", says Roy Lindelauf of the Royal Dutch Defence Academy, who develops software for intelligence agencies in the Netherlands. It turns out that the key terrorists in a group are often not the leaders, but rather seemingly low-level people, such as drivers and guides, who keep addresses and phone numbers memorised. Such people tend to stand out in network models because of their high level of connectedness. To find them, analysts map "structural signatures" such as short phone calls placed to the same number just before and after an attack, which may indicate that the beginning and end of an operation has been reported.

The capture of Saddam Hussein in 2003 was due in large part to the mapping of the social networks of his former chauffeurs, according to Bob Griffin, the chief executive of i2, a British firm which developed software used in the manhunt. Senior members of the Iraqi regime were mostly clueless about the whereabouts of the former president, says Mr Griffin, but modelling the social networks of his chauffeurs who had links to rural property eventually led to the discovery of his hideout, on a farm near his hometown of Tikrit.

From social to societal networks

Where is network analysis headed? The next step beyond mapping influence between individuals is to map the influences between larger segments of society. A forecasting model developed by Venkatramana Subrahmanian of the University of Maryland does just that. Called SOMA Terror Organization Portal, it analyses a wide range of information about politics, business and society in Lebanon to predict, with surprising accuracy, rocket attacks by the country's Hizbullah militia on Israel.

Attacks tend to increase, for example, as more money from Islamic charities flows into Lebanon. Attacks decrease during election years, particularly as more Hizbullah members run for office and campaign energetically. By the middle of 2010 SOMA was sucking up data from more than 200 sources, many of them newspaper websites. The number of sources will have more than doubled by the end of the year.

Once these societal networks of influence can be accurately mapped, they can be used to promote the spread of particular ideas – those that support stability and democracy, for example. In 2009 America's army, which jointly funds SOMA with the air force, began disbursing about $80m in five-year research grants for network analysis to promote democracy and national security. An authoritarian government, for instance, may have difficulties slowing the spread of a new idea in a certain medium – say, internet chatter about a book that explains how corruption undermines job creation. Diplomatic services can use this information to help ideas spread. Brian Uzzi of Northwestern University in Evanston, Illinois, who advises intelligence agencies on democracy-promotion analytics, says diplomatic services are mapping the "tipping point" when ideas go mainstream in spite of government repression.

SPADAC, a firm based in McLean, Virginia, performs such analyses on Egypt and other countries in Africa, the Middle East and South-East Asia. Clients include the United States, Mexico and various diplomatic services. Riots, bloody elections and crackdowns, among other things, can be forecast with improving accuracy by crunching data on food production, unemployment, drug busts, home evictions and slum growth detected in satellite images. Mark Dumas, the head of SPADAC, notes that societies with longstanding and strong social and business ties abroad weather change well. In relatively closed countries, like Egypt, rapid shifts in social networks can trigger upheaval, he says. In 2009 SPADAC's revenue reached $19m; in 2010 it is expected to exceed $27m.

Country analyses have great potential in peacekeeping and counterinsurgency operations, according to Kathleen Carley of Carnegie Mellon University in Pittsburgh. She is developing a societal model of Sudan with a team of about 40 researchers. Foreign aid workers and diplomats frequently stumble in Sudan because they fail to work out which tribal and political leaders they should work with, and how.

Dr Carley's model, known as ORA, analyses a decade of data on such things as weather, land and water disputes, cabinet reshuffles, reactions to corruption, court cases, economic activity and changes in tribal geographic maps. Within the information that emerges are lists of the locals most likely to co-operate with Westerners, with details of the role each would best play. This depth of insight, a demonstration of the power of network analysis today, will only grow.

This article was first published in *The Economist* in September 2010.

PART 5

The road ahead

CARL VON CLAUSEWITZ, a Prussian military theorist with extensive combat experience against the armies of Napoleonic France, described war as a "true political instrument". In the state-against-state conventional warfare that Clausewitz knew, victory on the battlefield works well, as he put it, to "compel our enemy to do our will". The calculus changes, however, in the messy, irregular wars against non-state groups that crop up all too often in today's weak or failed states.

Groups fighting technologically superior armies often seek cover by mingling with civilian populations. It is hard to force an enemy to bend to your will if its fighters cannot be found and killed or detained. Insurgents can hide among civilians even without having won their support. As numerous conflicts in Africa and elsewhere attest, armed groups may take refuge among a populace by coercing it, especially if the people are poor, with widespread robbing, raping, mutilating or killing.

Such, broadly, is the looming challenge for the West's advanced armed forces, the subject of the final part of this book. Victory, ultimately, is political, so military supremacy may mean little. The US military's counter-insurgency manual, FM 3-24, describes this sort of warfare as "armed social work". In counter-insurgency, you can win every battle but lose the war. By the end of the Vietnam war in 1975, the North Vietnamese and Viet Cong had prevailed in spite of losing more than three times as many soldiers as their American and

South Vietnamese enemies. When the Soviet Union withdrew from Afghanistan in 1989, the victorious mujahideen had lost at least five fighters for each Soviet soldier killed, according to one estimate.

Might the West fare better in coming years? Some believe so, for two broad reasons. First, during the past decade of far-flung American-led counter-terrorism and counter-insurgency efforts, technologists have designed more kit better tailored to irregular warfare. As preceding articles have shown, Western soldiers will benefit from improved physical protection, will be fed better intelligence and will wield more effective precision weaponry, including less-lethal varieties for fighting in civilian areas.

Second, the non-military technologies of globalisation will gradually make it harder for irregular forces to hide or thrive among non-combatants. The kit and software that facilitate communications, transport and business are also spreading stability and wealth by connecting poor and violence-prone "off grid" societies to better-functioning ones. As people become empowered and better informed they are more likely to reject insurgents and extremists in their midst.

Western powers, the thinking goes, will increasingly harness the spread of connectivity, courtesy of globalisation, to do more of the heavy lifting in peacekeeping or stabilisation efforts. Thomas Barnett, a former Pentagon strategist, says American officials increasingly consider this sort of "frontier integration" as crucial to peace in the longer term.

The swamp drains

Rather than seeking a decisive military victory, expeditionary forces can concentrate efforts on lubricating globalisation – by, for example, opening and securing trade routes and weakening obstructionists whose grip on power requires keeping others isolated, uninformed and disempowered. Today's insurgencies and extremist movements are to some extent a painful but transitional backlash of globalisation, or "Westoxification", as some see it, says Mr Barnett, author of a book about the subject called *Great Powers: America and the World After Bush*.

Might America, its allies and others now scale back, in

post-cold-war fashion – at least with the big-ticket "shock and awe" armaments that are of little or no use against non-state forces? In January 2009, Robert Gates, then America's defence secretary, told the Senate armed-services committee that the United States would shift resources to building counter-insurgency capabilities, accompanied by less investment in costly "99% exquisite systems".

Since then, however, defence thinking in America has shifted back to placing greater value on investments in expensive platforms – a view reinforced by the 2011 NATO campaign against Muammar Qaddafi's forces in Libya. Mr Gates, speaking to NATO officials in Brussels shortly before leaving office in June 2011, said inadequate spending by member countries on warplanes and other advanced equipment was pushing the alliance towards "collective military irrelevance".

Moreover, fears of state-on-state war have been growing in many parts of the world. A terror attack or skirmish, instigated by a government or not, could kick-start war between India and Pakistan. China has reiterated its claim to Taiwan and small disputed islands in the region. Fear of Russia has increased following its invasion of Georgia in 2008. North Korea has shelled South Korea and is thought to have sunk one of its warships. Western countries and others, including Saudi Arabia, believe Iran seeks nuclear weapons.

The upshot is that many countries will be under growing pressure to invest in expensive military systems for state-on-state conflict, in addition to manpower and kit for insurgencies large or small. Unfortunately for taxpayers, some countries will probably continue to purchase expensive weaponry even if unwarranted by the conceivable geopolitical threats they face, notes Alexander Ioannis, an export official at Ordtech Military Industries, a company owned by Greece's defence ministry that exports widely in sub-Saharan Africa, Latin America and East Asia. The explanation? The kit provides prestige and "looks good in national parades", says Mr Ioannis. Whether justified or not, spending on defence technologies, it seems, will not significantly decrease anytime soon.

18 The challenge of irregular warfare

After smart weapons, smart soldiers

Irregular warfare may keep Western armies busy for decades. They will have to adapt if they are to overcome the odds that history suggests they are up against

REBELLION IS AS OLD as authority itself, and so therefore is the business of putting it down. Nearly 2,000 years ago Jewish militants – known as Zealots, hence the English word – took up arms against the world's greatest power and terrorised those deemed collaborators. The Romans dealt with the revolt in Palestine in familiar fashion, laying waste any town that resisted, prompting many to commit suicide rather than suffer capture and, in 70AD, destroying the great Temple in Jerusalem and taking its treasures. "While the holy house was on fire," records Josephus, "everything was plundered that came to hand, and ten thousand of those that were caught were slain … children and old men, and profane persons and priests, were all slain in the same manner."

Modern Western armies cannot, as the Romans did, make a wasteland and call it peace. Modern wars are complex affairs conducted "among the people" and, as Sir Richard Dannatt, head of the British army, has put it, "in the spotlight of the media and the shadow of international lawyers". In Iraq in the 1920s, Britain's air force pioneered the use of "air policing" to put down rebellious tribesmen on the cheap; today the use of air power often carries big political costs. The greater the accuracy of modern weapons, the louder the outcry when they nonetheless kill or wound civilians. And the wider the reach of the internet, the bigger the impact of propaganda videos showing insurgent attacks against Western forces, regardless of civilian casualties. The British who fought the Mahdist religious rebels in Sudan in the 19th century had no need to worry about provoking attacks in London; today such a campaign would be seen as another front in the *jihad* against the West.

Such bewildering conflict is regarded by some military thinkers as the "fourth generation" of warfare, distinct from those of previous eras: the first generation, of line and column, which culminated with the Napoleonic wars; the second, of machinegun and artillery, which brought about the slaughter of the first world war; and the third, of manoeuvre with tanks and aircraft, which stretched from the second world war to the 2003 invasion of Iraq. Fourth-generation warfare, according to Thomas Hammes, a retired colonel in the American marines, involves loose networks, made more powerful and resilient by information technology. It does not seek to defeat the enemy's forces, but instead "directly attacks the minds of the enemy decision-makers to destroy the enemy's political will".

Related items

Many others, though, regard today's conflicts as variations on age-old irregular warfare, not least Mao Zedong's "protracted war" in China, the Spanish guerrilla attacks against Napoleon's forces in Spain, or even America's war of independence from Britain. Whatever the definition, "small wars" can have big effects. In the past six decades the British have been driven out of Palestine, the French from Algeria, the Americans (and French) from Vietnam, the Russians from Afghanistan and the Israelis from Lebanon.

Can America and its Western allies avoid similar humiliation in Iraq and Afghanistan? Martin van Creveld, an Israeli military historian, argues that insurgencies have been almost impossible to defeat ever since Nazi Germany failed to suppress Josip Broz Tito's partisans in Yugoslavia. Winning such wars requires one of two tactics: extreme restraint and patience, as shown by the British over nearly 38 years in Northern Ireland; or extreme brutality, as shown by Syria in 1982 when the army destroyed much of Hama, a stronghold of Islamist rebels, killing at least 10,000 people. Any other method, says Mr van Creveld, risks being too harsh to win the support of the population but not harsh enough to cow it into submission.

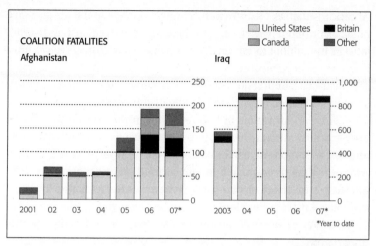

Source: iCasualties.org

FIG 18.1 Counting the cost

This rule is too stark. Experts point to successes such as the end of the insurgency in El Salvador, the collapse of the Shining Path rebels in Peru, the end of the civil wars in Mozambique and Angola, the demise of the Red Brigades in Italy and of the Red Army Faction in Germany. Much of this debate revolves around the meaning of victory and defeat, as well as the definition of counter-insurgency, civil war, counter-terrorism and so on. One school of thought holds that America's forces had largely defeated the Vietcong in Vietnam when its politicians lost the will to stop North Vietnam's conventional army from overrunning the south. That is to miss the point: in counter-insurgency one side can win every battle, yet lose the war.

Lessons unlearnt

Such arguments are a hot topic at Western military colleges, especially in America. More has been written on counter-insurgency in the past four years than in the previous four decades. The study of small wars was largely abandoned by the United States army in the 1970s as commanders promised "no more Vietnams" and concentrated instead on how to defeat the massed Soviet armies. America's humiliating retreats from Lebanon in 1983 and Somalia in 1994 convinced many

Americans that, as Colin Powell, a former general (and later secretary of state), once put it, America should not get involved in "half-hearted warfare for half-baked reasons". The swift ejection of Iraq's forces from Kuwait in 1991 reinforced such beliefs. Counter-insurgency became a secondary task undertaken mainly by American special forces, which sometimes offered training to friendly governments.

Given the difficulties in Iraq and Afghanistan, American officers are relearning the history of their own interventions in Latin America and, more important, the lessons of British imperial policing. Why, American experts asked, did Britain succeed against communist revolutionaries in Malaya in the 1950s, whereas America failed to defeat the communists in Vietnam in the 1960s and 1970s?

In his 2002 book "Learning to Eat Soup with a Knife" (a title drawn from T.E. Lawrence's "Seven Pillars of Wisdom", describing the messiness of waging "war upon rebellion"), John Nagl, an American lieutenant-colonel, concluded that British soldiers were better than the Americans at learning from their mistakes. General Sir Gerald Templer, the British high commissioner in Malaya from 1952 to 1954, argued that "the shooting side of the business" was only a minor part of the campaign. Coining a phrase, he suggested that the solution "lies not in pouring more troops into the jungle, but in the hearts and minds of the people". In contrast, says Colonel Nagl, the Americans in Vietnam remained wedded to "unrestrained and uncontrolled firepower", despite some work with small units that were deployed in border villages and civil-military reconstruction projects.

British officers are less impressed, saying their predecessors often repeated their errors. During the troubles in Northern Ireland, the arrival of British troops in 1969 was at first welcomed by Roman Catholics. But the army's heavy-handed methods, such as large cordon-and-search operations and the shooting of 13 civilians on Bloody Sunday in 1972, pushed many Catholics into the arms of the Provisional Irish Republican Army.

In any event, the American army and marines have produced a new counter-insurgency manual. One of its authors, General David Petraeus, is now in charge of the "surge" in Iraq. It may be too late to turn Iraq round, and Afghanistan could slide into greater violence. But the manual offers some comfort: it says counter-insurgency operations "usually begin poorly", and the way to success is for an army to become a good "learning organisation".

According to Mao's well-worn dictum, guerrillas must be like fish swimming in the "water" of the general population. T.E. Lawrence, helping to stir up the Arab revolt against Turkish rule during the first world war, described regular armies as plants, "immobile, firm-rooted, nourished through long stems to the head". Guerrillas, on the other hand, were like "a vapour". A soldier, he said, was "helpless without a target, owning only what he sat on, and subjugating only what, by order, he could poke his rifle at".

Western armies have unsurpassed firepower, mobility and surveillance technology. Guerrillas' main weapons are agility, surprise, the support of at least some sections of the population and, above all, time. The warren of Iraqi streets and the fortified compounds of Afghanistan compensate for the insurgents' technological shortcomings. The manual, however, attempts to change the army mindset: in fighting an enemy "among the people", it says, the central objective is not to destroy the enemy but to secure the allegiance of the citizenry. All strands of a campaign – military, economic and political – have to be strongly entwined.

Much of this thinking is drawn from the British experience in Malaya, but conditions today are vastly different. In Templer's day, securing "hearts and minds" did not mean just acting with kindness to win the people over; it also included coercion. Hundreds of thousands of ethnic Chinese, among whom the insurgents mainly operated, were uprooted and moved into guarded camps known as "new villages", where they were offered land. If the British could not find the fish, they resorted to removing the water.

They also sought to starve insurgents by restricting supplies of food to the population. In some areas rations of rice were handed out in cooked form so they would spoil before they could reach fighters in the jungle. Such measures are unthinkable today. Even the building of separation walls to reduce sectarian killings in Baghdad arouses Iraqi opposition. Checkpoints and curfews now have limited impact.

Templer was both the civil and the military boss. He emphasised policing rather than military operations, and the use of indigenous forces. The majority Malay population largely supported the British.

In a peninsula, the borders were relatively well controlled and the rebels had few external sources of support. Above all, the British had full sovereignty over Malaya. They could undercut the insurgents' claim to be fighting colonialism by guaranteeing equal rights, and by promising – and eventually granting – independence.

By contrast, the borders of Iraq and Afghanistan are permeable. Some neighbours are either hostile to the West (Iran) or unable to remove insurgent havens (Pakistan). The powers of America's Coalition Provisional Authority in Iraq lasted a year, long enough for America to make egregious errors, such as disbanding the Iraqi army and removing former Baathists, but not long enough to correct them.

Discontinuity of command

In Iraq the American effort is split between the military operations overseen by the generals and the civil and political work conducted by the embassy. In Afghanistan leadership is even more divided. There are two separate Western military commands – the NATO-led International Security Assistance Force, which provides the bulk of the troops, and the American-led Operation Enduring Freedom, which concentrates on hunting "high-value targets". Alongside these are a myriad of poorly co-ordinated reconstruction agencies.

Coalitions add further complications. Britain, America's only ally of any military significance in Iraq, is slowly leaving. And in Afghanistan, where boots on the ground are in short supply, NATO is wobbly. Many allies refuse to join a fight that has been waged mainly by American, British and Canadian forces, and several are under domestic pressure to bring their troops home. Overt colonialism has died, and with it have gone the large colonial armies. Counter-insurgency requires large numbers of security forces. But the West's all-volunteer forces have progressively cut expensive manpower in favour of technology. They have become infinitely better at finding and destroying things; but the best source of intelligence on the ground is often the soldier on the street with his "Mark-1 Eyeball".

Nationalist and pan-Islamic sentiments are much stronger than in the past. Information technology has helped jihadists spread the "single narrative" that Muslims everywhere are under attack, a contention reinforced by America's rhetoric about the "global war on terror". The internet provides a new and unassailable sanctuary from which to propagandise, organise and share tactics.

Still, the generals plead for more time. They point to Iraq's Anbar province, where Sunni tribes are turning against al-Qaeda. In Afghanistan, says Britain's General Dannatt, "strategic patience" is essential. American officers quote internal studies showing that it takes nine years on average (and often much longer) to defeat insurgencies. Yet perseverance is no guarantee of victory; many campaigns have taken as long, if not longer, to lose.

A growing body of opinion, both in the Pentagon and outside, has concluded that insurrections are best fought indirectly, through local allies. "It is extremely difficult for Western powers to defeat insurgencies in foreign countries in modern times," says Max Boot, author of "War Made New" (2006). "At the same time, there are very few instances of insurgencies overthrowing a local government. The problem is that Western armies lose the will to maintain imperial domination." Western forces always have the option of going home; for local governments, though, fighting insurgents is a matter of survival.

A better model than Malaya, argues Mr Boot, is the end of the Marxist insurrection in El Salvador in 1992. American forces did not lead the fighting. Instead, a small contingent of under 100 advisers from America's special forces helped the democratising government reorganise its army and avoid the fate of nearby Nicaragua, which fell to the Sandinistas in 1979. This approach has its own difficulties: America's reputation was tarnished by right-wing Salvadorean death-squads. In the end it was external political factors – the demise of the Sandinistas in Nicaragua, partly caused by an American-backed insurgency, and the collapse of the Soviet Union – that helped bring about a settlement and the incorporation of the guerrillas into a newfound democracy.

David Kilcullen, an Australian colonel and General Petraeus's main adviser on counter-insurgency, says fighting insurgencies in other people's countries is hard. "Running Baghdad is not like trying to police New York City; it's like the Iraqi police trying to run New York City." Tellingly, he says, Indonesian forces successfully put down an insurrection by the Islamist Darul Islam movement in the 1950s and early 1960s, but could not quell the resistance to their annexation of East Timor.

The dilemma for Western forces in Iraq and Afghanistan is that, though they may lack the wherewithal to win, the national governments they seek to help are unable to stand up on their own. At best, Western armies can create the political space to build viable governments. But this has proved difficult enough even where the fighting has stopped and the main political forces have been co-operative (or at least acquiescent) – as in Bosnia and East Timor. It may be impossible under sustained fire.

More brain, less brawn

Although most armies have now relearnt the limits of force and the importance of the "comprehensive approach", commanders complain that other branches of government have not. In a September 2007 article, General Peter Chiarelli, an adviser to Robert Gates, America's secretary of defence, says more money has to be spent not on the Pentagon but on the "non-kinetic aspects of our national power". He recommends building up the "minuscule" State Department and USAID development agency (so small it is "little more than a contracting agency"), and reviving the United States Information Agency.

As the American army expands, some thinkers, such as Colonel Nagl, say it needs not just more soldiers – nor even linguists, civil-affairs officers and engineers – but a fully fledged 20,000-strong corps of advisers that will train and "embed" themselves with allied forces around the world. The idea makes army commanders blanch, but they do not question the underlying assumption. Insurgencies may be the face of war for the West in the years ahead. Even if America cannot imagine fighting another Iraq or Afghanistan, extremists round the world have seen mighty America's vulnerability to the rocket-propelled grenade, the AK-47 and the suicide-bomber.

This article was first published in *The Economist* in October 2007.

Index

Figures are indicated in *italics.*

Hellfire missile 26, 104, 105, 110, 197
Henry L. Stimson Centre 131
High Energy Laser Technology
    Demonstrator 17
High Mobility Multipurpose Wheeled
    Vehicle (Humvee) 41, 44, 202
Hindenburg airship 115–16
hitmen 233–34
Hizbullah xvii, 94
    damages an Israeli corvette (2006) 12
    and drones 98
    and elections 267
    Israel sends bogus news flashes to
        mobile phones xvii
    and Israeli air power 90
    Israeli killing of Mughniyeh 230
    Katyusha rockets 17
    al-Manar satellite-TV signal pirated xvii
    scrambles signals from a French military
        satellite 143
Hiznay, Mark 84, 85
Hoffman, Professor Bruce 206
Hogervorst, Maarten 32
Holland, Steve 1, 27
Hollifield, Stephen 266
Hollis, Professor Duncan 174, 175
home secretary 255, 259
Hong, Dr Dennis 49
hostile-intent systems 223–26
Huang, Jen-Hsun 62
Huawei 180
Hughes, Nathan 13
Human Rights Watch 84
human shields 81
Hussein, Saddam xi, 6, 84, 93, 97, 191, 212,
    231, 267
Hutcheon, Dr Ian 76
hydrazine fuel 142
hydrogen bombs: nuclear fusion 66
hydrogen, in the *Hindenburg* 115–16
Hyperion Power Generation 73, 75
Hyperion Power Module (HPM) reactor
    73
hyperspectral imaging system 139

i2 211, 267
IABG 191
IBM 222, 264–65
    SPSS 266
Ibn Taymiyya 206
ICBMs *see* intercontinental ballistic
    missiles
identity cards 253
Identity Systems 222
identity theft 250, 256
IEDs *see* improvised explosive devices
image-recognition software 41
Imperial College, London 35, 54, 194, 240
improvised explosive devices (IEDs) 6–10
    blowing up 8

garage-door triggers 6, 7
    "hoax" wiring 6
    mobile-phone signals 7
    and predictive-analysis software 10
    responsible for two-thirds of coalition
        deaths 6
    shockwaves from 27
    squirting water into circuitry 8–9
    technological leap-frogging 10
    zapping with a laser 8
"impulse waves" 43
in-car navigation systems 58
In-Q-Tel 219, 261
India
    and BrahMos missile 12, 15
    and Pakistan 271
    progress as a space-faring nation 149
    and Sizzler missile xii, 12
Indonesia
    annexation of East Timor 279
    and Darul Islam movement 279
    submarines 14
    turboprops 113
    Yakhont missile sold to 12
information revolution 257
Information Warfare Monitor 154
informational warfare 153
informers 249
infra-red equipment 33
inks, electronic 56
innovation 4, 5
Insitu 101
Institute of Electrical and Electronics
    Engineers 121
Institution of Chemical Engineers 240
integrated circuits 108
Integrated Dynamics 99
intelligence
    agencies 202, 206, 222, 260, 261, 266
    air power used to gather 93–94
    Israeli intelligence in the occupied
        territories 94
intercontinental ballistic missiles (ICBMs)
    17
Intermat 34
Internal Revenue Service 213, 265
International Atomic Energy Agency
    (IAEA) 69–72, 151, 152, 168
International Civil Aviation Organisation
    124
International Experimental
    Thermonuclear Reactor, Cadarache,
    France 68
international human-rights laws and
    treaties 257
International Security Assistance Force
    9, 278
International Space Station 148
International Traffic in Arms Regulation
    (ITAR) 145–49